CW00482384

Napoleon

Napoleon

Alan Forrest

Quercus

For Rosemary and Marianne

First published in Great Britain in 2011 by
Quercus
55 Baker Street
7th Floor, South Block
London
W1U 8EW

A CIP catalogue record for this book is available
from the British Library

ISBN 978 1 84916 410 8

10 9 8 7 6 5 4 3 2 1

Text designed and typeset by Ellipsis Digital Limited, Glasgow

Printed and bound in Great Britain by Clays Ltd, St Ives plc

Contents

Introduction

Biography can be an inflexible medium, especially for the historian. It shapes a period, a country, a culture around the life of a single individual who may or may not be representative of it. It chooses, almost unavoidably, as its chronological span the dates of that individual's life and birth, telling the story of these years through the prism of his own experience as though, by implication, that experience had an importance that was wider, more all-encompassing, than the life of a single man, that it contributed in some significant way to the history of his times. And, in the case of Napoleon Bonaparte, it can help to give weight to a mythology, adding to the already well-established impression, created by a host of historical and biographical writings across the decades, that what mattered was the man himself, his vision and his ambition, more than the times he lived in or the circumstances he encountered. Few historical characters have had so much written about them, and few have been depicted in such emphatically personal terms, to the extent that the history of a whole era is often presented as the reflection of one man's power and pursuit of glory. Few have mixed history and legend more promiscuously. For that reason it may be wise to pause and begin this book with something approaching a health warning.

There are two ways of writing about Napoleon. One is to present the story of a titanic figure who dictated the history of his age and whose will alone determined the destiny of a continent. 'In the beginning', as Goethe famously wrote with the rise of German nationalism in mind, 'was Napoleon.' The other is to focus on the Empire, the political and economic system which it created and the cultural dynamic which it encouraged. Goethe probably did not intend the history of these years to be taken over by the personal life of one man, as many historians and biographers have tended to do. And the Empire, stretching across most of the European continent, was certainly not the work of one man. It was a collaborative enterprise that depended on the effort and vision of thousands of administrators, army officers, jurists and educators, a system that may have been conceived by Napoleon as an extension of French power, but which could only work with the active collaboration of others, Germans and Italians, Belgians and Dutch and Poles. The Empire as it had developed by 1806 was multinational, and multilingual, too. If Napoleon dreamed of recreating a Europe on the scale of the Carolingian Empire and looked back for inspiration to Classical Rome, others had to buy into that dream.

These were tumultuous years, dominated in France and beyond by the French Revolution and by the wars it unleashed, events over which the future Emperor had the most tangential influence. This, too, should make us pause and reflect on Napoleon's role, on the degree to which he was the product of the more individualistic, meritocratic society which the Revolution created, the product of his times as much as their creator. The history of this period is often presented as the reflection of his ambition, his vision, and his extraordinary imagination. It is a world conceived in the person of the Emperor, held together by his words and actions, as he lived it and as he recorded his reflections in his memoirs, dictated to his companions on Saint Helena. These do give the impression of a coherent and consistent programme, and of an idea of Europe and the Empire which he first forged and then ruthlessly enacted. Yet even interpreting these words and giving credence to his judgments is a delicate exercise; Napoleon's reflections on his career and his role in history were written to form opinion, not to reflect it. If there are few actual lies in his account, faithfully copied and published after his death by Emmanuel de Las Cases as the *Mémorial de Sainte-Hélène*, it is suggestive, often critical of others, and always highly partisan. It must never be forgotten that Napoleon fully appreciated the power of the written word and that he used it to telling effect: his despatches from the army, like his later laws and decrees, were penned with deliberation and an eye to his audience. He surrounded himself with journalists and spin-doctors long before it became a tradition of politics, aware of the importance of public opinion in the new polity he was creating. He wrote to impress his generals and his political allies, and to forge the views of the political elites, both in France and abroad. But he also, from an early age, wrote with future generations in mind, determined to provide justification for his actions and to burnish his image for posterity.

Seeing the history of these years through Napoleon's eyes offers a coherence forged by one man's ideas and vision, but this may be deceptive. It may be more useful to think of the Empire less as the personification of Napoleon's will and imagination than as a complex political system characterised by a sophisticated legal code and a developed administrative structure, which depended for its success on the cooperation of others and on the convergence of ambitions. Of course

Napoleon's own ambition played a crucial role here, just as his military prowess and his vision of Empire were critical to the success of the enterprise. But seen in this light, the Empire was much more than one man. It was a military and civil system of government, a triumph of conquest and administration that demanded allies and collaborators, kindred spirits and disciples. It was the response of a generation of lawyers, politicians and generals who had lived through the revolution, who had in many cases administered and directed that revolution, but who had now, in the first years of the nineteenth century, concluded that revolutionary institutions had run their course and that what France needed, above all else, was order and stability.

Napoleon's major achievement was to create a civic and legal order that inspired loyalties and, in many parts of Europe, survived after he himself had been banished to Saint Helena and the Empire was no more than a memory. It was less the work of one man, however grandiose his ambitions for empire, than the creation of a generation of Frenchmen brought up on a diet of enlightenment and humanism, and trained to regard good government and justice as essential attributes of a modern state; a generation, moreover, that had come to maturity and had, in many cases, been given undreamt-of opportunities during the decade of the French Revolution. They did not find themselves held back by questions of privilege or prevented by the chance of their birth from taking their place in the service of the state. Nor were they among those whom the Revolution picked out for persecution or excluded from citizenship: those who saw their allegiance to the King as more binding than their loyalty to the republic, who rated their Catholic loyalties above their duties as Frenchmen, who put private profit before public service, or who allowed themselves to be lured by the temptations of counter-revolution or federalism. For some, clearly, the French Revolution had spelt danger and personal catastrophe, and it split entire communities along factional lines. But for the vast majority of Frenchmen, and for some at least among the educated elites of Europe, it brought unrivalled opportunity, expanded the public sphere and offered the possibility of advancement. It was to this generation that the young Napoleon Bonaparte instinctively belonged, a generation ready and eager to grasp the opportunities which meritocracy held out to them. In France and across the Empire jurists and public officials responded to the challenge, accepting posts in the imperial administration, and bringing justice, the Code and efficient bureaucracy to peoples who had never before benefited from them. There is little doubt that for many the advantages of Napoleonic rule far outweighed the burdens of state taxes or the shame of defeat and invasion. They responded to the challenges they were offered and accepted their role in the modernisation of the polity, identifying with the Empire and assuming their part in implementing the Napoleonic dream. The history of these years was a collective enterprise, as much their story as his.

It is not, however, as such that it is primarily remembered. Napoleon inspired great loyalty and equally great hatred, among contemporaries and for posterity, and from the moment of his death in 1821 his reputation continued to grow, as a man of the people and the saviour of his nation. Stories abounded, some claiming that he had superhuman, even supernatural powers. Rumours circulated that he would rise from the dead, and return to lead France to further exploits and glory. Among former soldiers of the Grande Armée a cult of the Emperor developed which spread to civilians, to novelists, and to politicians once the Bourbons had been dethroned and expelled in 1830. The new king, Louis-Philippe, sought to link his own reputation to that of the Emperor in a bid to extend his popularity among peasants and artisans and in the small towns of provincial France. Napoleon's words, as they had been recorded by his companions on Saint Helena, were dissected by his admirers as they told and retold the story of his campaigns, a story that rapidly became subsumed into legend. In 1836 Parisians flocked to admire the newly unveiled Arc de Triomphe, honouring the men who had died in Napoleon's service. Four years later they turned out again to welcome him home, as his ashes, exhumed from his island grave and conveyed by ship from the South Atlantic, were carried with due pomp and dignity up the Seine and through the heart of Paris to a final resting-place at the Invalides.

Paris, 1840

Parisians turned out in force to hail their Emperor's return, on a cold December day in 1840, when his body was solemnly carried on a riverboat from Courbevoie on its final journey to the Invalides. It was a moment that Paris had eagerly awaited, though when it was first announced it had met with a mixture of joy and surprise. Many feared that the British would seek to keep the Emperor's body under their control rather than risk the new explosion of French nationalism which his memory might rekindle. They doubted that their king, Louis-Philippe, would take such a political risk at a time when his regime was under attack from republicans, legitimists and Bonapartists: was this really a way to reconcile the different political factions, they asked, or would the ceremony further undermine his own legitimacy?[1]

In fact, Louis-Philippe's political judgment was sound – at least in the immediate term – in that the Return of the Ashes redounded to the credit of the Orleanist regime; and at the same time succeeded, albeit temporarily, in eclipsing other, less glorious foreign policy issues in the national headlines. And though their Emperor's return may have encouraged some of the electorate to indulge in nostalgic dreams of glory, most Frenchmen believed that the government was fulfilling a debt of honour in carrying out Napoleon's final wishes. Had he not famously declared, in a codicil to his will, that he wanted his ashes to be returned to France and buried 'by the banks of the Seine surrounded by the French people whom I have loved so dearly' – a phrase that was sure to endear him to most of his fellow countrymen? In life Napoleon had been somewhat preoccupied by thoughts of his death and of his final resting place, and Paris was certainly one of the sites he had singled out. But there were others, most notably by the side of his ancestors in the cathedral at Ajaccio. What really alarmed him was the thought that the British might try to bury him in London and make political capital out of his death. After murdering him in Saint Helena, he declared, the least his enemies could do was to 'return my ashes to France, the only country I have loved'.[2] His words would leave a powerful mark on future generations of Frenchmen.

Napoleon's final return to his capital was minutely planned and choreographed. It required the exhumation of his body in Saint Helena, which was, of course, the property of the British crown; the despatch of a naval vessel to bring the Emperor's ashes back to France; and a long and potentially hazardous sea voyage of several thousand miles from the South Atlantic. The plan involved diplomatic niceties as well as considerable logistical subtlety. The voyage was prepared in full consultation with the British government, with the French Prime Minister, Adolphe Thiers, taking overall charge of the mission.[3]

The venture did not come cheap. Louis-Philippe put aside the sum of a million francs from the 1840 budget for the transportation of Napoleon's remains to Paris and the construction of his tomb in the traditional resting place of military heroes, the Church of the

Invalides, whereupon the Chamber of Deputies, overcome with patriotic emotion, voted to double it. The choice of the Invalides was explained by the Minister of the Interior, Charles de Rémusat, in a statement to the Chamber on 12 May. Napoleon's body, he explained, needed a 'silent and venerable location', which ruled out the choice of a public square in central Paris. 'He was an Emperor and a King; he was the legitimate ruler of our country. In this regard, he could be interred at Saint-Denis.' But, the Minister went on, an ordinary royal sepulchre was not fully appropriate for Napoleon. He must 'still reign and command in the precincts where the soldiers of our country go to repose, and where those who are called to defend it will always go for inspiration'.[4] His final resting place should be both a statement of his legitimacy and a reflection of his patriotism.

Other possible destinations had been considered and rejected, and the choice of resting place had been widely debated in the press. It was a matter of great public interest and caused a flurry of pamphlet and newspaper campaigns. In his report to the Chamber on 26 May, Marshal Clauzel outlined the most obvious candidates: '. . . the Pantheon which is home to all great men; the Madeleine, which is currently unclaimed and could justifiably be reserved for Napoleon; the Arc de Triomphe, which would provide him, as an epitaph, with the names of all his generals and a list of all his victories; the Column which was his work and his alone and, finally, the Basilica of Saint-Denis which has claims on him as a legitimate sovereign and which has stood ready for thirty years to receive him into the tomb which he himself had ordered'. But there were strong reasons for preferring the Invalides. It provided a dignified and prestigious setting that discouraged tumult and protest, and, besides, Napoleon had had a long association with the building. He had ordered that France's great military heroes Vauban and Turenne be buried there. He had decorated the church with the flags of his victories. And he had chosen the building for the very first ceremony to confer the Legion of Honour.[5] It was an easy decision to take.

Creating a tomb for the Emperor that would fit seamlessly into one of Paris's most famous churches posed major problems for the man who emerged triumphant from the public competition to select a design for the monument: Louis Visconti. The church was part of a coherent group of buildings that formed the Hôtel des Invalides, designed by the architect Jules Hardouin-Mansart to receive and care for French officers from Louis XIV's wars, and was one of the most prestigious building projects in late seventeenth-century Paris. It was a recognised masterpiece of baroque architecture and one of the great domed spaces of Europe, to be compared with St Peter's in Rome or Westminster Abbey in London.[6] It was into this space that Visconti was charged in 1842 to insert a commemorative tomb to the Emperor and a dignified last resting place for his ashes – one that would testify to Napoleon's greatness without jeopardising the dignity of the baroque building.

It was a difficult commission, especially as the popular mood in 1840 risked sinking into a jingoistic adulation of Napoleon and the military glory he had brought to France. The Emperor's ashes were to rest under the great dome with its 1706 painting of Saint Louis, a Crusader king who had brought civilisation to heathens and infidels.[7] In the words of the royal decree, 'The tomb will be placed beneath the dome, which will be reserved, along with the four side chapels, for the burial place of the Emperor Napoleon.' And it was stipulated that the area should for all time be devoted to this purpose only: no other coffin could be placed there in future.[8]

Visconti's crypt would not be completed until 1861, eight years after his death. Napoleon was not only being brought home to Paris at state expense, but he was also being given the dignity of a state burial. There were some who argued that the choice of the Invalides was an ambivalent one which, while reflecting Napoleon's military greatness, played down any claims to legitimacy which might have been embarrassing to Louis-Philippe. What is certain, however, is that he had been accorded a permanent place in the collective memory of the nation.

The first step had been to persuade the British government that it was in their own interest to allow the French to bring Britain's greatest enemy home to Europe, despite the risk that the celebrations that would accompany Napoleon's return might unleash new waves of nostalgia, and dreams of imperial glory such as had united the rest of Europe against the Emperor in his lifetime. Thiers briefed the French ambassador in London, François Guizot, himself a future prime minister, to whom he handed full responsibility for negotiations with the British. He informed Guizot that the King was committed to the plan, and that he counted on the cooperation of the British government. For, Thiers explained, Louis-Philippe could see no honourable reason to refuse France's request, since 'England cannot tell the world that she wants to keep a corpse prisoner'. Thiers went on, rather curiously, to expand on this view. 'When a condemned man has been executed, his body is returned to his family. And I ask pardon of heaven for comparing the greatest of men to a criminal hanging from the scaffold.'[9]

Guizot transmitted his government's request, emphasising the compassion due to those who had fought for Napoleon and wished to see him returned to his native soil. It was presented as a human-itarian appeal from one monarch to another. The French king, explained Guizot in his despatch to the Foreign Office, very much wished to see Napoleon's remains returned to French soil, to 'this land which he defended and which he rendered illustrious, and which maintains with respect the mortal remains of so many thou-sands of his companions in arms, both officers and soldiers, who devoted themselves at his side to the service of our country'.[10] The British government agreed with only a minimum of delay. Lord Palmerston added rather mischievously that such rapid cooperation should be taken as a sign of Britain's willingness to wipe away any lingering traces of the animosity between the two nations, which 'during the lifetime of the Emperor had pitted the French and British nations against each other in war'.[11] More pertinently, it was also an olive branch through which Palmerston hoped to win French coop-eration in the Levant over a current political crisis. The Pasha of Egypt, Mehemet Ali, was seeking to extend his somewhat fragile hegemony in Syria, a move that met with the support of the French government but with considerable opposition from Britain. For both the British and the French, therefore, the return of Napoleon's ashes could serve as a useful diversion at a moment of high political tension.[12] In fact, as France would soon discover, Palmerston had no intention of allowing himself to be distracted; in the weeks that followed, Britain would pull off a diplomatic coup by getting Russia, Prussia and Austria to join her in issuing an ultimatum to Mehemet Ali and, in the process, leaving Louis-Philippe dangerously isolated.

Once these diplomatic exchanges had been completed, the expe-dition to Saint Helena could be mounted. Two vessels, the frigate *Belle-Poule* and a smaller corvette, *La Favorite*, left Toulon on 7 July for the South Atlantic. In charge of this delicate mission was Louis-Philippe's son, the Prince de Joinville, who held the rank of ship's captain in the French navy, and who was pulled out of active service in the Algerian campaign to head the expedition. The crew numbered around five hundred men, and the expedition included a number of those who had accompanied Napoleon during his exile, most notably two of the Emperor's most loyal marshals, Generals Bertrand and Gourgaud; his priest, Father Coquereau; five of his former valets and personal servants; and Emmanuel de Las Cases, the son of Napoleon's secretary on Saint Helena, who had been a boy when he had last been on the island in 1821. The two ships anchored on 8 October in the harbour at Jamestown before a substantial welcoming party of islanders, who had been informed of their arrival some days before by the crew of a passing British ship. Las Cases expressed what he felt as he looked around the island at the objects that surrounded him, scarcely daring to believe his eyes and 'feeling what you feel when you wake up from a dream: my memories were as acute and as real as if the captivity had only ended the previous day'.[13] On the following day de Joinville obtained the agreement of the governor that the honours due to a monarch should be extended to Napoleon's body and that the coffin should be opened to allow official verification of the identity of the corpse.[14] This contrasted sharply with the Emperor's earlier interment in 1821, in an obscure grave shaded by two willow trees, in a little valley on Saint Helena. On that occasion, on the instructions of the British Colonial Secretary, Lord Bathurst, the only honours he was accorded were those that were routinely given to an officer of the British army.[15]

The real work, that of exhuming the body, then got under way, overseen by the surgeon of the *Belle-Poule*, Rémi-Julien Guillard, who left behind a detailed account of what happened. Digging was carried out at night when the air was coolest, and rumours that the grave might have been disturbed were soon discounted. He noted that, as the earth and stones were removed from the ground, they encountered neither foul smells nor an exhalation of gas; and when the chamber was opened, he went down inside it and found the Emperor's coffin, intact, below. 'The mahogany planks that formed the coffin still retained their colour and their hard texture', he reported, 'and there was neither solid nor liquid matter around it on the ground. The outer casing was held shut with long screws which we had to cut in order to remove the lid; underneath was a lead casket, which was closed on all sides and enveloped a mahogany casket that itself was perfectly intact; after that was a fourth casket in iron whose lid was soldered onto supports which folded down inside.' Guillard then describes the care with which they approached the body.

'The soldering was slowly cut open and the lid carefully removed; then I saw a whitish cloth that hid the inside of the coffin and prevented us from seeing the body; it was quilted satin and was used to decorate the inside of this casket. I lifted it by a corner, and, rolling it back from the feet to the head, exposed Napoleon's body, which I immediately recognised as it had been so well preserved, and his face retained such a lifelike expression'.[16] Such decay as had taken place was entirely consistent with the effect of nearly twenty years in the soil, the doctor confirmed, and he noted that if the uniform Napoleon was buried in had become dull and blackened during its years in the ground, his golden crown and his cross of an officer of the Legion of Honour still retained much of their glitter, while the two silver vases that had been buried with him, one of them capped with an imperial eagle, were closed and intact. Having exhumed the body and satisfied themselves that it had not been tampered with, the French secured it in six different coffins and caskets and loaded it on board the *Belle-Poule* for repatriation to France.[17]

With Napoleon's body on board, the *Belle-Poule* headed directly back to Europe, completing the voyage in around six weeks before docking at Cherbourg, where the Emperor's coffin lay on board for a week before being transferred to a river-steamer, the *Normandie*, for its journey up the Seine. In Cherbourg, more than a hundred thousand people came to kneel by the catafalque, which the city council had voted to adorn with a golden crown.[18] From Cherbourg, river boats took over, and the voyage began to resemble a festival parade as they escorted the coffin by planned stages towards Paris. At every staging-point, crowds gathered to join in the celebrations; flags were flown, and programmes of patriotic celebrations were organised. The *Normandie* carried the coffin from Cherbourg to Le Havre on 8 December and, on the following day, to Val de la Haye where it gave way to a flotilla of river boats with a shallower draught for the last stages upstream through Vernon, Mantes and Maisons-Laffitte, arriving in Courbevoie on 14 December. Throughout the journey huge crowds lined the river banks and bridges were turned into triumphal arches; salvos were fired, units of national guardsmen paraded, and military bands played martial music. The seven-day journey had the joyous atmosphere of a public festival, and those towns where there was no scheduled stop – notably Rouen – protested loudly at what they saw as a cruel and deliberate slight.[19] Their Emperor was coming home to France, and everyone, it seemed, wanted part of the action.

Prominent among those who took part in these celebrations were Napoleon's former soldiers, their enthusiasm for their old leader seemingly undimmed after a quarter of a century. Along the route they crammed on to landing-stages and lined up on bridges; many of them felt that this was their day, a time to celebrate their victories and sacrifices and to draw them to the attention of the civilian population. But it was primarily a moment to pay tribute to their Emperor and to remember the glory and drama of the long years they had spent criss-crossing Europe in his service. At Courbevoie, freezing in ten degrees of frost, Louis-Philippe's new Prime Minister knelt before the coffin, deep in thought and reminiscence: Jean de Dieu Soult who, in an earlier life, had been promoted by Napoleon to be Marshal of France, who was at his right hand at Austerlitz, and a major-general at Waterloo.[20] Progress on this last stage of the Emperor's journey had visibly slowed, in large measure to allow the architects and an army of tradesmen time to complete their work so that Napoleon's body could be received with due pomp and dignity. But it also allowed ordinary citizens and local authorities along the route a chance to pay their own respects and to produce celebrations worthy of an emperor.

In Paris, as news arrived of the approach of the flotilla, excitement spread, not least among survivors of the Grande Armée. Among those veterans who were housed in the Invalides, it was reported that 'joy spilt over into lunacy: it seemed that they were being taken back to the battles and glory they had been involved in before. The poor old wounded soldiers forgot their pain and their suffering; they sang, laughed, brushed their uniforms and polished their swords as though they were about to be reviewed by their great commander'.[21]

By the end of the week, when the flotilla had docked in Courbevoie, all eyes turned to Paris. The day assigned for the final cortege and the burial of Napoleon's ashes, 15 December, would be one of huge pomp and celebration as the funeral procession passed through the city. Contemporary reports are unanimous in describing the popular enthusiasm across Paris and the joy and pride that were reflected in the faces of the crowds. As the cortege moved through the streets of the capital, this enthusiasm at times risked becoming politicised, with some of the crowd bursting into prolonged chants of 'Vive l'Empereur' as a way of expressing their displeasure with the grey world they had come to associate with the monarchy. But most Parisians did not dwell on the political significance of the event, preferring to treat it as an additional holiday and revel in the colour, the music, and the artillery fire. They saw the moment as one to celebrate, as a popular festival in which they had a part to play. Some went further, seeing it as a moment of national reconcili-ation, a milestone in forging France's collective memory and estab-lishing the identity of the post-revolutionary nation. The republican and left-wing press reflected the generally popular enthusiasm and patriotism and praised Napoleon both as a military commander and as the heir to France's revolutionary traditions. Only the monar-chist Right had reason to quibble, reminding their readers that the return of the ashes did nothing to give Napoleon legitimacy, and that for them he would always remain a 'tyrant' and a 'usurper' of the Bourbon throne.[22]

Paris was sumptuously decked out for the funeral procession on a morning when the barometer recorded fifteen degrees of frost. Even some of the soldiers assigned to the ceremony found their resilience sapped by the cold. Yet the freezing temperatures did not deter the crowds, who turned out in their hundreds of thousands to watch the Emperor parade in the midst of his people. This was the traditional role of royal funerals of the sort France had become accustomed to witness during the Restoration, and which customarily had a religious as well as a political character, linking the recent death of a monarch or his martyrdom during the Revolution to the promise of salvation in another world. Under the two Bourbon kings they had been called to celebrate members of the Royal family lost to the Terror: the transfer of Louis XVI and Marie-Antoinette to Saint-Denis, the state funerals for Louis XVI and the Duc de Berry.[23]

In Napoleon's case, of course, the promise of eternity may not have been the message that the authorities most wished to convey, but this was the meaning that was usually encoded in the ceremonial of these royal occasions, and would certainly have reflected what the onlookers read into it. There was another difference, though, in that the Emperor had long been dead, and that there was no cause for lamentation. This was not a funeral in the strict sense of the term, but a reburial on French soil; onlookers were entitled to treat it as a source of celebration and jubilation rather than of more traditional mourning.

Napoleon's ashes were carried in their casket on a funeral barge, before being transferred to a huge golden coach drawn by sixteen horses and draped in purple cloth decorated with Imperial bees, with the figures of fourteen armed Victories, and with Imperial eagles in submissive pose. It was over thirty feet high and weighed thirteen tons, and was, depending on the taste of the individual spectator, either dazzlingly magnificent or overly heavy and cumbersome. It certainly had the disadvantage of hiding from view what most had come to see – Napoleon's coffin.[24] But the coach surely impressed the crowds as it rumbled across the cobblestones past the Arc de Triomphe and down the Champs-Elysées before crossing the Seine on its way to the Invalides. The streets were thick with onlookers, all hoping for a final glimpse of the Emperor as the long and colourful funeral cortege passed by. Appropriately, perhaps, in the light of Napoleon's achievements, the procession was overwhelmingly composed of soldiers, whose bright uniforms and martial music added to the sense of spectacle and to public enjoyment of the occasion.

The decoration of the streets matched the celebratory mood. In the symbolism and imagery of the decor, prominence was given to Napoleon's victories and to his acknowledged status as a military hero, the image of the Emperor that lived on in the Napoleonic legend and in the popular imagination. This was the hero of Marengo and Austerlitz rather than the originator of the University and the Code Napoléon. The streets along the route and the bridges over the Seine were lavishly decorated with symbolic statuary and triumphal arches that reflected the mood of the occasion. On each side of the Champs-Elysées, eighteen winged statues of Victory alternated with columns bearing an Imperial eagle. The Pont de la Concorde was decorated with four triumphal columns and eight statues representing the achievements of the French people – Wisdom, Strength, Justice and War on one side, Agriculture, the Arts, Rhetoric and Trade on the other – before the cortege reached the Left bank of the river where it was met by a huge statue representing Immortality. In front of the Invalides, as the procession approached from the Seine, it passed a bronze statue of the Emperor himself, while along the Esplanade thirty-two hastily created plaster statues of past French heroes gazed down approvingly.

The choice of those honoured as heroes was instructive, if somewhat eclectic. Monarchs were well represented, going as far back as Clovis, Hugh Capet and Charles Martel, though there was none more recent than Louis XIV. Military leaders of the past took their places beside them in the roll of honour: Joan of Arc was there, of course, along with Duguesclin and Bayard, Condé and Turenne. The great specialist in siege warfare, Vauban, was there too, as was Napoleon's greatest rival in the French revolutionary armies, Lazare Hoche. But so, more significantly, were seven of Napoleon's marshals, the generals who had served him in his great campaigns in Italy and Germany, Spain and Russia. They, too, appeared as heroes to be compared to the great soldiers of the past. Kellermann, Jourdan, Lannes, Masséna, Mortier and Macdonald were all included in the guard of honour, as, more surprisingly, was Ney, executed for treason for supporting Napoleon during the Hundred Days, but now rehabilitated for the occasion by Louis-Philippe.[25] In all, the manufacture of the decorations and sculptures had employed fifty of France's leading artists of the day.[26]

The ceremony continued inside the church with the solemn handing over of the ashes by the Prince de Joinville and their acceptance by Louis-Philippe 'in the name of France'. By this gesture Napoleon was accepted back into the nation, an act which, his supporters argued, gave him a new legitimacy in the turbulent history of French political regimes. On the coffin were placed, with an almost religious dedication, three objects sacred to his memory: a cross of the Legion of Honour, the famous hat he had worn at Eylau, and the golden sword he had brandished at Austerlitz. Then, once the coffin had been placed in the catafalque, the funeral service could begin, to the music of Mozart's mass for the dead, performed by six hundred musicians, singers and choristers.[27] It had been an eventful day. What had begun as a memorable effusion of popular joy ended in a mood of almost religious solemnity.

The Return of the Ashes offers eloquent proof of the French people's continuing fascination with the Emperor, and many in the crowd made no secret of their admiration for what Napoleon had achieved or their nostalgic memories of the Grand Empire. The celebrations were etched sharply on the public memory, and they were passed on to future generations in paintings, lithographs, poems and popular songs. Paris theatres offered operas which exalted the style and glory of the Empire, and they played to packed houses. More than a hundred poems were written and published to mark the ceremony, the most famous by Victor Hugo, and the vast majority singing the unquestioning praises of France's dead hero.[28] Painters vied with one another to depict the scene at Napoleon's graveside on Saint Helena, the arrival of the *Belle-Poule* in Cherbourg, and the colour and pageantry of the final procession across Paris. Some emphasised the beauty of the landscape and the dignity of the cere-monial to add lustre to the occasion. Others turned to allegory to give a more explicitly political interpretation of events, often mixing real and fictional characters or presenting the martyred Napoleon as a new saint in the Christian pantheon.[29] Artists such as François Trichot and Horace Vernet suggested that Napoleon even possessed divine attributes: they present him rising from the dead, resurrected like a new Christ to return to his people, or drawn in a chariot by an eagle towards an eternal paradise.[30] Caricaturists profited from the moment to recall the glorious victories of the Grand Army or to contrast the achievements and ambitions of the Emperor with those, far more modest, of the current regime.

The ready availability of prints and lithographs meant that within hours of the events in Paris, images of them were being distributed in all parts of the country, thus involving the people of provincial towns and rural hamlets in a moment of Napoleonic fantasy from which many felt they had been unfairly excluded. The exploits of the Emperor had long been a favoured theme of the popular prints produced by Charles Pellerin in Epinal and distributed throughout peasant France at fairs and markets. Pellerin used the opportunity to depict to his fellow countrymen the full wonder of the ceremonial, the size and opulence of the funeral carriage, and the huge and enthusiastic crowds that had lined the streets and blocked off central Paris. No detail was omitted, ensuring that the Return of the Ashes became one of the best-known and best-loved scenes in nineteenth-century French history, one that helped keep the Napoleonic legend alive for future generations.[31]

The legend had gained renewed popularity following Napoleon's death in 1821. It was constructed around his illustrious and multi-faceted life as soldier and statesman, a revolutionary general who had gone on to conquer Europe, a man of talent who rose from the ranks of the army to become the unchallenged leader of his country after the division and factionalism of the revolutionary decade.

That life began in 1769, on the island of Corsica.

2

Corsican Beginnings

Lapped by the warm waters of the Mediterranean, and with a landscape dominated by rugged mountains and precipitous ravines, Corsica
could appear a secretive place, wild and even hostile, to the eighteenth-century traveller accustomed to the undulating hillsides of
Tuscany or the Roman sites of the Midi or the Rhône valley. Clouds
often obscured the mountain tops, and the rich scrubland vegetation
of the interior provided natural cover for guerrillas and partisans, to
say nothing of brigands and outlaws. The island, indeed, already
enjoyed a somewhat lurid reputation for its fiery individualism, its
lack of governability, and the people's propensity to insurrection and
rebellion. These were not just political affairs: violence between individuals, families and communities was endemic in eighteenth-century
Corsican society – to which the persistently high murder rates bear
witness – and vendetta and banditry had already become central to
the popular image of the island.

In the early nineteenth century this image would be popularised
in romantic literature, with French writers from Maupassant to
Mérimée taking pleasure in describing the place of family honour
in daily life in what they termed 'the land of the vendetta'.[1] Court
records confirm this image. The murder rate on the island was

regularly four or five times that of departments in metropolitan France, and comparable only with those other heartlands of Mediterranean honour, Sicily and Sardinia. Long into the nineteenth century, Corsican society remained steeped in a tradition of blood vengeance which lingered, in defiance of all French attempts to punish honour killings and eradicate the culture of the vendetta. The central place of family honour was inscribed in proverbs and folklore; and the only way to repair dishonour, and wipe away the shame which it brought on the family, was to 'wash it away by blood'.[2] It would take many decades to undermine values that were a central plank of Corsican culture. Indeed, Stephen Wilson suggests that France's early attempts to control family feuding by introducing laws and state controls into the established system of blood vengeance only served to exacerbate violence, at least until policing and administration became sufficiently respected to replace the social controls imposed by family and clan loyalty.[3]

During its turbulent history, Corsica had been seized and annexed by successive states and empires, belonging at one time or another to the Etruscans, the Carthaginians, the Byzantines, the Saracens, and the Papacy. Yet none of these invaders had succeeded in imposing on Corsica any enduring tradition of administration, policing or justice; and since the middle of the sixteenth century their place had been taken by the republican city-state of Genoa on the west coast of Italy, which, after long years of strife, did manage to impose some semblance of order on the population in 1551. But it remained more of a semblance than a reality. Foreign government had never been easily accepted by the islanders. Corsica remained torn by faction-fighting and clan rivalries, a land of priests and warlords whose struggles were, by the eighteenth century, tinged by more than a suggestion of ideology in the form of Corsican nationalism. This was a place where it would never be easy to establish peace or achieve consensus, and with its strategic value clear to all its larger neighbours, it was never likely that they would leave the islanders to their own devices. Long before 1789 Corsica was an ideological battle-ground for more powerful neighbours; indeed, just as the 'Eastern Question' would engage the European powers in the nineteenth century, there was a 'Corsican Question' throughout much of the eighteenth: a question that would resurface every time the major European powers found themselves at war.[4]

Since at least the middle of the sixteenth century France had, unsurprisingly, been concerned to control Corsica. Indeed, with the long series of dynastic and colonial wars that characterised eighteenth-century Europe, it was perhaps inevitable that the island should once again become a pawn in relations between the great powers. Corsica was situated too close to the French coast and offered too good a vantage point across the western Mediterranean for French governments to leave it in the hands of potential rivals. Britain, in particular, was suspected of looking for further bridgeheads and naval bases in the Mediterranean and, as France's most powerful commercial and colonial rival, would have been a threatening presence so close to France's southern flank. Under the circumstances, Genoese ownership might almost have seemed to offer an acceptable solution in that it did not pose a threat to the French, yet usefully filled a potential power vacuum. Britain, in turn, viewed France's interest in Corsica as deeply sinister, proof of designs in Versailles to build up French naval dominance in the Mediterranean, and hence to attack Britain's position in India.

Conflict simmered just below the surface. In 1731 English ships arrived carrying supplies for Corsican rebels; in 1738 London reacted swiftly when there were signs that the French might be preparing to invade the island; and in 1755, on the eve of the Seven Years War, Corsica again figured high in Great Power diplomacy. In response to an English attack on the French fleet, the French Marshal de Noailles sent advice to the French king that he must hit back strongly, attacking British shipping and fortifying Dunkirk and the colonies. Noailles added that it was vitally necessary to secure the Mediterranean, 'to take early measures in order that the English do not seize Corsica', which the French, with an eye to the Levant and to India, rightly saw as a pawn in a wider Anglo-French imperial struggle.[5]

Genoa did not have sufficient military authority to offer a sure defence of the island, and when the Genoese went on to become embroiled in European warfare Corsica was left to the mercy of others. Besides, Genoese rule did not go unopposed among the Corsicans themselves. Administration and justice were poorly enforced, policing was primitive, and the island was often left prey to warring factions. The threat of violence and rebellion was never far away. In 1729 the Corsicans had risen in revolt against the Genoese – a revolt that had matured into a full-blown, if unsuccessful, revolution – and years of warring and factionalism had followed until 1755, when both France and Genoa were distracted by the wider conflict of the Seven Years War. It was then that the Corsicans seized their independence by armed struggle. This was, quite naturally, a campaign waged not by modern, disciplined armies, but by armed bands, village guerrillas, brigands and smugglers turned freedom-fighters in support of a traditional warlord. Yet in Corsican history as it would be written and celebrated by the islanders, the struggle assumed the guise of a national awakening, embodied in the person of Corsica's great national hero, Pascal Paoli. For the next thirteen years, until 1768, the Corsicans would have their own government, independent and liberal if somewhat paternalistic, under Paoli's leadership. The guerrilla leader was rapidly transformed into a statesman and constitutionalist.

Paoli became lionised by his fellow Corsicans. They admired his military prowess as well as his gifts as a lawgiver, his courage in fighting both Genoese and French, and his role in establishing Corsica as an autonomous republic. He was seen, too, as a thinker and philosopher of European standing, who had mastered and adapted the key texts of the French Enlightenment.[6] Corsicans were fascinated by the legend of one of their own who had risen to become the toast of the enlightened world, a man who had made Corsica a state and its people a nation; who had drafted a constitution that had attracted the admiration of Rousseau, and who had won plaudits from men of letters and from enlightened despots from across Europe. Frederick of Prussia, who was counted among Paoli's more enthusiastic admirers, praised his work as a lawgiver and honoured him with the gift of a sword. Paoli was routinely described as having steeped himself in the democratic traditions of the Ancient World and as being a natural successor to the leaders of classical Athens and Sparta. His image entered popular culture, too: he was depicted in over a hundred and sixty paintings and etchings, always with his faithful dog at his side to signify his unquestioned status as a man of the people.[7] And with Paoli's image, that of Corsica also enjoyed a new vogue. For eighteenth-century Europeans, Corsicans were not only wild shepherds given to feuding and clan warfare, but also the kind of primitive savages who were so admired in salon society, whether in the Alps or the Apennines, in Ireland or the Scottish Highlands. They were characterised also by a strongly republican and constitutional tradition that marked them out as one of the most progressive countries in Europe.

Paoli enjoyed a particular cult following in Britain. No doubt this was partly because he was an Anglophile and an impediment to French expansionist ambitions; but partly also because of his close friendship with the biographer of Samuel Johnson, James Boswell. Boswell spent three years on the island during the 1760s, during which he developed an affection for and understanding of the Corsican people, and his *Journal of a Tour to Corsica*, which he published on his return, captured the mood of the moment for travel literature and for a taste of the wild and exotic. The *Journal* was an instant best-seller in Britain, going through three editions in 1768 and 1769 alone; there were also three Irish editions of the book, and translations followed in German, Italian, Dutch and, despite opposition from Versailles, French. Boswell did nothing to hide his love of Corsica or his admiration for the spirit of sturdy independence which, he made clear, was personified by Paoli. The book excited the imagination of a European readership that was more and more attracted to the ideal of the romantic hero. It ensured that Pascal Paoli became a household name across Great Britain and much of Western Europe, and his Corsica a beacon of hope and freedom in a world still dominated by power struggles and dynastic ambitions. In a period marked by revolution in the city-state of Geneva and violent colonial resistance in America, it made the cause of Paoli and Corsica synonymous with the desire of men everywhere for the pursuit of liberty and independence.

Corsica, in other words, had established its place in European consciousness and in the European imagination – a place it owed in part to the Enlightenment and in part to the spirit of romanticism which wallowed in its rugged landscape and tales of feuding and banditry. But independence proved short-lived; France found it impossible to stand by and allow such a strategic island to rally foreign support and become the plaything of European diplomacy. In 1769 thirty thousand French troops invaded Corsica to suppress the independence movement, winning a decisive battle over Paoli's army at Ponte Nuovo and annexing Corsica to France. Corsican nationalists were dismayed at the demise of the independence project, lamenting the death of Paoli's regime as the end of a democratic republican idyll. But with the French regime established in Bastia and Paoli himself forced into exile, the patriotic movement was effectively dead, abandoned to its romantic dreams and poetic nostalgia. The rest of Europe had not intervened to help, as some had idealistically hoped; from this point on Corsica would remain a part of metropolitan France, with no real prospect of regaining its independent status.

Not all Corsicans, however, viewed the annexation in a spirit of negativity, since for some it spelt access to the cultural and career opportunities which metropolitan France could offer, including postings in the army and service in the state administration. To take advantage of these it was, of course, necessary to be of noble stock, just as it was for the French themselves; for Corsica followed France in being a society stratified by legally defined estates that were accorded greater or lesser levels of privilege. The principal privileges were accorded to the nobility, who could not be taxed and who enjoyed a monopoly of offices in the army and the royal service.

As in France, nobility did not have to be justified on grounds of merit or utility; it was self-evident to those who possessed it, and passed on down the generations. In William Doyle's words, it was 'a quality inherent in persons and their progeny, and inalienable except in clearly defined circumstances of forfeiture'. It was, he continues, 'a genetic trait inherited at birth, and extinguished only with life itself'.[8] Nowhere was this trait more consistently defended than in the officer corps of the army. In 1781, in an attempt to limit entry to officer rank to scions of old military families, these restrictions were further tightened, allowing access to the officer class only to those with four noble grandparents. France clearly offered opportunities, but these were reserved for an elite few within Corsican society, and for those who were prepared to trade their Corsican patriotism for a new metropolitan identity, a political price which bitterly divided the population and which many saw as unacceptable. And not all were. The cause of national independence was not confined to romantics and intellectuals; indeed, for many Corsicans, their status as a nation had been a matter of pride and honour, whose loss they continued to resent after the French annexation.

Men from all social backgrounds, including from some of the most prominent families on the island, were to be found among Paoli's supporters. Among them was Napoleon's father, Carlo Bonaparte, a lawyer in Ajaccio and a man of reasonably comfortable means, who had been one of Paoli's closest confidants at Corte during the independence years. He had never doubted his Corsican roots or denied his strong cultural links with Italy, and had counted himself as a Corsican nationalist. He spelt his family name in the Italian manner, 'Buonaparte', as his son would continue to do throughout his adolescence, only amending it to a more characteristically French spelling in 1796.[9] But like many others, Carlo had not followed Paoli into exile; he had preferred to stay on in Corsica, testing the political mood and attempting to further his legal career under French rule. He was not prepared to put a political cause above the material interests of his family, interests to which he devoted himself with commendable single-mindedness.

The Bonapartes belonged to one of the oldest established families of Ajaccio, one that had produced a long line of lawyers and public office-holders in the city, and whose 'nobility' had been recognised since the middle of the sixteenth century – at least in terms that commanded respect on the island. It is indicative of the ambiguous status of Corsican nobility that it was only imprecisely defined in law and difficult for outsiders to interpret. After annexation, the France of Louis XV had been forced to face up to this problem, and insisted that those Corsicans wishing to claim privileged status must prove their claims and produce documentation that would satisfy French officials. Carlo had little difficulty in doing so; he was an established notable on the island, and recognised as such in Genoa and beyond. In 1768 he obtained from the Archbishop of Pisa the right to use the title 'nobleman' and was declared a 'patrician of Florence'.[10] And in 1771 his noble status was officially recognised by the upper council of Corsica, which allowed him to enjoy a noble's privileges and to be elected to the Estates of Corsica[11] as a deputy for the nobility of Ajaccio.

This sounded grand, of course, but there is considerable doubt about what it meant in practice. Corsican definitions of nobility were not comparable to the French, and the Bonaparte family had neither the credentials, nor yet the resources, that would allow them to be recognised as nobles on the mainland. They belonged to an educated elite founded in judicial and military office in a society where such distinctions, combined with a degree of material comfort, were enough to define nobility. But they were not wealthy, certainly not to the degree that French high society would demand: Carlo was paid a salary of nine hundred *livres* a year as assessor for the royal jurisdiction of Ajaccio.[12] And the family certainly did not 'live nobly' according to the criteria demanded of the nobility in France. In reality, at various moments they fell deeply into debt, and Carlo expended a great deal of effort in petitioning the French authorities for grants and subsidies, most particularly in order to give his sons a respectable French education.

With a large family to support, and concerned to maintain appearances and mix in the right social circles, Carlo Bonaparte flagrantly lived beyond his means.[13] Though he was not the irresponsible spendthrift that some have made him out to be – family legend had it that to celebrate his doctorate he threw a party that cost nearly twice his annual income[14] – by the time of his untimely death from stomach cancer in 1785, at the age of only thirty-eight, he left his family drained of resources and dependent on the support of others. Late in his life, Napoleon would himself join his father's critics when he noted disapprovingly that Carlo had gone off on too many costly trips to Paris which further damaged the family's somewhat precarious finances.[15]

This was the world into which the young Napoleon Bonaparte was born in 1769, in Ajaccio, one of only two or three towns of any size on the island. If we believe what he himself would later say about his Corsican upbringing, there is little reason to doubt that his early years were happy ones. His childhood was blessed by a natural playground in the Corsican landscape, and he was surrounded by a large and supportive extended family to which he later declared himself devoted. His mother was Letizia Ramolino, a woman of great conviction who would be one of the defining influences of his childhood, and a source of support and strength in the family that would be all the more necessary after the early death of his father. On Saint Helena his biographer Las Cases would claim that the young Napoleon learned from her everything he would ever know about pride and fortitude, and Napoleon continued to acknowledge throughout his life his debt to the qualities shown by 'Madame Mère'. She was by all accounts a forceful woman, determined and passionate, and she instilled many of these qualities into her children. Levels of infant mortality in the eighteenth century remained high throughout the Mediterranean world: of Carlo and Letizia's thirteen children, only eight survived childbirth.

Napoleon was the second child in the family, though two elder children had already died in infancy and the next two children (both girls), born in 1771 and 1773, did not live more than a few months. The other survivors were his older brother Joseph, born a year before him in 1768; three younger brothers, Lucien, Louis and Jérôme; and three sisters, Elisa, Pauline and Caroline. Of the younger children, Lucien was born in 1775, Elisa in 1777, and Louis the following year; the others did not arrive until the next decade, with Jérôme, the youngest, not born until 1784.[16] The difference in their ages was such that the young Napoleon spent the greater part of childhood with Joseph, to whom he felt the greatest lingering loyalty; by the time the younger children were born he had already left Corsica for schooling in France. Family ties would prove strong, however, as was traditional in Corsican society, and once in power Napoleon would not forget the loyalty he owed to his family. He was concerned to maintain his sisters in style and comfort, while all four of his brothers would be promoted to duchies or kingdoms across Europe during the years of the First Empire.

The Bonaparte family, as we have seen, enjoyed considerable prestige in Corsica, partly through Carlo's role in public life and his friendship with Paoli. His social ambition was not without a suspicion of political opportunism, and after the annexation it would be among the French, not the Corsican nobility, that he sought to establish the reputation of his family. By 1779 he had committed himself politically to France, dropping the Italian 'Carlo Buonaparte' in favour of the aristocratic French 'Charles de Bonaparte', in the hope that his claims to nobility would be recognised in metropolitan France as well as on the island. He did not hesitate to seek out powerful French patrons to further his ambitions, the most notable of whom was the Comte de Marbeuf, the French military governor of Corsica, whose brutal repression of any vestige of rebellion against French rule in 1769 left a long legacy of bitterness and anti-French sentiment on the island.

From 1770, Marbeuf and Napoleon's father appear to have become friends and political allies, the governor recognising in Carlo the kind of Corsican nobleman who might be ripe for integration into the French nobility. It is clear that Marbeuf made generous gifts to Carlo and his family; that he visited their home in Ajaccio; and that he was a particular admirer of his young wife. Indeed, there were strong rumours that he had an affair with Letizia, who was nearly forty years his junior, and in whose presence he was noted taking the air, playing card games, and attending social gatherings, among them receptions at the governor's house in Corte.[17] The inevitable gossip followed.

Marbeuf would continue to take an interest in the family's education after Carlo's death; indeed, it was his intervention that finally provided Napoleon with the royal bursary that would take him to the cadet school at Brienne, near Troyes, where his military career could be said to have begun. But that still lay in the future. Carlo sorely needed Marbeuf's patronage, since his family's prestige would not in itself have opened doors for him in France. His relative prominence in the closed society of Ajaccio counted for little outside Corsica. It would have been insufficient, for instance, to get his son a place in the royal administrative service or entry to officer rank in the infantry or the cavalry – a social disadvantage of which the future Emperor was only too well aware. For this reason Carlo directed Napoleon towards the artillery, since this was the one branch of the military where a firm mastery of mathematics and engineering was indispensable, and where educational attainment could compensate for a lack of legal privilege or noble status.

Officer rank in the artillery was a career to which men of bourgeois backgrounds might legitimately aspire, even before 1789, always provided that their ambition was backed by real ability. To take one distinguished example, Lazare Carnot, the future revolutionary general and Minister of War, was a prize-winning mathematician in provincial Dijon who succeeded in making a solid career in the artillery of Louis XVI, gaining successive promotions but still failing to rise to the very top, something that he himself attributed to his status as a commoner. But at least Carnot could enjoy a career as an artillery officer at a time when he could not even have imagined being received into an infantry or a cavalry regiment. In the event, he had to wait till 1789 and the legal abolition of privilege under the early Revolution before his career really took off.[18]

It was in the artillery and in the service of France that Carlo Bonaparte sought a career for his second son. To this end the youth had to be given a good French education, which his father saw as far superior to anything that was available in Corsica itself at that time. And so in 1778, still less than ten years old, young Napoleon set sail for the mainland – 'the continent', as it was referred to in Corsica – accompanied by his father and his brother Joseph. For Carlo the mission was part political, part financial. As a deputy for the nobility of Ajaccio, he went to Versailles to press Corsican inter-ests on the French government, while at the same time trying to obtain scholarships to cover the cost of his sons' education in France. Both boys were admitted to the local college in Autun, where Joseph was to start his studies for the priesthood and Napoleon to prepare for entry to military academy. He did not have to stay there for long. Within three months his scholarship application was successful, and the brothers were parted. Joseph stayed on at Autun in the care of the priests, while Napoleon moved to the more prestigious surroundings of the military academy at Brienne – one of the twelve provincial cadet schools established by Saint-Germain in 1776 – to begin his secondary education and work towards a commission in the royal corps of artillery.

The five years he spent at Brienne were to prove critical both for Napoleon's intellectual development and for his sense of identity: a sense of who he was and of where his future loyalties lay. The broad-ranging curriculum included three languages (French, Latin and German), and a number of artistic and cultural subjects that prepared the young students for some of the social demands of the officers' mess (music, dancing and fencing).[19] Napoleon is portrayed to us as having been an enthusiastic student, at least in those subjects that fired his imagination. He enjoyed reading history and geography and excelled in mathematics; his teachers, members of an order of Franciscan friars, were universally complimentary about his work, while several of his contemporaries recalled his commitment to his studies and his voracious appetite for reading.

But the school was not noted for its high academic standards or its outstanding teaching, and Napoleon's education remained limited. The Third Republic schoolbooks that portrayed him alone in the school yard, holding back from the games of his classmates to devour some classical text, may have been exaggerated for educational effect, as schoolmasters tried to persuade their reluctant charges of the crucial importance of their schoolwork;[20] but his studious image did spell out one essential truth. The young Bonaparte had made his way in life and in his military career through hard work as much as through family ties or his father's assiduous social networking. At Brienne there were suggestions that he was something of a loner, a rather sullen and depressive young man who preferred the company of his books to that of his fellows; others claimed that the young Corsican remained taciturn and angry. But these accounts were generally written many years after the event, most often after the fall of the Empire, by which time few commentaries on his formation and personality were neutral or unbiased. Suffice it to say that he survived his school years, performing adequately in most subjects and showing promise in some. And he won the highest accolades from his teachers when, in 1784, he left Brienne and gained entry to the prestigious École Militaire in Paris, at which point he was replaced at the school by his younger brother, Lucien.[21]

The decision to seek a military career in the service of the French crown was in no sense an innocent one. For the Bonaparte family it represented a conscious choice as they prepared their sons for honour and advancement in France. It was a choice that would have momentous consequences for both Joseph and Napoleon; and a decision that would lead them both to assume new identities as Frenchmen, in the process abandoning the cause of Corsican nationalism. There was, of course, an alternative for young men of good Corsican families born around the end of the 1790s, which the Bonaparte brothers could have chosen: they could, as their father had done in his youth, have asserted their Corsican roots and joined Paoli's resistance to France's imperial ambitions. And there is plenty of evidence in Napoleon's own youthful writings that the choice he was making was a difficult and, at times, a painful one; that he remained deeply Corsican in his emotions and his psychology, deeply aware of what distinguished his island from the rest of France. In particular, he remained resentful of the elitism of French society, especially the society he encountered at Brienne, with its sneering contempt for his impulsiveness, his emotionalism, and his fractured French. He felt pangs of homesickness in a France which, to his eyes, never wholly accepted him. His experience was not always easy. It separated him from his family and his childhood friends. It presented him with new challenges but also exposed him to jeers and ridicule, not least on account of his imperfect French and his Mediterranean accent. The sons of the French aristocracy who passed through Brienne were overwhelmingly from the provinces of central and northern France and could be unremitting in their mockery.

Napoleon continued to study the history of Corsica both from exile in France and during his sojourns on the island. He read Boswell's *Journal of a Tour to Corsica* with evident enjoyment – the book had achieved a new popularity in its French translation[22] – and in 1786 he wrote to a bookseller in Geneva, Paul Barde, beseeching him to send him the later volumes of the *Histoire des révolutions de Corse* by Abbé Germanes, adding rather plaintively that 'I would be obliged if you would let me know of any works you have on the island of Corsica or which you would be able to get for me promptly.'[23] He showed a passionate interest in his Corsican roots – indeed, his first known piece of writing, in 1786, was a sketch on the history of Corsica in which he aligned his loyalties firmly with his own people. The Corsicans, he declared, 'had been able, by pursuing all the laws of justice, to shake off the yoke of Genoa, and they can do the same to that of the French'.[24]

The ambivalence in Napoleon's loyalties at this stage of his life is clear, and it is at least plausible that the pain and resentment of these early years were important factors in developing his person-ality and deepening his commitment to his new nation. Not many men get to choose the state they will serve, and they rarely do so with such deliberation, or such consequence, as the future Emperor. Though he never rejected his origins and retained deep affection for both the island and the members of his immediate family, he made no secret of the fact that he now saw his future in France. His ambition to be an army officer, to hold command and seek personal glory, was one that required him to commit himself to his adoptive country. It could not be satisfied in an independent Corsica.

In Paris at the École Militaire Napoleon's education became more technical, more focused, in preparation for a career as an army officer. He was no longer a schoolboy: the students were taught about the science of fortification, and their studies were supple-mented by classes on drill, musketry, and horsemanship. At first sight his results might appear unremarkable. There were two hundred and two candidates in his year from the various military schools in France, of whom one hundred and thirty-six passed the final examination, fourteen of them for the artillery. Fifty-eight were admitted to the rank of second lieutenant – in most officers' eyes the real proof of quality – and Napoleon was among them, classed forty-second in the *promotion*.[25] This was an impressive achievement for a young man who had spent so little time in classes and on the training-ground. Whereas it took most cadets two or three years of study to qualify for a commission, the young Bonaparte passed out at the end of his first year, at the age of only sixteen.[26]

On 10 January 1786, less than eight years after he had first arrived in France, he passed out as a commissioned officer, a second lieutenant in the artillery regiment of La Fère. His first army postings involved fairly routine peacetime work – garrison duties in modest provincial towns like Auxonne and Valence, postings which inevitably brought their share of lethargy and tedium. Nor do his duties there seem to have been particularly exacting, as he was absent from his regiment for lengthy periods. Within months of assuming his post he received permission to return home to Corsica to deal with family matters that had lain unresolved since his father's death. He would stay there for over a year, only returning to his regiment in September 1787. But again his service was of short duration, as he was granted a further six-month leave in December and immediately went back to Corsica.

He would return to the island for a third visit from September 1789 till February 1791, visiting family and immersing himself in writing, and again, for a fourth and final time, from September 1791 to May 1792. During these later visits he took an interest in the political situation in Corsica – he had not yet at this stage of his life lost his youthful passion for Corsica and its history – writing both to Paoli and to the royalist leader, Matteo de Buttafoco, and attempting to gain Paoli's confidence. He took part in the electoral campaign of 1790, and manoeuvred, unsuccessfully, to get his brother Joseph elected to the Legislative Assembly the following year. He took his place in the battalion of the National Guard in Ajaccio, where he was elected lieutenant-colonel and second-in-command. But there, any vestiges of sympathy for Corsican autonomy ceased. His Guard battalion, called out to defend the citizenry of Ajaccio and their property against violent attack, was forced to confront riots in the city, and the memory of his using violence against his own people finally destroyed any lingering bond he may have had with the Corsican people. Of his first six years in the French army he spent nearly four back in Corsica.[27] These years proved a form-ative period in his life and left him disillusioned with Paoli and the nationalist cause, which he increasingly dismissed as romantically unrealistic in its ambitions. They cemented the earlier decision by his family to throw in their lot with France.

Throughout his youth Napoleon's reading reflecting his wider interests in philosophy and political sovereignty – he read and re-read Rousseau during the later 1780s – and most especially in history. In pre-revolutionary France he could not but be affected by the literary and political tastes of the times, and his early writings include short works of political philosophy of a generally radical and enlight-ened persuasion. This outlook distinguished him from most of the young noblemen he encountered at school at Brienne. Whereas they expressed royalist beliefs and obedience to the Catholic Church, the future emperor was already expressing humanist sentiments and anti-clerical prejudices. He savoured the great classical authors like Cicero and Caesar, and enlightened works by Voltaire, Diderot, and the Abbé Raynal, often adding his own responses to their texts and praising the virtues of patriotism. In all these early reflections he showed consistency in arguing the need for a strong state to protect the weak from the exploitation of the rich and powerful, and demonstrated a healthy scepticism of the clergy and their teachings.

In 1817, he would tell Bertrand on Saint Helena that his crisis of faith had come early, when he had listened to a Catholic sermon at school which declared that Cato, Caesar and other great figures of Antiquity were condemned to eternal damnation. He was, he said, no more than eleven years old, but it had left an indelible mark. 'I was scandalised to hear that the most virtuous men of Antiquity would be burned in perpetuity because they did not follow a religion of which they had never heard.'[28] The clergy he held in disdain for their condemnation of the Enlightenment and of men whom he regarded as progressive and patriotic, men whose opinions he respected and cherished. For Napoleon already thought of himself as a writer, and of his early works as contributions to a broader humanist debate. At the age of eighteen he wrote to the fiercely anti-clerical Raynal, whom he regarded as something of a mentor, introducing himself as a young author, a philosopher who needed advice in order to get established. He claimed to share many of Raynal's views and went on to submit one of his more serious youthful works, his *Corsican Letters*, to him for advice and feedback.[29]

Though in later life Napoleon undoubtedly exaggerated the extent of his belief in enlightened ideas, there seems little doubt that he read widely in the philosophy of the day and formulated his own views on public events. In his early writings we find him declaiming against the Church and the iniquities of the clergy, denouncing religion as a force for tyranny whose ideas ran counter to the liberties of the people and obstructed the will of the people, and declaring his belief in, and love for, his *patrie*, whether French or Corsican, with all the passion of the late eighteenth century. He declared that the clergy were independent of the state and destructive of its unity. Moreover, he argued, 'from the fact that Christianity breaks the unity of the state should we not conclude that it has been at the root of the many troubles that have destabilised Christian countries?'[30] These ideas were not uncommon in the eighteenth century, and Bonaparte may not have been the most original of writers – many of his political views seem highly derivative – and the views he expressed were often shared by a large number of the educated youth of his generation. But he was largely consistent in his opinions. He was impatient with the world around him, radical and often angry in his denunciation of the elites and their reluctance to seize the initiative, their tendency to lassitude. He was critical of authority where he thought it had failed, but was no friend to anarchy or disorder. In this he shared the views of many who lost patience with the Bourbon regime.

In one of his best-known tracts, his 'Dissertation on Royal Authority', written in 1788, he repeated Rousseau's view that for a State to enjoy authority it must represent the general will; and, more memorably, he declared that monarchy was, almost of necessity, a flawed system on which to construct the government of a people. 'There are', he declared with a certain flourish, 'very few kings who have not deserved to be overthrown.'[31] Already the young Bonaparte had evolved a confident rhetorical style, born of the rationalism of the Enlightenment and turned against his enemies, a rhetoric that would continue to serve him well in the years ahead.[32]

He had also developed a suspicion of established elites and a scorn for their prudence that led him to praise men of action like Frederick the Great, to identify with the new revolutionary regime after 1789, and to hitch his star to the Jacobin cause. This he would do most explicitly in 1793, in *Souper de Beaucaire,* a play he published about the political friction that had developed in the South, in which he did nothing to conceal his republican sympathies.[33] But it would be rash to go further, or to suggest that he was in any way a committed Jacobin. There is no evidence that he joined any political club, or declared his specific affiliations, during the republican moment of 1792–94.

Already in his writings during the last years of the Old Regime we can see the limitations of his political vision and his impatience with the accepted views of others. Bonaparte was neither a committed republican nor a terribly original thinker, but as an avid reader with a capacity to devour whole libraries – which Annie Jourdan has colourfully described as 'bulimic'[34] – once he had made up his mind on an issue he would defend his opinion with a consistency that at times approached stubbornness. Above all, he showed an early interest in the sorts of issues that would dominate the political agenda during the revolutionary decade: in particular, questions of constitutional rights and the role of government in the pursuit of a fairer society and a universally respected law. To that extent, his early writings are suggestive both of his political ideas and of the restless temperament that lay behind them. But they do not add up to a political manifesto. Many of his youthful outpourings before the Revolution wisely steered away from politics, concentrating instead on the safer world of ancient history and the Classics. Once in the army he continued to write about those things that affected him or where he felt he had expertise – Corsica, of course, but also military regulation and the deployment of the artillery. But it did not go beyond that, and years of absence meant that he was only superficially informed of the nuances of the new political situation.

Now that he was back in France he had to decide how he would align himself with the new politics of the French Revolution.

3

Son of the Revolution

Napoleon's rise owed everything to the French Revolution, to its ideals of liberty and equality, the meritocracy that lay at its roots, and the huge institutional changes that it wrought. Without the events of 1789, France would have retained the restrictive legal order of the Old Regime, with its emphasis on privilege and inheritance, its passion for nobility and hierarchy, and a social order that – while cherishing ideas of honour – excluded commoners from positions in the officer corps of the army or in the royal administration. In pre-revolutionary France, Napoleon's horizons would have been limited and the bounds of his ambition severely curtailed. 1789 therefore was a year of hope, a year when social walls and barriers seemed to fall with a devastating ease that echoed the dramatic surrender of the Bastille before the onslaught of the Paris crowd.

For Napoleon and thousands like him the changes that were being made in the name of the French people opened the door to brilliant careers and rapid social advancement – as Napoleon himself began to realise. He had spent his schooldays in the company of the sons of French aristocrats, who were destined for officer rank in the military, and he encountered the same sorts of men in the army – men whose social values he could not share and whose disdain and snobbery he bitterly resented.[1] There was much about *ancien régime* France for which he had little affection and with which he could not identify. The ideals of the early Revolution were far from being anathema to the young officer.

Napoleon's letters during the summer months of 1789 may talk deprecatingly of looting and pillage by the populace since, as a soldier, he emphasised the importance of keeping order, and thus the need to side with the authorities against popular violence. In the town of Auxonne where his regiment was stationed, rioters had sounded the tocsin from the parish church, attacked public officials and burned the tax registers; moreover, many of the troops sympathised with the rioters, and in August soldiers in Napoleon's regiment mutinied and indulged in an orgy of drunken violence.[2] His main duty, he wrote to his brother Joseph, had been to contain the violence after the rioters had broken down one of the gates of the town, and his general had given him responsibility for haranguing the mutineers, subduing the rebels and safeguarding property in the city.[3] No army officer could condone such indiscipline, and Napoleon did not seek to do so; but he could not entirely conceal his excitement at the implications of what was happening around him. Writing to Joseph from Auxonne in early August, reporting rumours that were circulating amongst the garrison, he announced that 'all over France blood had been spilt'. But, he added, 'almost without exception it was the impure blood of the enemies of Liberty and the Nation, those who had long been getting fat at their expense. We hear that in Brittany five people have been killed and their heads sent to Paris'.[4] The tone of his letter is more one of wonderment than of condemnation, a realisation that the meeting of the Estates-General heralded a new political era and that the events unfolding around him were more than just another banal manifestation of the rebelliousness of the French.

It must be remembered that at this time Napoleon's world still revolved around Corsica, and it was to Corsica that his thoughts immediately turned. There, talk of liberty meant something very different from the new meanings it had acquired in France: it meant the independence and political autonomy of the island, freedom from French control, and the right of the Corsican elites to rule their island in accordance with their own traditions. To many islanders, that liberty had been synonymous with the nationalist rhetoric of Paoli, now living in exile in London, and they saw in the French patriots in 1789 and 1790 men who might help them to achieve their goals. Inevitably, Corsican reaction to events in Versailles and Paris was coloured by Corsicans' own aspirations; for many of them liberty remained inextricably linked to a desire for Corsican independence.

Napoleon, from his army post in France, expressed his hopes for the future freedom of his island in a letter he wrote to Paoli in early June. Clearly his mind was still on Corsica; his dreams were of giving the Corsican people the sort of liberty that was being so widely discussed in metropolitan France. And despite their differences, he did not conceal his hope that Paoli might return from exile to provide the Corsican people with the leadership and inspiration they now lacked. 'General', he wrote, with reference to Corsica's loss of sovereignty in 1768, 'I was born at the moment when our country perished. Thirty thousand Frenchmen thrown up on our shores, drowning the throne of liberty in waves of blood, that was the odious sight that first met my eyes.' When Paoli left

Corsica, wrote Bonaparte, 'all hope of happiness went with you; slavery was the price of our submission; oppressed by the fetters of the soldier, the jurist and the tax collector, our fellow-citizens find themselves despised by those who administer them'. And while the purpose of his letter was modest – to seek Paoli's approval for the history of Corsica which he had written during his periods of leisure from the army – the language in which he expressed himself and the bluntness of his condemnation of French rule implied that, in the new political context provided by the outbreak of the Revolution, he had not lost his youthful faith in the patriot leader.[5] That he still wrote to him may seem surprising in view of Paoli's earlier political career and Napoleon's own decision to throw in his lot with France. It was scarcely the language of a loyal officer in the French army whose commitment to the cause of the French people seemed unquestioning.

By June 1789 that commitment was indeed firm, but he kept his contacts in Corsica, where he appears to have retained political ambitions of his own. As the son of a notable local family, recently returned from the mainland and well connected to the most prominent political factions on the island, Napoleon enjoyed something of a public profile. As mentioned before, since receiving his commission he had spent more time in Corsica, through a series of extended leaves, than he had in France itself.

By September 1789 he was back in Ajaccio, engaged in politics with other members of his family, helping to form a local unit of the National Guard, welcoming Paoli back from exile, and establishing a patriotic club on the model of the popular societies that were beginning to appear across France. Locally, public opinion was volatile, ready to respond to outside challenges and aggravations, and news of developments in France only served as a catalyst for further demands. Popular anger was aroused by high grain prices and the scarcity of bread, as it was everywhere in the French provinces, but the anger also reflected more parochial Corsican concerns and social antagonisms inherited from the *ancien régime*. Corsica used the language of the French Revolution to express itself politically, but its leaders and its political priorities were often specific to the Corsican nation. The young army officer, Napoleon, knew how to appeal to local interests and to interpret the factional politics of the Revolution on the island.

Enthusiasm for more radical politics came with news of the fall of the Bastille and of the Night of 4 August, when members of the privileged orders had excitedly forsworn privilege before a packed session of the National Assembly. The city of Bastia, inspired by the Corsican deputy to the Assembly, Christophe Saliceti, came to be seen as one of the most radicalised cities in provincial France.[6] By returning to the island, Napoleon was able to exercise a political influence that would have been denied him on the mainland. But he was also able to understand the reality of Corsica's politics and the conservative position of many Corsicans. It was this that led him to understand that he faced a choice, and ultimately to break with Paoli. It also led to his first and most polemical political pamphlet in the Corsican context, his *Letter to Matteo Buttafoco* of 1791, in which he made clear his unshakable attachment to France and to French ideas.[7] He castigated Buttafoco for his continued adherence to monarchy and to feudal values: 'Your favourite plan', he wrote accusingly, 'was to share out the island between ten barons. Not content with helping to forge the chains with which your country was restrained, you wanted to go further and subject it to the absurd regime of feudalism!'[8]

In both his rhetoric and his political ideas, the young Bonaparte displayed a passion that was no longer capable of entertaining any hint of compromise; he had become a committed devotee of the Revolution, even a convinced republican, and therefore on the radical wing of revolutionary politics at a time when France was still a constitutional monarchy. Already in June 1790, in Ajaccio, he was driven by his radical convictions to support popular action and participate directly in a popular uprising. This expression of revolutionary enthusiasm could only drive a further wedge between the young army officer and his erstwhile hero, Paoli, whose anti-Parisian posturings were increasingly coming to be identified with the political Right and the rejection of republicanism.[9]

In the early years of the Revolution, during which he continued to enjoy long periods of leave from his regiment, Bonaparte divided his time between France and Corsica, finding inspiration in the ideological and political changes voted in in Paris while pushing forward the revolutionary cause on his native island. Here there were signs of pragmatism to which other members of his family, in particular his brother Lucien, were temperamentally unsuited: a desire to appease opposing factions and accommodate an increasingly intransigent Paoli. But where Napoleon had no intention of compromising was over the complete integration of Corsica into France – a process that was concluded by the decree of 20 January 1790 – and the polity of the French Revolution. Increasingly, he moved away from his previous Corsican patriotism to adopt the new revolutionary model that was emanating from Paris. There was no longer any place for either autonomy or independence for the island, no special statute or devolutionary concession: it was to be a department of France, like any other area of the interior.

The Committee of Division recognised, however, that Corsica did present unique challenges: it had sufficient territory to justify its division into two departments, whereas it had a sparse population that could be encompassed in one. Besides, there were few towns of any size on the island; its economy was underdeveloped, and it was divided down the middle by a chain of mountains. Finally, the National Assembly concluded that Corsica should be a single department, with its administrative centre in Corte, but divided into nine districts in order to take account of its social and economic diversity. Integration into France, it was hoped, would help end the excessive poverty and depopulation that characterised Corsican life, and provide the basis on which to build a programme of economic regeneration.[10] In accepting this logic, Napoleon could not but lose the sympathy of large sections of the Corsican electorate. It meant taking sides with the French against most of the Corsican warlords, foremost among them Paoli himself, now allied to the British in what was becoming an internecine fight between power brokers and bandit leaders.

For Napoleon, it was a dangerous environment in which to operate and an even more dangerous one in which to leave his mother with her tribe of young children, and the Bonaparte family did not emerge unscathed. By the summer of 1793 they found themselves caught in crossfire between the opposing factions, and the family home in Ajaccio was attacked and pillaged. Letizia and her children were warned by a friendly bandit leader that it was time to get out, and they rapidly found themselves reduced to the status of refugees, homeless and penniless and hurriedly leaving the island for the south of France. It was a harrowing moment: the mother and her young family, scurrying through the night to the protection of a French ship, one of several hundred Corsican families forced to flee to the mainland, abandoning all their possessions to be pillaged by Paoli's henchmen. They took refuge in the small town of Saint-Maximin, not far from Toulon, with the help of funds obtained through the good offices of Saliceti.[11] It had been a disturbing and disruptive experience, and though he was not there in person, Napoleon was deeply affected by it. He was hurt and bruised by his rejection from his own people, while the memory of his family – fearful, shivering and reduced to temporary indigence – would continue to haunt him.

In the early period of his career, Napoleon found the desire of the revolutionary authorities to pass sweeping measures to renew the fabric of the nation refreshing and energising. He was a convinced believer in the benefits of meritocracy and applauded the boldness of the revolutionaries in abolishing nobility, selling church lands and reforming a society rooted in privilege. In print, he mocked the corruption of the old order and lambasted the privileged idleness of many members of the nobility; and there was nothing in his actions to suggest that he was disaffected with the revolutionary regime. He did not emigrate; he continued to serve in the army; he took the oath of loyalty to the constitution of 1791.[12] With the passage of time, however, his letters suggest a growing disquiet at the violence and extremism of some elements of the population, in particular the Jacobins and the Paris crowd. In June 1792, in a letter to Joseph, he quoted Lafayette's moderate stance with obvious approval, and sided with the army against the more radical factions in the Assembly. Lafayette had written to the Assembly warning of the extremism of the Jacobin Club, a warning that Napoleon found 'very powerful'. He went on to explain that

'M. de La Fayette, a majority of the officers in the army, all honest men, the ministers, and the department of Paris are on one side; the majority of the Assembly, the Jacobins and the populace are on the other'. The Jacobins, in Napoleon's view, were 'madmen who are lacking in common sense'. They had abused Lafayette and had stirred up the crowd; indeed, they did not hesitate to promote popular violence. Only a day or two before, he noted, an armed crowd seven or eight thousand strong had forced its way into the Tuileries and demanded an audience with the King, forcing him to drink to their cause and to wear a red liberty cap. When he heard of Louis' humiliation, Napoleon wrote that such action was both unconstitutional and dangerous. The crowd was armed with axes and pikes, sticks and guns; and all that the National Guard could do was to stand by to make sure that the King was not harmed. 'It remains very difficult to guess what will become of his authority in such a stormy atmosphere.'[13]

Although he remained a French patriot, seemingly committed to the revolutionary cause, here he wrote with the unease and confusion of a man who felt that he was being overtaken by a stream of events which were changing the political landscape before his eyes.[14] In particular, that image of the crowd – threatening, insulting and volatile – was one that remained with him throughout his life. He might have been a Jacobin in Corsican politics; but back in France he comes across as a moderate republican, a man of order, protective of authority, and with an abiding distrust of popular violence.

He was also, of course, a career officer, with an eye on promotion and a keen concern for his position within the army. Politics, even Corsican politics, remained secondary to military questions, and from 1792 the condition of the army became more pressing with the declaration of war against Austria and Prussia, to be followed the next year by its extension to include Britain and Spain. The French military seemed poorly equipped to take on the rest of the European continent, in large measure because the army which had served the Bourbon monarchy was so ill-suited to the demands placed on it by the revolutionaries. The officers, as we have seen, were all drawn from the nobility and had taken a personal oath of loyalty to the monarch. Would they fight with equal alacrity for the sovereign people – especially after the King was suspended and put on trial and the country turned into a republic in September 1792? The answer quickly became obvious: noble officers resigned their commissions during the first years of the Revolution, many passing discreetly across the Alps or the Pyrenees to spend the rest of the revolutionary decade in political exile. By 1792, a third of army officers had already tendered their resignations, often in response to particular stimuli – the abolition of noble privilege, the ending of seigniorial dues, the institution of constitutional monarchy, or the example set by the King when he fled from Paris in June 1791, only to be intercepted by the National Guard at Varennes.[15]

The morale of the men in the ranks was often not much better. Whole regiments mutinied in 1790 at Nancy, Perpignan and elsewhere, in protest against low pay and poor conditions of service; others again, sent to impose order during crowd troubles and market disturbances, made it clear that their sympathies lay with the people they were supposed to police. If the Revolution was to create an army that would be capable of defeating the finest regiments in Europe, and one that was not wholly incompatible with the values and ideology of the regime, root-and-branch reform was urgently needed.[16] The army of the Bourbons had failed too often in the

European wars of the eighteenth century. Now France would be plunged into a series of conflicts that would see the great powers of Europe join forces against her in a succession of coalitions that would last, almost unabated, for over twenty years; wars so costly and draining of the country's resources that historians have compared them to the Great War of 1914–18 and been tempted to call them 'the first total war'.[17]

War was not imposed on France against the wishes of her leaders; indeed, those who spoke out against it were largely confined to radicals like Maximilien Robespierre, who feared that it would leave the door open to counter-revolution and conspiracy at home. His was a minority voice in late 1791 and the early months of 1792, when many in Paris clamoured for war, seemingly confident that the revolutionary spirit of the French people would make their armies invincible. Or else, like some of the King's ministers, they sought war for tactical reasons, to increase royal authority and deflect attention from failures at home. But the Austrian and Prussian leaders, too, had every reason to welcome a war with France at a moment when the French army was so obviously weakened that victory seemed assured. The first engagements in the summer of 1792 confirmed the worst fears of the French commanders; after their armies capitulated at Longwy and Verdun, the road to Paris lay unprotected for the first time since the seventeenth century. France's frontiers were breached and the Revolution itself was endangered, spreading both rumour and panic in the streets of the capital. The situation was saved, temporarily at least, by dogged French resistance at Thionville and Montmédy in the east, and by the failure of the Duke of Brunswick's Anglo-Prussian army to press home its advantage over a poorly trained French force at Valmy in September. It was not a classic military victory – some nine hundred lives were lost on each side – but the Austrian army scattered, Paris was saved, and Valmy went on to enjoy a special place in French republican mythology.[18]

Though the new army was grafted on to the line army inherited from the old regime, it would prove to be a very different animal, both in the ranks and in the officer cadres. Before 1789 soldiers were recruited for long periods, usually from among the poorest and most rootless members of society; they were pressed into service at fairs and markets, lured by a signing-on bounty, or trawled from poorhouses and prisons. Many were mercenaries from other countries, pressed into the service of the French king. Voltaire was not alone in dismissing the men who fought in Europe's armies as the lowest of the low, the dregs of civil society. But these methods were insufficient to provide either the numbers the new armies required, or men who could be trusted with the mission of defending the Revolution and the nation. From 1791, therefore, the revolutionaries called for volunteers; by 1793 they were demanding mass levies from across the population; and in 1799 they turned to full-blown conscription without even the possibility of buying a substitute to fight in one's place. The professional background and social configuration of the troops changed dramatically, and the army, for a few short years, became predominantly French as the government relied on its own people where, previously, it had bought soldiers from other states. The ideal of the 'nation in arms' was proclaimed, and with it the notion that every citizen had a duty to play his part in the defence of the republic.

For officers, too, change was sudden and tangible. Junior officers were elected by their units, and there was, for the first time, direct promotion from the ranks. Officer rank was no longer restricted to noblemen, but was conferred on the basis of experience in the field and merit. Aristocratic concepts of honour were also revised, and were replaced by concepts of personal internalised honour and by the reputation one established with one's peers.[19] Because of the high turnover of officers – both through heavy casualty rates in battle and as a result of resignations and emigration – promotion could come rapidly and at a very young age. Recognition was there to be won for those with flair and talent, and a new generation of officers, men like Hoche and Moreau, did nothing to conceal their professional ambition or their thirst for glory. They identified strongly with the French Revolution, with French patriotism; they did not hide their republican sympathies; they sought patrons among the country's political elite, and they competed to serve the Nation at the highest level. Prominent among such officers was Napoleon Bonaparte, who came back to France in 1793 to report for duty with the Fourth Artillery regiment, stationed in Nice. There he was fortunate to find as his commanding officer Jean du Teil, whose brother he had known during his early garrison duty at Auxonne. Napoleon quickly got himself noticed, and he was assigned to Avignon to organise ammunition supplies.[20]

The political climate in France was tense in the summer months of 1793, a period dominated by an uncompromising struggle between the two principal republican groups, the Girondins and the Jacobins, which ended in violence and the Jacobin seizure of power. During this period the government found its authority challenged not only by the foreign armies camped along the frontiers but also by dissension in many parts of the French provinces. Already in the spring a Spanish force had broken through in Catalonia and briefly captured the city of Perpignan, while in the north Dumouriez had abandoned his army and gone over to the Austrians.[21] In the Vendée and along the valley of the Loire the countryside had erupted into open warfare, with a counter-revolutionary force declaring itself loyal to Church and King, defying the Revolution's recruitment demands and uniting the greater part of the West against the government. It would take military intervention and ruthless repression to restore law and order to the region. Meanwhile, several of France's largest cities had risen in revolt in the summer against what they saw as oppression from Paris, with Caen and Bordeaux, Marseille and Lyon all taking back their share of national sovereignty and declaring that they no longer felt bound by the decisions of the republican assembly in Paris, the National Convention. It was August before most of these revolts, condemned by the Jacobins as 'federalist' and aimed at destroying the unity of the Republic, could be suppressed, and the retribution that followed was often bloody. There were six hundred executions in Marseille, two thousand in Lyon, as these cities were restored to the authority of the state. Right across the Midi the atmosphere remained highly charged.

Was there a degree of cynicism in Napoleon's professed republicanism and his preparedness to identify with Jacobins like Saliceti, who had shown favour to his family and helped to advance his military career? Were his expressions of political attachments also exercises in opportunism? While it is clear that he remained sympathetic to many of the ideals of the Revolution, it is impossible to dismiss these accusations entirely. He was conscious of the importance of patronage and showed himself skilful in using it. He took care to pay due homage to those in political authority, and such attentions helped bring his name to the notice of the Committee of Public Safety in Paris. And even at this early stage of his career he showed symptoms of that gift for self-publicity that would become so important in the years ahead. It would be wise, therefore, to approach Napoleon's public utterances on politics with a degree of caution – especially the most famous, *Souper de Beaucaire*, the pamphlet which he published within weeks of his return to France. It is in many ways a work of the romantic imagination, a dramatised discussion between the author, a soldier in the army of General Carteaux in the Midi, and three other characters, from Marseille, Nîmes and Montpellier, who had witnessed the political convulsions in the south and lived through the federalist interlude. But in it, he also takes care to show his own political colours by denouncing the extravagant ambitions of the Marseillais in challenging the authority of Paris, and by warning of the consequences that await them if they continue to defy the forces of the republic.

The work is notable for the open exchange of views which it presents, even views favourable to the rebel cities, though inevitably it is the opinion of the soldier and the pragmatic patriotism of Napoleon himself which emerges triumphant. He makes it all sound so easy. 'Shake off the yoke of the small number of rascals who are leading you into counter-revolution', he advises his new friend from Marseille; 're-establish your legal authorities; accept the Constitution; give the deputies back their freedom, so that they may go up to Paris to intercede on your behalf; you have been misled, and it is not new that the people should be misled by a small number of conspirators; since the beginning of time the ignorance and compliance of the masses have been at the root of most civil wars'.[22] It may sound like common sense; but it was also extremely partisan advice, and exactly what Paris and the Jacobins wanted to hear said.

Carteaux succeeded in retaking Marseille on 24 August, and terror and mass executions followed. The lesson was clearly spelt out that the government would tolerate no further dissent from provincial republicans, and that insurrection would be met with severe punishment. The capitulation of Marseille left only one major city in the Midi in the hands of the rebels: Toulon, the main Mediterranean naval port, where the federalist authorities sought to ensure their safety by handing over the dockyard and the port installations to the British and Spanish fleets, a move which was seen by Paris as a craven act of treachery that must be defeated. Its potential to inflict catastrophic damage on the French navy cannot be doubted. When the Royal Navy and Admiral Hood reached Toulon they found anchored in the *Grande Rade*, equipped and ready to sail, a French fleet of seventeen ships of the line, five frigates and eleven corvettes. Refitting in the New Basin were a further four ships of the line and a frigate; while in the Old Basin, in various states of repair, were eight more ships of the line, five frigates and two corvettes. Hood was presented with the opportunity to knock out at a stroke a major part of French naval strength, though in the event the British and their Spanish allies left the job only half completed. Many of the ships surrendered at Toulon were repaired and would sail again under the French flag in later campaigns,[23] but the French were in no position to foresee this outcome, and they responded with a predictable show of force. In the later summer of 1793 Carteaux's army, around ten thousand strong, was directed against Toulon and its rebel authorities.

The expedition against Toulon presented Napoleon, newly promoted to the rank of captain, with his first major opportunity to impress his superiors in the heat of battle. Toulon, protected by a series of detached forts, was one of the strongest defensive positions in Europe, yet Carteaux had only a weakened army and woefully inadequate artillery. In all, he had a few field guns, two twenty-four-pounders, two sixteen-pounders and a few mortars; he had expected to attack by bombarding the Allied fleet, but that proved to be beyond the range of his guns, and the French plans seemed highly flawed. Carteaux was a brave and experienced officer, but he was no expert in the use of artillery, and he failed to give his gunners sufficient resources. This was Napoleon's opportunity. He interceded with the deputies-on-mission from the Convention, explaining his tactical ideas and stressing the advantage of surprise and the value of artillery, given the topography of Toulon. And though many in the military remained dubious about these tactics, the deputies gave him their support, and Napoleon was rewarded with the post of 'commandant of the artillery of the army before Toulon', an appointment that he interpreted as giving him absolute autonomy over the artillery and its deployment.

At his command, guns and supplies were quickly shipped in from across Provence, gunners were taught to man them, and young officers learned to take command. His plan was to take the English positions and gain control over the roads without resorting to a siege; he preferred to take advantage of the manoeuvrability of his light artillery and to direct maximum fire at the English redoubt to dislodge them from their position of strength on the hilltop of Le Caire.[24] Executing this plan was necessarily risky and involved great feats of bravery, but on the night of 16 December the British were finally dislodged from their fort, and on the following day the Republicans entered Toulon. Philip Dwyer is right to note that in the dispatches from the city the principal credit is given to the commanding officers, most notably Dugommier, the new commander-in-chief.[25] But the victory was Napoleon's, and his talent came to the notice both of his army superiors and his political masters. He was rewarded with promotion to the rank of brigadier-general (*général de brigade*).

The Revolution demanded not only talent from its officers, but also political loyalty. The political leadership had had too many painful experiences with officers who proved untrustworthy, socially conservative, or whose loyalty was to the king or to the Catholic Church before it was to the French people. There is little reason to doubt that Napoleon's reputation as a good revolutionary, even in some circles as a Jacobin, helped secure his rapid rise. Toulon had been a highly political campaign, the siege of a French city in revolt, an act in a civil war which pitted Frenchman against Frenchman and where political disaffection could easily lead to defection or treason. That, too, had its dangers. In the south-east Napoleon relied on his standing with – and, to a degree, his cultivation of – several key Jacobins, among them deputies-on-mission from Paris, whose reputations would be scarred by the brutality of the repressive measures unleashed against Toulon once the city surrendered. At the height of the Terror it was clearly useful to have men like Fréron and Saliceti, Paul Barras and Augustin Robespierre, among his cheerleaders and protectors. But when the Jacobins were in their turn toppled by a palace revolution in the Convention on the Ninth of Thermidor (27 July 1794), the political landscape was transformed. The younger Robespierre was sent to the guillotine with his brother on the following day; while Barras and Fréron, after successfully conspiring against Robespierre, scurried to realign with the anti-Jacobin cause.

Napoleon found his political position dangerously exposed, and his friendship with Augustin Robespierre a particular source of embarrassment. For a few days his life may even have been in danger: his arrest was ordered on a charge of treason, and he spent a fortnight under house arrest. He expressed his outrage in a letter to deputies-on-mission to the area, protesting that the charge that hung over him was an attack on his honour and reputation. 'Declaring a patriot suspect', he declared, 'robs him of his most precious attributes, public confidence and esteem'.[26] But the moment of crisis passed, thanks once again to the intervention of Saliceti and to the praise heaped on him by his army commander. Napoleon could point to the sacrifices he had made for the Revolution and the support he had provided in pursuit of its goals. He could also show that his contribution to the fall of Toulon had been a purely military one, and that he had not taken part in the often gratuitous cruelty that followed. In the event he was exonerated and did not have to stand trial.[27]

The revolution of the Ninth of Thermidor did not immediately abolish the 1793 constitution; nor yet did it undermine the republican character of the regime. What it did do was to purge the Convention of those deputies most closely identified with the politics of the Terror and to rid France of the exceptional laws and jurisdictions that had defined it. In fact, the regime remained strongly republican, intolerant of the aristocracy and the clergy, and profoundly committed to the ideal of a secular state. Over sixty of Maximilien Robespierre's closest allies were purged – purging was a favoured ploy, the figurative cleansing of the body politic – yet some of the men who had served under the Jacobins were called back to office, while more moderate republicans, among them many who had sympathised with the Girondins, resumed political life. On the other hand, the new regime remained suspicious of those whom it adjudged to be tainted with terrorism, or with violence that had become closely associated in their eyes with Jacobin extremism. Their aim was to end the spiral of revolution, to draw up a new and lasting constitution, end the state of emergency, and create a republican stability which so far had eluded French lawmakers.[28]

The army, because of the danger it posed, was subjected to close surveillance, and officers deemed too close to Robespierre were investigated or stood down, especially those radical *sans-culottes* who had been promoted in 1793 and 1794. The Thermidorians looked instead to appoint men of proven military talent, but also men on whom they could depend, who would not question their orders and could be trusted to fight in the name of the Republic. This would become even more pressing in the months that followed when the regime was threatened by military plots – from the Right as much as from the Left – and the army was exposed to the blandishments of royalists and counter-revolutionaries. It was imperative that the officer class should remain loyal to republican institutions at a time of increasing political turbulence within France, when the revolt in the Vendée had not yet been extinguished and popular violence threatened in Paris.

After his success in Toulon, Napoleon might have hoped to profit from the new order, but his career was anything but assured. He dreamed of spreading revolutionary war across Italy and encouraging the people of Genoa to throw off the yoke of the House of Savoy. But this was not the government's aim, and Lazare Carnot assigned the Italian campaign to older, less headstrong generals, leaving Napoleon out in the cold, his future uncertain. The new

Minister of War, Aubry, showed particular vigilance in removing those with known Jacobin sympathies, and despite interventions on his behalf, Napoleon was denied the command he felt to be his due. And when he did receive an assignment – to command an infantry brigade in the civil war in the Vendée – he made no effort to hide his disappointment, protesting about the unsuitability of the posting and even engaging in a bitter altercation with Aubry which he must have known he could not win. There was little glory to be gained from the campaign in the Vendée, essentially by this stage a final clearing-up operation against the last of the rebels, and Napoleon felt little enthusiasm for the kind of work it entailed. He did not go to the West, but took refuge behind permissions and sick notes, staying on in Paris into the summer of 1795 with such fellow officers as Junot and Marmont, and enjoying the artistic and social life – theatre and opera, salons and café society – that the city offered. His enjoyment was not, however, unqualified. What he really aspired to was military action and a command in Italy.

He was rescued from this enforced idleness, and from facing a possible charge of insubordination, by the intercession of friends and political allies who were to play an increasingly important part in his career. The most significant of these was Paul Barras who, like himself, had started out as an officer-cadet in the royal army of the 1780s, before resigning in favour of marriage and the rather spendthrift lifestyle of a young nobleman. With the advent of the Revolution, Barras had thrown himself into radical politics, getting himself elected to the Convention and voting for the King's death in 1792. In the following year he was in Toulon, as a Jacobin deputy-on-mission, when he encountered Bonaparte, was impressed by his courage and temperament, and promoted him to captain. The two men remained on good terms after Barras was recalled to Paris, where he plotted against Robespierre and helped to overthrow him, taking power himself as one of the five Directors in 1795. He would prove a valuable and powerful ally: he trusted Napoleon and helped to advance his career.[29]

In August, Barras' intervention led to Napoleon's appointment to the new Topographical Bureau of the army under General Clarke. This was a group that had responsibility for strategic planning and which reported directly to the Committee of Public Safety. In Napoleon's eyes this was no more than a stop-gap appointment, but at least it might serve as a stepping stone to something better, and it diverted him, at least momentarily, from thoughts of resigning his commission. His anger and depression returned, however, less than a month later when he found that his name was omitted from the official army list of generals.[30] These were nervous and deeply unsatisfying months in Napoleon's military career, months when his morale was at its lowest ebb and when he seems to have contemplated suicide.[31]

Yet by the end of 1794 his prospects, and with them his temperament, had much improved and, thanks again to his political protector Barras, his career seemed to be back on track. The origins of his changed fortunes were once again political, as the Convention was faced with a popular uprising in Paris in Vendémiaire (5 October), the latest in a series of popular *journées*, days of rioting and violence that marked the history of the capital throughout the Revolution. These *journées* generally took their name from the month in which they occurred, as expressed in the new revolutionary calendar which the Republic had introduced in 1793 in a bid to rationalise the division of time. Not only was the new calendar stripped of all religious context; it also purported to be more logical and scientific, with the year divided into twelve months of thirty days, and each month subdivided into three ten-day units, or *décades*. Sundays and Saints' days were abolished, and Frenchmen were now given one day off in ten, on the *décadi*, which proved scant compensation. But it was not purely a propagandistic daily reminder to the population that they were living in revolutionary times. The Jacobin Gilbert Romme, who had proposed it to the Convention, took pains to tie the calendar to the astronomical year; each year would begin on 22 September, which had both natural and ideological significance as the date of the autumn equinox as well as the start of the First Republic. Interestingly, the calendar outlasted the Republic and remained in use until 1806 when, persuaded that French commerce was suffering from time differences across Europe, Napoleon returned to the same Gregorian calendar which the Revolution had abandoned.[32]

The disturbances in Vendémiaire had their roots, as was so often the case, in the government's failure to control the economy, leading to uncontrollable inflation and high bread prices. Seven of the city's sections – the forty-eight local districts into which Paris was divided in 1790 and which now controlled local political assemblies and units of the National Guard – rose in arms against the government. The difference this time was that the crowd was manipulated by the royalist Right, not the Jacobin Left as at the height of the Terror, so that the Republic once again was in peril. To make matters worse, the National Guard seemed likely to join the rebels, thus increasing levels of violence and leaving shops and homes unprotected.

Paul Barras had responsibility for public order in the capital and it was he who ordered the regular army to suppress the insurrection; he turned for support to former Jacobins and convinced republicans of the kind who had been largely excluded after the Ninth of Thermidor. Napoleon fell into that category; besides, Barras knew him, and admired him for his tactics in Toulon. Napoleon took full advantage of the opportunity he was given, taking care to demonstrate his value to the government. He responded efficiently and effectively, showing at Vendémiaire both the tactical ability to curb civil disorder and a clinical concern to maintain the peace, even at considerable cost in human life. To the Thermidorian administration he provided evidence that he was a man who would not flinch before unpleasant or sensitive missions: several hundred Parisians died in the fighting, and Napoleon would long be identified in the capital as 'Général Vendémiaire'. It was the first time the Revolution had used the army to quell popular agitation in Paris, and its impact was both immediate and dramatic. The days of the revolutionary crowds, as George Rudé reminds us, were 'over for many a year'.[33] The political landscape in the capital was permanently altered by Napoleon's 'whiff of grapeshot', since the army would remain in occupation throughout the years of the Directory which followed. As for Napoleon, he had proved himself the man of the moment and in a single day reconstituted his failing military career.

Napoleon's months in Paris were significant, too, in his personal life: during this period we learn far more about his sentimental relations with women than is known of his earlier career. It is true that he had written some rather ponderous prose about the nature of love, rather in the same style as his early enlightened writings. But at this time we know that he became romantically involved with Désirée Clary, the sixteen-year-old daughter of a soap-merchant, whom he had met in Marseille. His correspondence with her reveals a sensitive romantic spirit that had previously remained largely concealed. In his letters there is a pleading quality which suggests that he was pining for her company and seeking reassurances of her love and fidelity; though there is much, too, that seems rather stereotyped and drawn from the world of literary conceit. In April the pair apparently became betrothed, though their relationship was never straightforward, and was complicated, not least in her father's eyes, when he was faced with a second proposal of marriage linking the two families, between Désirée's older sister Julie and Napoleon's brother Joseph.[34] In the event Napoleon's fondness for Désirée did not result in marriage, though he would continue to visit her in Marseille, whereas Joseph and Julie were duly married in August 1794. Napoleon seems not to have been too upset by the outcome. Marseille was a long way from Paris, where, during his months of leisure, his social horizons were being considerably widened.

It was in Paris that he was inducted into metropolitan high society and a world of clubs and salons, and of salon hostesses such as the actress Thérésia Cabarrus. She, by then, was Madame Tallien, who, as the wife of a leading Thermidorian politician, was well connected to the cream of France's political leadership. It was a time of extravagant balls and parties, glamorous dresses and exaggerated coiffures; a time when Parisian society danced at the whim of the *jeunesse dorée* and swooned before the *merveilleuses*. Napoleon in later life would denounce the sumptuous fashions and the extravagant expenditure, as well as the social elitism and disdain for ordinary people, that were characteristic of these years. He admitted to friends that he had often felt ill-at-ease in high society and that he at times felt shunned by a world where his rough Corsican accent and occasionally clumsy manner with women had no place. In comparison with others, he believed, he was unlucky in love.

Perhaps he was. But he did make friends in Paris, and even female conquests. The most spectacular of these was a young woman of Creole stock, Rose de Beauharnais, six years his senior and now a widow, whose husband Alexandre, a former president of the National Assembly and of the Paris Jacobins, had been guillotined the previous year for allegedly allowing Mainz to fall to the enemy. Rose – born Marie-Joseph-Rose de Tascher de La Pagerie, on a sugar plantation in the commune of Trois-Ilets in Martinique – belonged to the minor nobility of the island; her father, Joseph-Gaspard de Tascher, had come to Martinique from the Perche.[35] Rose, too, might be thought vulnerable to arrest as a former noble: indeed, she had spent some time in prison at the height of the Terror, and on being released she seems to have thrown herself into a giddy round of balls and parties. Napoleon saw her frequently at Madame Tallien's house and at Barras's home; he quickly fell for her beauty and her noble bearing, the aura of balanced calm which he so much admired. In contrast, Désirée Clary, rather cruelly perhaps, would find herself rejected, left to fall by the wayside. Rose was now the sole object of Napoleon's desire, the person on whom he lavished his love and attention. It was he who took to calling her, affectionately, Josephine, and by March of the following year, 1796, they would become man and wife.[36]

Napoleon had found the partner he had so long craved, and his letters over the following years would leave little doubt that his was a genuine love affair, one that would survive the long absences that an officer's way of life entailed.[37] Josephine's feelings, however, remain something of a mystery, as she wrote few letters and showed little interest in his, sometimes not even bothering to open the stream of passionate eulogies that he sent her.[38] Her interest, it seemed, was less in Napoleon as a man than in his career, his potential success, and what she assumed would be his future wealth – in short, the social kudos which her association with him would bestow. There is little evidence of affection on her part, far less of love or devotion. When she met Napoleon she was drifting round the Paris salons, her reputation somewhat damaged by a series of short-term romances and one-night affairs. Nor did she show the least inclination to follow him to Italy, preferring to remain in the *beau monde* of Directorial Paris. None of this, of course, helped to reassure the Bonaparte family – particularly not Letizia – who did nothing to hide their disappointment with his new bride.

But neither Napoleon nor Josephine was to be deterred. He clearly was infatuated with her and was blind to her faults. As for Josephine, she had the marriage she had set out to achieve. She had shown little hesitation in accepting the advances of the young, rather dashing Corsican general whose charm was spiced with unpredictability and perhaps just a whiff of danger.[39] Bonaparte certainly would not disappoint her ambitions. The widow of the disgraced revolutionary general had already taken her first steps on a road that would lead her to the imperial throne.

4

Bonaparte in Italy

However much Napoleon Bonaparte's thoughts might turn back to Paris and to Josephine, these would be years of relentless campaigning for the young general – campaigning that kept him away from France for long periods of time. From late 1795 his military career took off quite dramatically. The long months of enforced idleness in Paris, and his tendency to depression and melancholia that accompanied them, became an increasingly irrelevant memory. For while the repression of the royalist insurrection in Vendémiaire may not have been truly significant from the viewpoint of military strategy, what it did demonstrate was his willingness to serve the political leadership of the day loyally and unswervingly, even against his own people. His period of disgrace – his refusal to serve in the Vendée, even his abrupt removal from the list of officers – was now over, and the gossip and calumny that he had suffered damaged him less. But the rumours persisted, so much so that on Saint Helena he could reminisce that once he became a major political figure, he was still attacked for his part in the Terror, with odious claims made about his responsibility for the bloodletting at Toulon. To answer such lies, he declared, would degrade him further, so he remained aloof and silent, taking solace in the promotions and the shows of public esteem that rained down on him.[1]

On the very day of the insurrection he had been restored to his previous rank of brigadier-general, and made second-in-command of the Army of the Interior. Before the month was out, a rather jittery government, preparing to apply the new constitution and make way for the Directory and desperate for an army on whom it could rely, rewarded Bonaparte with further responsibilities. First he was promoted to the rank of *général de division* in the artillery, his command extended to a full division rather than a single brigade; then, only ten days later, he found himself promoted for a second time, to *général en chef* of the Army of the Interior. For this post he remained in Paris, since this was the army that dealt with incidents of insurrection, public disorder and counter-revolution in France itself. It was a highly sensitive posting in political terms, one that might at any moment involve fighting and killing fellow Frenchmen in defence of the Directory and the interests of the French state. The position could not be entrusted to anyone whose loyalty was in any way suspect. Thus, from being a relatively obscure young officer whose reputation stemmed largely from a solitary success at Toulon, Napoleon suddenly found himself in a position of real power in the army, a position which reflected his political support and which attracted envious looks from those who felt themselves outmanoeuvred.[2]

October 1795 was a month of heady change and a seemingly vertiginous rise, though his letters to Joseph seem calm and factual, betraying little of the excitement he must have felt or the ambition with which he is so often credited. 'You will have read in the public prints everything that concerns me', he wrote on 11 October, shortly after his first promotion. 'I have been appointed by decree as second-in-command of the Army of the Interior'. Then, in the next breath, he added the words 'Barras having been appointed commander-in-chief'. Paul Barras was Bonaparte's patron, his supporter in the corridors of power, a voice and a source of intercession on whom he believed that he could rely. Barras was important to him, as the continual references in his correspondence with his brother surely demonstrate. On 20 October, he discusses the elections that are being held to renew the Convention, showing his close interest in the politics of the moment and noting, quite specifically, that 'Barras, Chénier and Sieyès have been selected in several departments'. He himself, he says, without complaint, is being kept very busy; his responsibilities are preventing him from writing at greater length.[3] But he clearly enjoys them, relishing the trust that has been placed in him, and keeping a close eye on the political manoeuvres in the capital. On 1 November, for instance, after barely drawing breath to tell Joseph that he has been placed in command of the Army of the Interior, he turns once again to the political situation in Paris: 'The councils of 250 and 500 have now met. The first of these has already drawn up its list of candidates for the Directory', he tells him, adding, almost incidentally, that among those nominated was Paul Barras.[4] The tone of his correspondence with Joseph, the brother with whom he had most in common and with whom he was most likely to share his feelings, shows not a shrill triumphalism, but a quiet satisfaction with his change of fortune and a realistic concern for the political future of the nation. Nothing in these letters was suggestive of vaulting ambition or of the political career that lay ahead.

Perhaps luckily for his military career, Napoleon did not stay long with the Army of the Interior, which was in some ways a poisoned chalice, a role always likely to be seen by the Republic's enemies as ideologically driven. Reliability and loyalty to the Directory were paramount, and in Bonaparte's case were only accentuated in the public gaze by his association with Barras, a man widely seen as lacking real political principle, a manipulator and power-monger tainted by a suspicion of corruption. In Paris Napoleon had no choice but to be the government's man. During the short period of his command there, he ordered the closure of the neo-Jacobin Pantheon Club, supervised the policing of the theatres – one of the traditional focal points of opposition politics – and purged royalists and right-wingers from the War Ministry.[5] To stay in Paris too long would of necessity mean a close identification with the regime, one that would risk him losing popularity and public esteem. In the meantime, French arms had chalked up some notable successes along the frontiers, so that a war which had started out as a desperate defence of the Republic from the assaults of its neighbours had turned into one of invasion, occupation and annexation by a triumphant Republic.

France had first aimed to secure the natural frontiers of the Rhine and the Scheldt, which had been the traditional foreign policy objective of every monarch since Louis XIV and had essentially been secured under the Jacobins. Thereafter, the main focus of attack was the German lands across the Rhine, electorates and city states which progressively came under French domination. By early 1796, the First Coalition had largely collapsed, so that only Austria, Britain and, somewhat waveringly, Piedmont remained at war with France. The international situation had swung dramatically in France's favour since the desperate days of 1793, when the Spanish had besieged Perpignan and the Convention had had to turn its armies against the rebels of the Vendée and the federalists of Lyon.

The War Minister, Carnot, saw expansion east of the Rhine as France's primary target, overrunning the various temporal and ecclesiastical territories that blocked the route of the advancing armies, annexing some directly to France, and elsewhere creating a series of buffer states, or sister republics, in what are now Belgium and Holland. Most of the territories they entered, from Aachen to Mainz to Cologne, had been part of the now badly fading Holy Roman Empire, and hence dependent on Austrian arms for their defence. It was for this reason that, in the spring of 1796, Carnot dreamt of opening up another front in Italy to attack Austria's possessions beyond the Alps – especially Milan and the rich Lombard plain. A new Army of Italy was established, a force of some fifty thousand men, to complement the main French armies in Germany and attack the Austrians in their northern Italian fastnesses. It was to the command of this army that Bonaparte, doubtless to his considerable relief, now found himself transferred. His ambitions for an Italian offensive were well known in Paris, and Barras was once again instrumental in pressing the claims of his protégé with the political leadership. For Bonaparte it was the chance to open a new phase of his career, offering him the possibility of victory, of riches, and of military glory. Looking back, he would see this move as critical, since there could have been no future for him in Paris. 'A young general of twenty-five could not remain any longer at the head of the Army of the Interior', was the terse, almost dismissive epitaph on his first command that he wrote twenty years later.[6] He was perhaps twenty-six rather than twenty-five in the spring of 1796, but otherwise his assessment surely stands as a measure of his restless ambition.

It is difficult not to be struck by the enormity of the risk that the revolutionary authorities seemed to be taking in choosing the young Corsican for his first operational command. Bonaparte might be favoured at court by Barras and his immediate circle, but that was hardly a guarantee of success on the battlefield. He was still only twenty-six – not in itself a disadvantage in the revolutionary army, which had something of a tradition of promoting its officers young – but he was little known in the high command, he had no field experience, and his only previous campaigning had been against uprisings and insurrections inside France. It might not seem the most appropriate preparation for the plains of Lombardy or the steep mountain passes of the Alps, where *barbets* – guerrilla troops indistinguishable from the bandit gangs from whom they were recruited – waited to ambush the advancing French armies. Yet not all the auguries were unpropitious. By 1796 the French were in the ascendant in Germany, having progressed from defence to offence during the months of the Terror and now pushing eastwards beyond the Rhine. And the Army of Italy, though deemed the least important of France's five armies and hence the least favoured in matters of supply and equipment, had at least the merit of being undefeated on the battlefield. Its low morale was due to hunger and neglect rather than to military experience.

Napoleon was aware, too, of other problems he might face with his own army. The product of a revolutionary *amalgame* in 1793, it had brought together in the same units line soldiers from the 1780s, tried and battle-hardened in the service of the King, and the volunteers and requisitioned men of the revolutionary levies. Discipline could often be lax, and the commitment to drill and training uncertain. Besides, the Army of Italy had necessarily been thrown together hastily, with soldiers transferred from other fronts which, as the French had learned in the Vendée, was not always a proven means of assembling the best and most committed troops.[7] In theory Bonaparte had over sixty thousand men at his disposal, but in practice, their numbers decimated by disease and the fatigues of war, they seldom amounted to more than thirty-eight thousand fit for active service. At any one time many thousands were absent, sent back to France to hasten their recovery.[8] This meant that they were, numerically at least, no match for the Austrians and the Piedmontese with whom the new young commander would have to engage. Nor were they well equipped or supplied. Here, as in many of the French revolutionary armies, too little attention was paid to military logistics; there were too few carters and horses, and insufficient mules to carry heavy supplies across the Alps. There were reports of troops without shoes, deprived of adequate stores, and paid months in arrears. Supply problems both undermined military effectiveness and drained the soldiers' morale.[9]

But we should not dwell overly on the shortcomings of the situation Napoleon inherited, for there was promise, too. Its leaders were men who, like himself, had achieved their promotions on merit rather than through birthright. Napoleon understood their attitudes and commitment, qualities that he was prepared to develop and exploit since he came to his command imbued with many of the reformist instincts of the later eighteenth century, the redrafting of military ideas that had been initiated by such noted authors and practitioners as Guibert, Servan and Gribeauval. He felt unconstrained by the more conservative tactics of the Bourbon army, believing instead in the virtues of rapid movement and the tactics of surprise, which he found especially valuable as a response to the slow-moving and largely predictable Austrians. Napoleon was well aware of the weaknesses of the Austrian army that was ranged against

him, and he believed that he could exploit them: a shortage of officers compared with the numbers in the ranks, a formalism that
could lead to a lack of flexibility on the battlefield, and a rather
cumbersome administrative structure. The Austrian army moved
slowly and stolidly, in part the result of its laboured decision-making
and communication.[10]

He also believed quite unshakably in his own judgement, in his
inborn talent as a strategist on the battlefield, and this belief enabled
him to be bold and incisive in his decision-making. Once installed
at the head of his new army, he lost little time in imposing his
authority on those under his command, in particular on the older
and more experienced officers who surrounded him, and who might
have maintained their own cliques and coteries had they been given
any leeway by their new commander. He impressed them with his
knowledge and bent them to his will, a vital step if he was to maintain unity in the ranks and guarantee a single, effective command.
And he gave them responsibility in battle, responsibility which the
younger officers, in particular, accepted with relish. For Italy was
not just the scene of some of Napoleon's greatest triumphs; it was
also the breeding ground for future marshals of the imperial army
like Augereau and Lannes, Sérurier and Masséna, who served under
him as divisional commanders.

But it was not just his officers who learned to trust his judgement; Napoleon also, and famously, took great care to cultivate the
men in the ranks. He did not forget that they too had fears and
frailties, and he sought to win their affection and devotion, playing
on his image as a general who had risen through the ranks and
who shared their fears and apprehensions. He made clear to his
troops just what he expected of them. He set before them clear

military objectives and strategic goals; and he knew how to flatter them when flattery was required to give them the self-belief they so badly needed. An army that has not been paid and lacks adequate food supplies cannot be expected to respond to hollow appeals to patriotism, as he well understood. So he harassed suppliers and military commissioners, exacting supplies for his men; in March 1796, for instance, he noted with satisfaction that several companies were now actively providing supplies of meat, grain and hay for his troops, while sixteen hundred mules were arriving to assist the artillery.[11]

He turned to oratory, too, in persuading his men that they had a general who was one of them, who shared their hardships and discomforts and who understood their everyday concerns. In a speech to the troops which he later crafted into a resounding – but sadly apocryphal – declaration, he described the plains of Lombardy as a land of conquest where they would find all the riches, all the food and drink that they could dream of. His words have become famous – or, at least, the words that he later recorded for posterity: 'Soldiers, you are hungry and naked. The government owes you much; it can give you nothing . . . I want to lead you into the most fertile plains on earth. Rich provinces, great towns will be in your power; there you will find honour, glory and riches.'[12] It was not quite an invitation to plunder, but it came close. It was a message that an unpaid, ill-nourished soldier would surely appreciate. Later, as the army prepared the assault on Mantua, he would add another promise, that of peace: 'The peace of Europe, the happiness of your parents, these will be the results of your courage. Let us do once more what we have done so often in the past and Europe will not challenge our claim to be the bravest and most powerful nation on earth.'[13]

But he did not promise riches alone; he also emphasised that he would lead them to honour and glory, which could only result from success in the field. For soldiers, victory is not just about medals and promotions, though Napoleon was quick to promise these, too. It was also the key to survival. Like all soldiers, everywhere, they admired a general who looked after their needs and rewarded them with victory on the battlefield, largely because victory raised morale, reduced casualties and saved needless slaughter.

Before arriving in Italy he had studied both the geography of the country and past campaigns that had been conducted in that theatre of war. He had also taken the first steps in securing the coast traffic on which military supply would depend,[14] and very soon he would achieve a dazzling reputation as a general in the field. Indeed, it was the Italian campaign that provided Napoleon with his credentials as a great military leader, a man who could turn a battle by brilliant tactical deployment, a sharp-witted strategist who could read a battlefield like a book and outpace his opponent. It was not that his tactics had fundamentally changed from traditional Old Regime armies: the composition of the armies was little different from that in the Seven Years War; their weaponry remained largely unchanged, and the drill manuals were the same as under Louis XV. What had changed was the speed of French manoeuvres and of their response to attack, a lightning speed that repeatedly took the enemy by surprise and which lay at the very heart of Napoleon's battle plan. It would underpin an unprecedented series of victories as Napoleon thrust into Lombardy, first defeating the Piedmontese – thus ending in the space of two weeks a stubborn war of attrition that had lasted four years – before turning against the main Austrian army.[15] Tactically it was an impressive start: he moved his army speedily and incisively, taking advantage of its greater manoeuvrability and the resort to lighter artillery to cut off enemy advances and mount surprise attacks.

He had had to act quickly. The Austrians tried to pre-empt his offensive with a surprise attack that resulted in Napoleon's first real battle, at Montenotte, on 10 April 1796. Victory here, and the seizure of the strongholds of Alba, Fossano and Cherasco, not only cemented the self-belief of the French but provided them with the supplies and provisions they so badly needed. They then crossed the Po and took the important crossroads city of Alessandria. For the Austrians, too, the psychological impact was important, for, even if the French usually ensured that they went into battle with superior numbers, this series of defeats sapped Austrian morale and left their commanders dejected and bewildered. They had lost the fortresses that could slow down the French advance, and had left the road to Milan exposed and undefended. Besides, news of this rapid series of defeats, combined with the fear spread by lurid stories of looting and plunder by the French armies, led King Victor Amadeus of Sardinia to sue for peace, and to withdraw his army from the coalition against France. As Napoleon told his victorious soldiers, they had achieved great things: winning six victories, taking enemy positions and capturing the richest part of Piedmont. They had taken fifteen thousand prisoners and killed or wounded more than ten thousand men. And they had done so in conditions of great deprivation. 'You have won battles without cannon, crossed rivers without bridges, made forced marches without shoes, drink or bread.'[16] But they were not finished. Milan was Napoleon's next objective, the capture of the Lombard capital being seen as a decisive strike against Austrian power in northern Italy.

The French march on Milan was interrupted, however, by an Austrian defence of the bridge at Lodi, over the river Adda, and battle was joined. For posterity, this would become one of the key engagements of the young general's military rise, and Napoleon himself would make much of it. But historians are agreed that this was a relatively minor battle, involving small forces and comparatively contained losses; and if it must count as a victory, with the French left in control of the bridge and the town, Bonaparte did not achieve all his objectives. His army had been held up on their march, and the Austrian commander, Beaulieu, managed to escape with his troops; Lodi cannot be said to have ended the war in Lombardy. On the other hand, Bonaparte could now enter Milan, while Murat took Genoa. By the end of the year, he had taken Modena, signed a treaty with Naples, and secured Verona. He had also engaged the Austrians in the more conclusive battle at Arcola, the site of another bridge which his campaign would make famous, and took the town after three exhausting days of combat.

The war ground on throughout the winter between two tired and battered armies until, in February 1797, Napoleon played his master card at Rivoli, dispersing the Austrians into the surrounding mountains and capturing the heavily defended fort town of Mantua. The consequences were decisive. An Austrian garrison of thirty thousand men surrendered; Napoleon forced the Pope to sign a treaty at Tolentino whereby he agreed to offer Austria no further aid; and he made as if to march against Vienna itself. At first the Austrian Archduke refused any truce or offer of peace, but in April he reluctantly accepted the terms that Napoleon held out to him. The Austrians agreed to cede Belgium and Holland to France, along with the west bank of the Rhine and the Ionian Islands; they also

agreed to recognise the Cisalpine republic, the sister republic which
Napoleon had fashioned out of the Austrian lands in Lombardy.
Back in Paris these terms were hailed as testimony to the brilliance
of the young general, though there were those in Italy who felt that
the treaty had been drawn up to impress public opinion back in
France, with little concern for Italian interests. In particular, there
was anger that Venice had been sacrificed in the peace negotiations
by being handed back to the Austrians – some would even use the
word 'betrayed' – so that the deal could be quickly sewn up.

The peace treaty was finalised the following autumn at Campo
Formio – a rare instance of a diplomatic treaty seemingly dictated
by a general in the field without referring back to Paris.[17] It was a
moment that demonstrated Napoleon's impetuous nature and his
disdain for conventional niceties or questions of diplomatic precedence. In conducting peace negotiations he was certainly exceeding
his authority as a general. But it also hinted at something else: political as well as military ambition. He was keen to achieve a settlement and to present Paris with a diplomatic coup to add to his
military triumph, a triumph that would show him in a new and
different light. Already he had forged a high reputation as a soldier.
Now he was also a diplomat and a peace-maker.

It was in Italy that Napoleon established his claims to military
genius, in his own mind as much as in the minds of those who
served under him. After his victory at Lodi, he would later recount,
'I no longer regarded myself as a simple general but as a man called
upon to decide the fate of peoples. It came to me then that I really
could become a decisive actor on our national stage. At that point
was born the first spark of high ambition'.[18] And though this may
seem an implausible claim – there were plenty of hints before Lodi

that the young Bonaparte had already had dreams of future grandeur
– it justifies closer examination. For what had Napoleon achieved
at this early stage in the Italian Campaign that could turn his head
to this extent? What did Lodi mean to him? In military terms it is
almost customary to dismiss the battle as a minor engagement, yet
it came to be at the heart of the Napoleonic myth which he himself
did so much to propagate. It was a hard-fought battle, but not a
major engagement of the two armies. And yet it was a first successful
illustration of the rapid deployment which was Napoleon's own
version of *Blitzkrieg*, and as such it could be seen to have had a
wider significance.

The English military historian Spenser Wilkinson, who does not
hide his admiration for Bonaparte as a tactician, describes the significance of Lodi in unambiguous terms, claiming that:

> The four weeks' campaign that ended at Lodi revealed a great
> commander. It contained the germ, and more than the germ, of all his
> future exploits. It exemplified all his principles: the original distribu-
> tion of the troops into three groups or camps about twelve miles distant
> from one another; their swift concentration by a forward march begun
> before dawn; the seizure of a central position from which to strike the
> separated portions of the enemy; the aim at the enemy's communica-
> tions; the spreading of the divisions like a net to enclose the enemy's
> flanks; the drawing in of the net to envelop the enemy; the combina-
> tion of a frontal attack with a surprise attack on the flank; the use of
> a river to mask a movement against the enemy's rear; the collection on
> the battlefield of a superior force; above all, the unprecedented rapidity
> of movement, and the incessant, never-ending energy of the action.[19]

If Wilkinson is right, then it is not difficult to see why Napoleon attributed such great importance to the battle, nor yet why the Italian campaign offered him such opportunities for building his reputation back in France, both with the Directory and in the eyes of a wider public. The process of mythologising, which would consume much of Napoleon's energy throughout his career, had already begun.

Of his many achievements during the Italian campaign, his adroit manipulation of the news and his command of propaganda were arguably as significant as his skills on the battlefield. Already he was demonstrating a command of words and an appreciation of the importance of heroic images that would not have shamed a political leader of a much later and more media-conscious age, a capacity to choose a telling phrase, or spin a story in a particular way that was guaranteed to capture the public mood of the moment. His sense of the popular pulse rarely deserted him; in that sense, as in many others, he would prove himself to be a singularly modern figure in an age of authoritarian monarchs, narrowly defined elites and restricted electorates. Notably, once he was established in power, he would manipulate both the arts world and the media, setting the topics for art competitions, leaning heavily on journalists, or restoring the monopoly of the Paris book trade. For a man who had claimed in his youth to be a true son of the Enlightenment, he would show a powerful desire to control expression, and he took little interest in encouraging free speech.

In 1796 in Italy his interest in the media was rather different. He sought to bolster his public image, to lay claim to heroic status, and to establish himself in the public imagination. And he believed that the various media that lay at his disposal had an important military role to play, whether in appealing to civilians, dampening enemy morale, or bolstering the confidence of his soldiers. His resort to propaganda was, then as later, multi-layered. Addresses to his troops, proclamations to the inhabitants of besieged cities, and newspaper articles strategically placed in the official Paris newspaper, the *Moniteur*, were all parts of a strategic campaign of self-promotion.[20]

Napoleon's message was quite deliberately directed at different audiences, and for different purposes, too. First and foremost was the army itself, where Bonaparte showed himself to be a creative publicist, using well-chosen news stories to bestow praise, raise confidence and improve morale. The military press was not his invention: the Revolution, and especially the Jacobin years, had seen the rise of a tradition of newspapers written by and for the army – papers like Carnot's *Soirée du camp*, which distributed its highly political message among the troops in all of France's armies, and the more local papers, limited in their news and circulation to a single army, and often a single frontier. The papers fed upbeat reports of developments elsewhere in the war; soldiers read them eagerly, and they played a significant part in spreading confidence and reassurance.[21] During 1797 Napoleon himself created and financed two such papers, both written from within the army – first the *Courrier de l'Armée d'Italie*, then, some days later, the more ephemeral *La France vue de l'Armée d'Italie*, both of which circulated among the troops, though they were aimed also at a political readership and excerpts and articles were reprinted from them in the Paris press.[22]

The papers were subtly different in tone: if the *Courrier* courted the new revolutionary elite, he issued a second paper specifically to reassure more traditional elements in both French and Italian society.[23] These papers helped to inculcate a spirit of pride and professionalism in the troops, and to keep them abreast of the principal political developments back in France. In the press that was produced from within the army, and also in the confident proclamations he issued to his soldiers, Napoleon established a powerful medium through which he could communicate directly with his men and stir their deepest emotions. This was the traditional function of newspapers in wartime: to reaffirm soldiers' confidence in the cause for which they were fighting, while troubling and undermining the confidence of the enemy.[24] It required a special language, one that created a special rapport.[25]

But the troops were seldom Napoleon's principal target for propaganda, even as battles raged around him. The newspapers also served to inform the public back home of the army's exploits in Italy, and in doing so they presented an image of Napoleon that came close to that of the classical hero. He was portrayed as a supreme strategist who would lead them to glory; as a military thinker who could outwit any opposing general; and as a man capable of sometimes impetuous but always incisive decisions that could turn a battle and decide the fate of thousands. As a political appointee himself, fully aware of his debt to men like Salicetti and Barras for his rapid preferment, he understood how important it was to make his achievements known back in Paris: his daring strategies, his blistering troop movements, his decisive victories in the service of government. He was astute enough to realise the value of a supportive press, one that would keep his name on the front pages and in the public eye. Italy was not the Directory's principal theatre of war, and without the oxygen of publicity Bonaparte risked being relegated from the headlines, dismissed as the general of a minor army in a secondary conflict. He had no intention of allowing this to happen. He chose as his editors men with experience of both journalism and revolutionary politics, men who still retained connections in the capital – the former Jacobin Marc-Antoine Jullien for the *Courrier*, and the more moderate Regnault de Saint-Angély for *La France*.[26]

News items were strategically placed in national newspapers back in Paris at moments that would achieve maximum impact. The policy was carried out with almost military precision. From the moment when the Italian campaign began in April 1796 Bonaparte's army appeared in the French press more often than any other in the field. Items featured in the official *Moniteur* as a matter of course, but they were also placed in more polemical newspapers. During the months following September 1796, for instance, the conservative *Nouvelles Politiques*, whose editorialists included the highly influential Charles Lacretelle, was well connected with a powerful group of moderate right-wing deputies on the legislative councils, and was hence seen as an ideal conduit for Napoleon's exercises in self-aggrandisement.[27] It gave news from all France's fronts, mentioning all four armies then on campaign. But the highest number of mentions was reserved for the Army of Italy, which was alluded to in sixty-six separate issues of the paper in a six-month period. And in thirty-one of these Bonaparte was reported as announcing some sort of victory. There were few indications of defeats or setbacks, with the result that it was difficult for readers of the paper not to associate the Italian campaign with an unbroken series of French advances, or to identify its young general with victory and military glory.[28]

This, of course, was Bonaparte's intention from the outset. Using the papers he controlled or financed through the army as a shameless source of self-promotion ensured that, in the bitter faction-fighting that characterised Directorial politics, his name was not allowed to become besmirched or, worse, forgotten. To intensify his press campaign he launched a further paper in February 1797, with the suggestive title *Journal de Bonaparte et des hommes vertueux*, printed and distributed in Paris. Again the paper heaped praise on the Army of Italy and its victorious commander, and made the speed of the army, its style of campaigning and the bravery of its men its recurrent themes. As for Bonaparte himself, his despatches are faithfully reproduced, and his genius lauded. From the very first issue the masthead of the paper was adorned with a caption comparing him to a legendary general of Antiquity (`Hannibal slept at Capua, whereas Bonaparte does not sleep in Mantua').[29] It also talked of the enemies it was challenging: royalists, with whom it urged no compromise, and *émigré* priests who, in Bonaparte's view, could safely be left alone as there was no law against their presence in Italy. From time to time the paper did not hesitate to criticise the Directory, or to compare the inactivity of France's politicians, and their corruption, with the vigour and incisive judgement of Napoleon himself.[30] The paper was rightly seen as far more than a vector of information to an admiring public. It was a mouthpiece for Bonaparte's growing political ambitions, with the qualities he displayed in Italy being vaunted as those of a leader and visionary, a man of grandeur and destiny.

He also turned to the talents of others, of artists and men of letters. Poets used their literary licence to burnish his image, using words like 'invincible' and 'immortal' in odes and eulogies addressed to him, while on the battlefield his impact was presented as immediate and always decisive. After Arcola, indeed, the unbeaten army was transformed into an unbeatable one, with the very appearance of Bonaparte sufficient to determine the outcome. He was being recreated as a providential figure, the image at the heart of the Myth of the Saviour of later years. 'Enemies flee, kings surrender, everything evaporates and trembles at the very sound of his name.'[31] What poets could do in print, playwrights could provide for the stage, for the world of the Paris theatre which had become, during the Revolution and the Thermidorian Republic, a hotbed of partisan politics and satirical attack. Even at this early stage of his career Bonaparte took an active interest in the Paris theatre, and was aware of the significance of his representation there. The year 1797 alone saw a whole raft of plays about Bonaparte's victories in Italy or set around the capitulation of Mantua, as the glory and colour of events in Italy were welcomed as a distraction from the rather drab political scene back in France.

By 1798, however, Paris theatregoers were equally enthusiastic in lauding the end of the war and the signing of peace at Campo Formio. Many in Paris seemed to tire of battles and killing; it was the prospect of peace that most vividly captured the public imagination, a peace won by military prowess and a spark of individual genius.[32] The Napoleonic myth assumed new forms, as he was increasingly hailed as the great peace-maker of his age.

Painters and artists also played their part in popularising the young general's achievements and turning his portrait into a widely recognisable icon among the French public. Although at this time Bonaparte lacked the opportunity and resources of the imperial years – when he would commission the finest artists in Europe and set the themes for prizes at the Academy – the glamour and excitement of the Italian campaign was sufficient to attract painters and engravers to Italy, most on their own account, eager to paint portraits of the victorious generals and to depict the most dramatic battle scenes. Indeed, while he was still in Italy, engravings, busts and statues were appearing in the salons of Paris, and some went on to be imitated by popular colourists eager to profit from the mood of the moment. No other general could compete with his popularity or his artistic exposure. In Italy, Napoleon was able to attract the interest of several outstanding young painters, among them the Milanese artist Andrea Appiani, and the young Frenchman and student of David, Antoine-Jean Gros. Appiani produced the first portrait of the young Bonaparte, an image which by early 1797 had been engraved and widely commercialised.

As for Gros, he was carefully courted by Napoleon, and more especially by Josephine, and became a sort of official portraitist, a regular in the elite circle, rather like a royal court, that surrounded Bonaparte at the palace of Mombello. His principal output in this period was a series of portraits of those close to Bonaparte, most notably Josephine and Berthier, and the iconic image of *Bonaparte on the Bridge of Arcole* that hangs in the Louvre.[33] This painting so pleased Napoleon that he offered Gros a sum of 250 louis to have engravings of it made, and these in turn helped popularise the future Emperor's portrait across Europe. But it did not appear in the Paris salon until the Consulate, in 1801.[34]

The signing of the Treaty of Campo Formio, with the congress at Rastadt that followed, did, of course, bring Napoleon's military activity to an abrupt halt, and peace was not something that necessarily augured well for an ambitious general. There was some diplomatic work to be concluded and the Directory sent him to Rastadt with full diplomatic powers. And no doubt he had some personal matters to sort out, too. From the moment he left for Italy, three days after his marriage, persistent rumours circulated that Josephine did not return his affection – she certainly did not reply to his letters – and that she was openly leading the life of a socialite in Paris, publicly admitting her lack of fidelity to her husband and seeking sexual gratification wherever it was offered. By the time of their return from Italy she had taken a lover, a young lieutenant in the hussars by name of Hippolyte Charles, to whom she remained devoted for at least another two years; she would break with him only in the summer of 1799, while her husband was away, this time in Egypt.[35] It all made for an uneasy homecoming for Bonaparte, despite the profuse praise that was bestowed on him and the adulation of the Paris crowds. He had a fear of idleness and a desire for military action that made any prolonged period of furlough hard to bear; meanwhile, there is evidence that some at least of the Directors were wary of his popularity and his ability to mobilise political support. But how could he best, and most safely, be deployed? They first thought to place him at the head of the new army that was being prepared for an invasion of England, a force that was to incorporate many of those who had fought in northern Italy.

But in March 1798 there was a sudden *volte-face*. The idea of a cross-Channel invasion was dropped, and the Directory decided to pursue another form of attack on Britain and her Empire, one that had the added advantage that the army's most overbearing general could be sent still further afield, beyond the limits of Europe itself. To disrupt the British in the Indian sub-continent, a new route to India had to be found, one that could be accessed without going round Africa and the Cape of Good Hope. So the Directory turned its attentions to the East, and the Mediterranean. In April it decreed the creation of the Army of the Orient, with Bonaparte as its commander-in-chief.

On 19 May 1798, he sailed out of Toulon for Egypt.

5

Lure of the Orient

The decision to despatch Bonaparte to Egypt, and to concentrate so much of France's renewed military effort on a colonial war, seemed bizarre to many, especially since the Directory had devoted so much effort during the previous months to planning a full-scale invasion of Britain. Britain had become, for the country's political leaders, the most dangerous and determined of France's enemies, a colonial power prepared to use its great wealth to deny French expansion on the continent and to assume the role of paymaster to counter-revolution across Europe. And the circumstances for an assault on Britain had seemed auspicious, with evidence of Radical subversion in London, the naval mutinies at the Nore and Spithead, and constant murmurs of rebellion from Ireland.

The Directors had had good reason to believe, in 1796 and 1797, that their moment had come, and that they might at last hope to break the resistance of France's most stubborn and affluent enemy. They were already pursuing an economic war against Britain, and they had become increasingly intolerant of what they interpreted as British intransigence over peace-making, a refusal to compromise over French gains in northern Italy and, especially, along the estuary of the Scheldt. This was the context in which Bonaparte had been appointed to head the Army of England, and to prepare invasion plans. But by 1798 there was good reason to fear that that moment – if it had indeed ever existed – had passed, and that a successful invasion of England would require the mobilisation of huge resources that were beyond the capabilities of the French navy.

The condition of the navy gave cause for alarm and Bonaparte, on a tour of inspection of the naval ports, was quick to conclude that the idea of a direct frontal assault from the sea was risky at best, and, at worst, sadly misconceived. On the other hand, as he reported to the Directors in February 1798, there were perhaps more hopeful alternative strategies for attacking the British and their interests. By land, he argued, the more practical policy would be to attack Hanover and Hamburg, which would harm British commercial interests in Germany and Northern Europe; or by sea England's colonies abroad, where the Royal Navy would be less concentrated and Britain's armies more stretched. The third strategy, Napoleon suggested, would be to mount an attack on the Levant that would disrupt British command of the Eastern Mediterranean and 'threaten her trade with the Indies'.[1] At this moment he gave no hint of his own preference, but he had sown the idea in many people's minds that one way of staunching the flow of wealth to Britain was to cut off its communications with its colonial possessions, especially the richest among them, India. An attack on Egypt could be a mechanism for destroying British power in the Indian subcontinent; it would also provide France with a delicious dose of revenge for the repeated colonial defeats she had suffered at the hands of the British in the course of the century. The Directors – or at least a majority among them – would seem to have been convinced by this argument, especially since the number of ships and mobilisation of resources required for an attack on Egypt was a fraction of what had been discussed for an invasion of England.

Since the reign of Louis XIV the French had periodically dreamed of conquering Egypt. Choiseul had considered it following the loss of French Canada and of colonies in India; Vergennes, though, had opposed the idea, preferring to offer French support to the American colonists against Britain in 1778.[2] Bonaparte himself was clearly attracted by the idea of leading a military assault on Egypt, whether in order to advance his own interests or to promote a new colonial policy that could be achieved without resort to slavery. His enthusiasm for this policy is attested to by contemporaries, and especially those in his more intimate circle. One of the most faithful of these was Bourrienne, a former classmate at Brienne, who went on to become his personal secretary and who left what he claimed to be a faithful account of his master's thoughts and utterances, though many of these have been exposed as pure fiction.[3] Already in 1797, he has Bonaparte claiming, with apparent prescience, that 'the time was not far distant when, if we are really to destroy England, we must seize control of Egypt'; and writing to the Directory's new foreign minister, Talleyrand, reminding him of the strategic value of Egypt and adding that it was a power vacuum waiting to be occupied, a territory that 'belongs only to God Himself'.[4] What is certainly true is that Napoleon was an early convert to the strategy of mounting an assault on the Eastern Mediterranean. Even while he was still in Italy, preparing the terms of Campo Formio, he is reported by a much more reliable source, Miot de Melito, to have been discussing a possible invasion of Egypt.[5]

Talleyrand, ever the schemer, was an eager player in this particular diplomatic game, quickly won over to the grand dream of making the Nile into a French-controlled waterway and thus cutting England off from its richest colonial possessions. He realised, too, that for political reasons it must be he himself, and not Bonaparte, who took policy initiatives, since the Directors were jealous to guard political power for themselves and instinctively distrusted the young general who had dictated peace terms at Campo Formio. They were not, of course, so naïve as to be deceived by the political manoeuvres of Talleyrand, which were fairly transparent, nor yet by the two reports he submitted to them exaggerating the threat posed by Turkey to justify a French attack on the Levant.[6] But they did allow themselves to be convinced of the value of a campaign in North Africa, though, when they finally gave their consent to the expedition, they did so with the deepest misgivings. Napoleon had made no secret of his boredom back in Paris or his impatience for another glorious campaign. The last thing they could afford was to hand the political initiative to their over-ambitious general.

But where did Napoleon's own dreams of the Orient – and his apparent passion for the idea of an Egyptian adventure – originate? The whole enterprise was far removed from the military world he knew, a world of land armies and long marches, of artillery attacks on towns and fortifications – a world punctuated by Alpine passes and the wide plains of Lombardy. Now his army would face an entirely different and very unfamiliar landscape: a landscape of sand and desert, but also of temples and pyramids, tombs and sphinxes, and marches in a blazing heat that few Europeans had experienced. The Egypt they sailed towards was not just a foreign country. It was a culture of which the French understood little, but which held a unique fascination for them; an ancient civilisation of closely held secrets and strange religious rituals, locked houses and walled courtyards, veiled faces and sweeping robes. It was above all, as Napoleon's friend and cultural advisor, the engraver Vivant Denon, observed after landing in Alexandria, a land of deep silence. There was, it seemed to the French, no conversation in the streets, no laughter, no scampering children or barking dogs. Egypt seemed profoundly melancholy, unwelcoming and inward-looking, and for many of the French soldiers this was the dominant image they would retain of North Africa – particularly of Islam. 'The first image that came into view,' Denon wrote of Alexandria, 'was of a vast cemetery, covered by countless tombs of white marble against a white soil; a few skinny women, draped in long, torn clothing, were like ghosts as they wandered among these monuments; the silence was broken only by the screeching of kites as they circled over this sanctuary of death.' It was a bleak image that, in the minds of the French, contrasted starkly with the colour and gaiety of the European cities they had left behind.[7]

But that image only took shape once the French army had reached Egypt and become acquainted with the country and its people. Before they left French soil there is abundant evidence that – like Napoleon himself – they shared the fascination with the Orient that so typified Western Europe in the second half of the eighteenth century. They were not talking of a poor society, or an under-developed one: Egypt in mid-century was a rich and artistically sophisticated nation, part of the Turkish Empire of the day, and carried on a flourishing trade with Europe, especially France. The country was famed for its delicate carved woodwork and its skilled craft culture, and visitors from Europe returned home with tales of opulent palaces and bustling markets, most particularly in the cities such as Cairo, Rosetta and Alexandria. Cairo, indeed, was a true southern capital, a great trading city with commercial links all round the Mediterranean. But these privileged conditions were changing rapidly, a consequence of chronic political instability. The old Egyptian empire had long given way to rule as a province of Turkey, with instability a permanent threat. In 1766 the country was rent by the rising of Emir Ali Bey to throw off the Turkish yoke and establish his own autocratic rule. Political crisis followed: he was assassinated in 1773, resulting in further political instability and economic decline, and leading, in 1786, to a short-lived attempt by the Turkish ruler, the Sublime Porte, to re-establish his nation's control. As a consequence, by the time Napoleon and his men arrived they found not the luxury and general prosperity they had read about in earlier travellers' accounts, but an economy in tatters and a populace reduced to dire poverty.[8] Many had nurtured hopes of finding an exotic paradise steeped in precious objects and gilded fabrics; they were to be bitterly disappointed.

Napoleon undoubtedly left France with a romanticised notion of what he would encounter and an imperial vision of the great civilisation he was about to conquer. His reading of history had stood him in good stead: he knew about the ancient civilisations of Egypt and Persia, just as he had read the great classical authors of Greece and Rome, and he was already conscious of the awesome step he was taking in trying to annex an ancient empire to the ascendant star of revolutionary France. Bonaparte was not modest about either his talents or his ambitions. In correspondence he compared himself to Alexander the Great, imposing a new, modern civilisation in place of one that had become decadent and outmoded. Indeed, the belief that Western Europe was an empire in the ascendant, facing the last corrupt vestiges of past civilisations, would seem to have intoxicated him.[9] When he left for the Orient he took with him an impressive array of the great works of his own century, notably those of Montesquieu, Voltaire and Rousseau, as well as some of the authors of Antiquity. These may have been predictable, the standard texts of any well-read man of the Enlightenment, but it is interesting that he thought to read them on campaign. He also took the *Voyages* of Captain Cook, one of the most influential texts of exploration and the discovery of the exotic; Goethe's romantic and melancholy *Sorrows of Young Werther*; and, significantly, the Koran, with which he sought to familiarise himself before beginning his talks with the Egyptians. All in all, it was a fairly catholic mixture, but one that showed a man immersed in the transnational culture of the late eighteenth century and excited by an encounter with a great, though poorly understood, extra-European civilisation.[10] There was far more to his fascination with Egypt than a desire to cut Britain off from its colonial possessions.

His fascination with the culture of the Orient took other forms, too, and though his critics have often been deeply cynical about his real motives, a thirst for military glory and an enlightened curiosity about one of the world's great civilisations can sometimes go hand in hand. We know that Napoleon's youthful reading of the Classics had left a deep mark on him, and that it was not out of character for him to read Livy, Plutarch or Tacitus on campaign. Nor was it so exceptional, in an age when the officer corps of European armies were still moulded with aristocratic values, for army commanders to be cultivated, and sometimes well-read, men. In the Peninsula, for instance, British officers read the most recent novels of Walter Scott; while the most literary of France's generals, Choderlos de Laclos, is perhaps better remembered as the author of one of the most provocative novels of the eighteenth century, *Les Liaisons dangereuses*. Laclos may have been a libertine and, in the eyes of his detractors, a pornographer, but he was also, until his death in Napoleon's service near Naples in 1803, a dedicated artillery officer.[11] To his contemporaries there was nothing strange or contradictory about these roles. So, with Napoleon, few would have pointed to any tension between his success as an army officer and his avowed interest in the Ancient World, any more than it would have seemed strange that an artillery officer should claim to be a talented mathematician.

What is clear, however, is that he went to somewhat excessive lengths to ensure that his intellectual gifts were recognised by the public, and to win such esteem and kudos as associations with science could confer. Thus in 1797, following the departure of Carnot – a fellow artillery officer – Bonaparte assumed the seat he vacated at the French Academy; he thereafter took care, when in Paris, to be seen in the company of the most prominent intellectuals of his day. In the eyes of many of his biographers, and some contemporaries, this was a step too far, a distinction that could in no way be justified, but a blatant attempt to win over France's intellectual elite.[12] Such criticisms counted for little with Bonaparte himself; he flaunted his membership of the Academy and routinely placed 'Member of the Institute' first among his various titles and honours, even before his military rank.[13]

For all this though, the main objective of the Egyptian campaign was the conquest of a faraway land, very different from the revolutionary mantra of defending the fatherland, of fighting for *la patrie en danger*. Some of the more revolutionary of the generals remarked on this, and there is little doubt that those such as Kléber, who still held firmly to republican ideals, were uneasy about the morality of this new development in French diplomacy that condemned them to fight what they saw as imperialistic wars, wars that had no evident significance for the safety of the French civilian population.[14]

But Napoleon allowed himself no such doubts. He would talk afterwards of the Egyptian campaign as a war conducted in the interests of civilisation; and in his correspondence at the time he did not conceal his desire to be understood by the Arab world as the saviour of a glorious civilisation. Writing from Cairo to the Governor of Syria, Ahmed Djezzar, in August 1798, he explained, in a passage that recalls the sensibilities of the Revolution, that he was in Egypt not to attack the people or their beliefs but only to punish their rulers. 'I have not,' he said, 'come to make war on Moslems.' When he had landed in Egypt, he added, 'I reassured the people and offered protection to the muftis, the imams and the mosques. The pilgrims to Mecca have never been welcomed with greater warmth and friendship, and the Festival of the Prophet has been celebrated with more splendour than ever.'[15] The intended inference was clear: here was a Western leader who did not come with assumptions of innate superiority, who had studied the Koran and would treat Islam as the equal of Christianity, and who could be trusted to respect the cultural treasures of Ancient Egypt. It made for a powerful propaganda offensive, though it did not deceive the Egyptians for long.

There was certainly something mildly exotic about the military expedition that set sail from France on some three hundred ships in the spring of 1798, an expedition which Napoleon had assembled and, in the case of many of its participants, personally inspired.

The thirty-six thousand troops included units drawn from the armies in Germany and Italy, armies which had had very different traditions and whose relations were marked by a degree of rivalry. They were well supplied with officers, over twenty-two hundred in all. Bonaparte's own entourage, unsurprisingly, was drawn from officers he had come to know and trust in Italy and who continued to operate as an inner circle on this new campaign.[16] They were competent – often brilliant – soldiers, who succeeded in the very challenging task of adapting quickly to the fighting conditions they encountered in North Africa.

But it was not the presence of the army that was most remarked upon in Toulon, but rather the incorporation of around a hundred and sixty of France's most distinguished scientists, archaeologists and engineers, men whose duties in Egypt had nothing to do with the progress of the military, but who were charged with exploring Egyptian monuments and pyramids, archaeological sites and ancient inscriptions. Their task was to investigate every aspect of Ancient Egyptian culture; to record its splendours and catalogue its remains, to transcribe its languages and identify its species of animals and birds. They were there because of Bonaparte, and Bonaparte alone. It was his idea to adapt the expedition for cultural as well as military goals, and his personal prestige which had led scientists from all over France to agree to participate in the first place. It was his conception, too, that from the outset military conquest and scientific discovery should be closely associated, twin pillars of the same imperial enterprise. The idea was not wholly without precedent. The eighteenth century had been a period of ambitious scientific exploration, including circumnavigations of the world by two great Frenchmen, Bougainville in 1766–69, and La Pérouse in 1785–88.[17]

And there were, of course, classical precedents to follow: Napoleon was very conscious of the fact that he was following in the footsteps of a great predecessor, and that in his marches to Egypt, Persia and India, Alexander the Great had taken with him a band of learned men and philosophers to explore the lands they passed through. There is little doubt that Napoleon saw himself as a new Alexander.[18]

Not everyone in the army was persuaded of the wisdom of this approach, which they interpreted as a dilution of their military endeavour, especially since their general seemed to favour *les savants* and their work over the military targets of the expedition, while the costs of archaeological work and hiring artists to record the monuments came out of the military budget. But there was a longer-term political goal here which cannot be overlooked, since it was this that allowed Bonaparte to present himself not just as a military conqueror but as the bearer of civilisation. Indeed, almost his first action on arriving in North Africa was to create an Institute of Egypt in Cairo, a place where scholars could meet and discuss cultural matters, and where a new science of Egyptology could be evolved.[19] There was more than a hint of diplomacy in this, as well as an immediate publicity coup. He came to Africa with an understanding of culture and antiquity, concerned to discover and cherish Africa's heritage, whereas the British – whose fleet had withdrawn from Egypt only the previous year – were presented as new barbarians, a trading people whose only interest in Africa lay in opportunities for profit and commercial exploitation. Of course, in reality, Napoleon's own motives were far more complex and in no sense altruistic. For him it was about control, and power: what Edward Said would represent as the European pursuit of the total knowledge of and total control over an Oriental society, as 'the original sin in the modern nexus of hegemonic Western power and knowledge'.[20]

The military campaign did not go smoothly; this was to be no repeat of the rapid succession of victories that Napoleon had enjoyed against the Austrians in Lombardy, although the first action of the advancing fleet was an undoubted triumph. The French bullied and bribed the Knights of St John to surrender their fortress city of Valletta and seized the strategically placed island of Malta for France. They then sailed on to the coast of Africa, where they faced a very different army, a force of Mamelukes with traditional battle tactics and little sense of European strategy. They were distinguished in European eyes by their oriental uniforms, their curved scimitars, and their disorganised conduct on the battlefield. Against them the French won some notable battles, fought against memorable and exotic backdrops, most particularly the Battle of the Pyramids in July 1798, where French losses of three hundred contrasted dramatically with the Mamelukes' two and a half thousand. In open battle the French enjoyed a clear advantage, which they maintained even after the Porte declared war and they had to face Turkish as well as Egyptian forces in the field. In 1799, for instance, they celebrated comprehensive victories at Mount-Tabor and Aboukir, pressing home their advantage in a succession of engagements.

But these were the high points of a campaign that spelt mixed military fortunes for Napoleon. His navy was effectively destroyed by the British under Horatio Nelson when the two fleets met at the Battle of the Nile in the first days of August 1798. As a consequence of these victories the British were handed effective control of the Eastern Mediterranean and denied the French the possibility of getting supplies and reinforcements to their armies, which proved a decisive blow. On land Bonaparte found his tactical options dramatically reduced. He was forced to move north into Syria to face the Turks, but he found his army fatally weakened by fevers and, worst of all, by bubonic plague which struck his troops in Jaffa. Morale plummeted, desperation set in, and they were cut off from supplies of food and water. He besieged Saint-Jean-d'Acre, but this time his temerity and incisiveness were not enough, for the city was supplied by the British from the sea. It was a galling defeat for Bonaparte, and one which led him to renounce his objective of taking Acre and retreat with the remnants of his army across the sun-baked desert to Cairo. An expedition that had started so promisingly had ended in failure, despite the fact that the French had won a series of lightning victories and had destroyed two Turkish armies. In military terms it had been an impressive performance, though the work of the army was undermined by French naval weakness, and by the crushing British naval victory at the Nile. But Napoleon could justly feel that his achievement went beyond the purely military. In his dealings with civil society he had impressed upon Egypt and its people his interest in them and their land, his concern for the ruins of their past, and his evident interest in Islam. Just as importantly, he had built up solid working relations with local people, and had laid the foundations of a French colony in Egypt.

Yet the retreat from Acre was that of a beaten army: stragglers were cut down by Turkish fighters, while many of the men, their bodies weakened by plague or raddled by disease, fell by the wayside. Dying soldiers sought opium to end their sufferings; others, in despair at what they were living through, committed suicide in front of their officers. At Jaffa, some twelve hundred of the most seriously ill were placed on boats to be transported to hospital in Damietta.

Those who were able to walk were forced to march on, with the bedraggled and demoralised remnants of the army, blowing up the defences of every town they passed through and taking hostages from among the local population.

When they finally reached Cairo, they were dirty, exhausted, and often mortally weakened by plague, glad only that their hell was over and that food and a change of uniform awaited them. The campaign, it might seem, had ended in disaster, sufficiently so for Bonaparte to order the burning of some of the expedition's records. But that was not the way it was made to appear. At the approach to Cairo, the French were greeted as conquering heroes: Napoleon had already taken steps to ensure that the impression of victory was maintained whatever the true cost of the campaign might have been, and that the sheiks of Cairo were outside the gates to welcome them with gifts of horses, camels and slaves. His soldiers must have been confused to hear that theirs had been a brilliant triumph, that 'the enemy army which was marching to invade Egypt is destroyed'; or that the decision had been taken to turn back from the castle of Acre because it 'is not worth the loss of any more time'.[21] It was all untrue, of course, but Napoleon had already learned the principal rule of the propagandist: that he should never feel constrained by the truth. His reputation for invincibility was in jeopardy – all the more so when he then abandoned his army, defeated and demoralised, in Egypt to return to France. He understood the importance of winning over opinion back home, of making his fellow Frenchmen aware of what he had achieved in North Africa and proud to count the campaign in Egypt as a notable French success. But to do that he had to conduct another campaign, one shaped in words and images.

As had become clear in Italy, Napoleon was ever aware of the esteem and kudos that could accrue from his military talents, and he had never hesitated to make the most of his achievements, parading them before the army and the French people alike. But in Italy he had had a succession of remarkable victories to present to an admiring public, whereas presenting Egypt in similarly triumphal terms might seem well-nigh impossible. However, the very distance between Paris and Cairo, and the colour and exoticism of the desert, were peculiarities of the Egyptian campaign that he could manipulate, and which ultimately played into his hands. Here he did not need to dwell at length on the outcomes of battles, but could put added emphasis on the cultural mission which he saw himself fulfilling, a mission that ensured France's place among the great civilisations of the world.

As he had in Italy, he published two news sheets from Egypt, each with a distinct audience in mind. The *Courrier de l'Egypte* was targeted primarily at the troops, which allowed Bonaparte to present his own version of events and to dismiss damaging rumours. Again, there was a clear emphasis on cultural policy, with historical and cultural articles, pieces about the new improved administration, and articles praising the high quality of the Islamic elites and boasting of their cordial relations with France. But after the initial issues, published in France in the weeks before the fleet sailed to North Africa, poor communications and long distances ensured that the *Courrier* was little read back home, though excerpts from it were sometimes reprinted in the *Moniteur*, always to Napoleon's advantage. His second publication, *La Décade Egyptienne*, was more uncompromisingly scholarly, its mission to report on the work of Napoleon's Institut d'Egypte and to discuss Egyptian antiquities with the scientific community in France.[22] In both papers Napoleon was depicted as a multi-talented figure, at once soldier and diplomat, religious and cultural leader, and the representative of civilisation in a foreign land. Against exotic backcloths, surrounded by Mamelukes, sphinxes and pyramids, he represented France and the spirit of the *Grande Nation*, the embodiment of French republican values exported to far-flung lands.[23] Science stood side by side with ancient architecture, religious faith with exoticism. His supporters would even claim that he 'worked miracles in Egypt', going so far as to imply that he 'was close to being talked of as a successor to Mahomet'.[24]

It is interesting how the strangeness of the landscape and the richness of Egypt's heritage contributed to the construction of Napoleon's new identity, and how far he had come since the days when he was seen exclusively as a brilliant general. For already in Egypt it is clear that he was seeking to present himself as a statesman, a diplomat, a man of honour and compassion, and a leader totally at ease in the diverse cultures of the world. He was aided in this by Vivant Denon, whose real interests were always more artistic than military and who confessed that, close-up, he found little in war that was of real beauty. Denon was overwhelmingly grateful for the privilege of accompanying the expedition. The publication of his journal, detailing the wondrous discoveries they had made and the antiquities they had uncovered in their marches across Egypt, was a major literary event in Paris, and played a significant part in popularising Orientalism in Western Europe. Napoleon lavished praise on the ingenuity of the scientists and men of letters who had accompanied the expedition, and by so doing he helped to introduce French readers to a hitherto unknown world of Egyptian antiquities.[25] A new generation of Imperial artists would perpetuate the sense that Napoleon had conducted himself in the Levant as a civilised Frenchman: a man of the Enlightenment and a man of reason and sensibility.

The Paris art market, liberalised during the Revolution, was restructured in the early years of the nineteenth century, with government-inspired themes for competitions at the Salons and generous prizes donated by the state. Large-scale history paintings were again in vogue, and artists vied with one another to present Bonaparte's victory at the Battle of the Pyramids, for instance. Such a subject offered a heaven-sent opportunity to combine a eulogy to the regime with a splendidly exotic backcloth of Arab horses and scimitars, palm trees and camels. Or else they rushed to portray victories at Aboukir and Nazareth. These were battle scenes, but battle scenes enriched by their novel and exotic setting. Napoleon's artists did not, however, restrict themselves to questions of tactics or military triumph. They also captured moments of generosity, sympathy, or forgiveness that suggested symptoms of true greatness.

Two incidents that were taken from the campaign in the Levant provided striking examples of another side to Napoleon's nature. One was his readiness to forgive his enemies once they had surrendered to him – a principle to which he did not religiously adhere throughout the campaign, though after the insurrection against the French in Cairo, there was one such moment. It was well captured in *Napoleon Pardoning the Rebels of Cairo*, a canvas of 1808 by Pierre-Narcisse Guérin, which underlines the simple nobility of the pardon, and the power of life and death that had lain in Bonaparte's hands.[26] In a series of pictures, many inspired by Denon's sketches, Antoine-Jean Gros, a painter who was fascinated by the East and deeply regretted that he had not been asked to take part in the expedition, paid his own tributes to Napoleon. The most memorable focused on a second incident, when Bonaparte had visited the sick and dying in the hospital during the outbreak of bubonic plague at Jaffa, evidencing heroism of a quite different kind. In his *Bonaparte Visiting the Plague-stricken in Jaffa*, Gros depicts the revolutionary general consoling plague victims, speaking to them about their woes, even touching their wasted bodies. It was an extraordinarily iconic image, which would be repeated many times in popular lithographs and cheap prints. And for Napoleonic art, too, it would have important effects. The enormous popular success of the painting in the 1804 Salon 'established once and for all the viability of large-scale propagandistic representations of contemporary events depicted in the language of classical history painting'.[27] By then Napoleon had become fully aware of the value he could extort from representations of this kind.

But science was about more than propaganda, and there is no reason to suppose that Bonaparte's interest in Egypt stemmed from nothing more than cheap cynicism. He shared the enthusiasm of his linguists and artists for the treasures of Egypt, the tombs and temples, gates and sphinxes; he expressed curiosity about its languages and inscriptions; and he revelled in the exotic landscape of the Pyramids. The most enduring, and in many ways the most impressive, outcome of the whole campaign was the publication back in Paris of the *Description de l'Egypte*, a series of twenty-four lavishly illustrated volumes produced by the *savants* after their return. These detailed the scientific discoveries made during the expedition and unveiled to the world the wealth of the antiquities that had been unearthed by the French in Egypt. Most of the antiquities remained in Egypt, though some were seized by the French and brought back to Paris for exhibition in the Louvre; the most famous of all, the Rosetta Stone, would be plundered for a second time by the British as part of the final peace treaty and would find its home in the British Museum. The *Description* is a work of breathtaking ambition, introducing to Europe a world of temples and tombs, inscriptions and sculpture, of which they had little knowledge. Of the forty-three authors, only two were specially co-opted after the expedition returned; the others were all veterans of those months in the desert, pioneers who had volunteered to accompany Bonaparte on this great adventure and who had explored ancient Egyptian civilisation from the Mediterranean coast to the desert of the interior, and up the Nile to Luxor and Karnak. They produced hundreds of engravings and entire volumes of plates, dividing the work into three discrete sections on 'Antiquities', 'The Modern State', and 'Natural History', and showing as great an interest in recent change and the modernisation of the Islamic world as they did in the remains of a world long lost.[28]

The propaganda value of the *Description*, like that of the artists, would be greatest in future years, when it would help to cement Napoleon's image once he had already seized political power in France. By then it played on a familiar theme, for it conveyed, in a fuller and more scientific form, the same message that he and his acolytes were sending back to Paris from Egypt at the time, a message that praised his diplomacy as much as his soldiering, his appreciation of ancient ruins and exotic cultures, his tact and understanding and wisdom. This message would have a powerful effect on opinion back home, quite apart from fulfilling the more obvious task of ensuring that he was not forgotten, exiled beyond the furthest extremities of Europe and abandoned to oblivion.

The correspondence from the Army of Egypt could itself be turned to the purpose of glorifying Napoleon's role, and of emphasising the high level of respect he commanded among the Egyptian elite. On 23 July 1798, for instance, the national newspaper *Le Publiciste* ran an item on the hymn of praise sung by a Coptic choir in the Grand Mosque of Cairo 'to celebrate the entry into the city of Bonaparte at the head of the Braves of the West'. The paper obligingly hailed Bonaparte as the 'new Alexander' and commented that the style of his letters was as inimitable as that of Julius Caesar himself.[29] These, we may safely conclude, are comparisons of which Napoleon would have approved; he may even have suggested them in the first place. They played an important part in preparing the reception that would await him when he disembarked in Fréjus from the ship that bore him and a few selected counsellors back across the Mediterranean. They would also serve a valuable purpose in preparing the Napoleonic myth for future generations.

Though the military expedition ended in defeat – Bonaparte was never able to offset the crippling blow inflicted by Nelson at Aboukir Bay, which left him unable to guarantee the supply of his army – the Egyptian adventure cannot be dismissed as a simple failure. The scientific achievements would ensure that the French and their young general continued to be seen as explorers, humanists, men of science bringing the glories of an ancient civilisation to the notice of the modern world. Administratively he brought to Egypt many of the benefits which he had already bestowed on Italy: laws, courts of justice, ready access to administration, and an administration that was not sapped by corruption. And in the longer term the expedition helped to reshape France's relations with Egypt long into the nineteenth century. French engineers stayed on after the army pulled out and helped to staff the country's administrations.[30] So, in the short term, did Kléber and Menou, left by Napoleon to maintain French rule in Egypt, and their regime was talked of as bringing progress and modernity. They succeeded in finding Egyptians ready and willing to serve France; but they could not turn around the war, or deter the British from attacking the last remnants of the French army. In all, French rule lasted a mere nine months. Kléber was to die in Egypt, murdered by a patriotic student at the Azhari mosque in Cairo after repressing a popular rising in the city;[31] Menou, on the other hand, was able to negotiate the safe departure of the last units of the French army before returning to France in 1802.[32] They left behind a tradition of administration that was honest and efficient so that, ten years later, when Mehmet Ali ran the Mamelukes out of Egypt and established a strong, authoritarian state, he did not hesitate to borrow from the administrative practices which Bonaparte had established.[33]

In this respect Napoleon's Egyptian legacy was not destroyed along with the remnants of his armies. He helped to establish French interests and government practices in Egypt, and he has some claim to be acknowledged as an innovator and as a pioneer in colonial governance. Some French historians during the first half of the twentieth century went rather further, seeing in the colonisation of Egypt the beginnings of France's nineteenth-century empire and a prologue to the colonisation of Algeria in 1828.[34]

6

First Consul

Though Napoleon's propaganda machine proclaimed the Egyptian campaign a resounding triumph, it was a difficult boast to sustain in reality. He had suffered significant reverses and his thrust north into Syria had proved unexpectedly costly with the loss of around six thousand men to the enemy, plague and physical exhaustion. He had been forced to accept defeat at Acre and had retreated south, only to see the British navy land an Ottoman expeditionary force near Alexandria. The gloom was only lifted by the brilliant cavalry charge unleashed by Murat against the Ottoman army that had occupied Aboukir, an attack that scattered the enemy and delivered the city. For Bonaparte it at least meant that his campaign in Egypt had ended with a victory which would raise spirits and confirm his reputation back in Paris; as usual he made sure that the Paris newspapers buzzed with excitement about the scale of his supposed triumph. But he couldn't fool himself. He had already concluded that this would be a long and difficult campaign, punctuated by setbacks and reverses, and this realisation may have contributed to his decision in the late summer of 1799 to return to Paris and the faction-ridden political world of the Directory. He appointed General Kléber to take military charge in North Africa, informed the Directory of his decision, and emphasised the importance of Egypt to French security. And in the most paternal language he passed his soldiers into Kléber's care, writing to the General thus: 'The army which I am entrusting to you is entirely composed of my children; even in the midst of their greatest sufferings I have always had marks of their affection; maintain them in these sentiments; you owe me that because of the esteem and the special friendship in which I hold you, and for the real feelings of attachment that I have for them'.[1] The message was, of course, sent on to Paris; Napoleon's sense of publicity did not desert him. The soldiers could be excused if many of them judged his departure rather more harshly.

He set sail for France on 23 August together with his chosen companions, among them several of his future marshals, in a small flotilla of naval ships, consisting of just two frigates and two sloops, commanded by a French vice-admiral, Ganteaume.[2] He left behind the bulk of his army and a majority of his officers and scientific advisers. He even abandoned Pauline Fourès, his mistress during his time in Egypt (Josephine, it would appear, did not enjoy a monopoly on infidelity); it was widely rumoured that she responded defiantly to his act of desertion by transferring her affections to the new commander, Kléber.[3] When they heard the news of his return and realised that he had abandoned them on the other side of the Mediterranean, many of the troops were understandably indignant, though they were soon won over to his successor, who commanded a wide degree of respect in the ranks and who many hoped might negotiate them a return to France.

But what are we to make of Bonaparte's actions? Despite allegations that he had betrayed his men, he had done nothing wrong in terms of military etiquette, and could reasonably argue that he was now more urgently required in Europe than in Egypt, where there was little that he could now achieve. Though some historians continue to present his departure as a shameful retreat, one that salvaged Bonaparte himself but left his army at the mercy of the Egyptians, the Turks, and increasingly the British, he had other, more positive reasons to return to France in the summer of 1799. In Egypt he felt marginalised from Directorial politics and decision-making, even from regular news contact with the mainland. Indeed, during the seventeen months he spent on the campaign to Egypt, he was often dependent for news on chance encounters with foreign merchants or, after the surrender at Aboukir, on the packet of European newspapers he received from Sidney Smith, the British naval commander whose ships had supplied the besieged garrison at Saint-Jean-d'Acre.[4] These contained worrying news about the pursuit of the war in Europe; he learned, most notably, that France faced a second coalition of hostile powers, and the gains which he had made in Italy seemed increasingly to have been put at risk. As he reported to the Directory from Aix the day after his return to French soil, it was through these papers – English papers – that he had learned of the defeats suffered by Jourdan in Germany and Schérer in Italy – defeats that left France's sister-republics in tatters (`I left immediately, that very hour,' he wrote somewhat melodramatically).[5] Bonaparte was probably right to believe that he could contribute little more from Egypt and that his talents could be more usefully applied back in Europe. He found his isolation from politics increasingly insupportable, and his return was motivated less by his desire to flee the war in Africa than by ambitions that could only be satisfied in France.

His ship docked in Fréjus, along the coast from Toulon, on 9 October, having made a brief stop in Corsica to allow him to visit his relatives. It was the last time he would ever set foot on the island, a final glance at the boyhood world he had come to reject. From now on his focus would be firmly on France, its government and governability, its security and, especially, its pursuit of war.

For Napoleon had always been a political general, keenly aware of the cause in whose name he fought and of the importance of political power struggles back in Paris. Through continued propaganda and seizing opportunities for self-publicity he had ensured that his name remained on the front pages of the Paris news sheets; and his upbeat reports on his campaigns in Egypt and Syria ensured that he remained in control of the popular pulse back in France. As a consequence, he returned to France a hero, just as he had from the Italian Campaign, a conqueror who had taken the French standard to the most exotic lands of the Orient. His landing at Fréjus and his triumphant reception in Aix were only the start of a hero's return; in Lyon, they even composed a play in his honour, titled *The Return of the Hero*.[6] By the time his entourage reached Paris, the people of the capital were expectant and excited; what Jean Tulard has termed 'the myth of the saviour' – a myth that would sustain Napoleon through the next sixteen years – was born.[7] The political class were drawn to him, while the workers of the Paris *faubourgs* sang street songs to fête his return. War had made him a national figure and supplied him with the reputation he now needed to make his mark on politics. War had elevated him to a position and a status above politics, and at the same time had helped to undo his possible rivals. Of his fellow generals, Joubert and Hoche were dead by 1799, while Moreau was severely compromised. At a time when the Directory appeared increasingly jaded and stale, the cards seemed to have been somewhat fortuitously stacked in his favour.[8]

Bonaparte went out of his way to reassure the political class that his return to France was not part of a plot, that it was not premeditated, not the consequence of vaulting political ambition. His decision, as he presented it, was an immediate response to a political crisis which he had read about in the newspapers passed to him by Sidney Smith; these, he claimed, provided the catalyst that induced him to abandon North Africa. What he termed 'extraordinary circumstances' had persuaded him to return to Europe. The renewal of the war on the continent had turned public attention away from Egypt, while the fact that the army in Egypt risked defeat made its contribution seem suddenly peripheral. Napoleon was not slow to express his contempt for the politicians who had sent it there. He dismissed their capabilities with a single stroke of the pen: 'Everything is ignorance, stupidity or corruption with them. I am the one, I alone, who have carried the burden, and who, through a string of successes, have given purpose to this government, which, without me, would never have been able to raise itself or to maintain itself in power. With me absent, everything would crumble. Let us not wait until that destruction is complete: the damage would be irreversible'.[9]

These words are revealing, but do they really explain the circumstances of Napoleon's return from North Africa? What they do convey is his arrogance and his complete faith in his own abilities; they may also suggest something of his sense of his own destiny. But the idea that his return was a sudden, impulsive gesture, a decision taken in an instant on the basis of a few newspaper cuttings, is far less credible, especially given the publicity trail he had carefully laid in advance of his return and the web of plotting into which he was drawn as soon as he reached Paris.[10] Once in the capital, he did not retire into private life or seek to escape the glare of public attention. He had a number of friends and allies who helped him to keep in touch with the popular mood, to feel the pulse of the nation. And that pulse told him two things: that people were tired of a politics which they increasingly equated with drift, self-interest and the abandonment of republican ideology; and, even more strongly, that they were tired of war and ready to turn to anyone who promised to restore peace and normality.

As for the political class, they still saw Bonaparte as 'General Vendémiaire', the military leader to whom they had turned earlier to save the conservative Republic against its radical adversaries. This of itself made him a political figure. Now, when he returned and surveyed the political scene, he found that much of the sense of purpose that had characterised the early Republic was sadly lacking. The years of the Jacobin Republic, characterised by a hatred of privilege and a ruthless desire to purge the body politic of counter-revolutionaries and political moderates, had ended in the excesses of the Terror and the Republic of Virtue; and since 1794 much of the government's energy had been given over to establishing political stability and consolidating republican institutions, as politicians who had previously been bitter opponents united around a new constitution.

But stability was easier to talk about than to enact. The process of ending the Terror had been fraught with difficulty: memories were long and politics became enmeshed in vengeance and recrimination.[11] The lower house of the legislature, the *Conseil des Cinq-Cents*, was seriously rent by faction, with the regime once more a prey to battles between the more conservative republicans like Sieyès and neo-Jacobins like Joseph Fouché. The renewed strength of the Jacobin cause during the early months of 1799 aroused anxiety among conservatives, a change signalled in Paris by the new and central role played by a political club, known first as the *Société du Manège*, later (taking its name from the street where it met) as the *Société de la Rue du Bac*, which gave the movement greater cohesion and was a symptom of its more developed organisational capacity.[12] Neo-Jacobins were especially strong in the upper echelons of the army, where radical and often highly capable men, frustrated by political horse-trading or threatened with exclusion from the political forum after the fall of Robespierre, had sought to make a new career and serve the Republic in a different way. Their presence in the army gave them a new form of power and authority, as Napoleon was only too aware.[13] It also threatened to destabilise still further the already stuttering Directory.

It was not Bonaparte alone who masterminded the conspiracy that overthrew the Directory in Brumaire of Year VIII. When he returned to Paris, that conspiracy was already being planned by some of the Directory's most prominent politicians, republicans like Sieyès and Fouché and Napoleon's old associate, Paul Barras – men who believed that change was needed to restore the authority of the government. They saw the Directory as fatally weakened by the compromises it had been forced to make after previous periods of crisis, most especially after the violent insurrections of 18 Fructidor and 30 Prairial, and believed that its claims to constitutionality were sorely flawed. As Fouché noted, the constitution of Year III had become inoperable, so that 'from a purely constitutional regime we had moved to the dictatorship of five men: and that had not proved successful'. Worse, in his eyes, was what had followed, for 'now that the very essence of the executive has been mutilated and weakened, everything indicated that we would pass from the despotism of a few men to the turbulence of the crowd' if something were not done about it without delay. [14]

In particular, Sieyès and his fellow plotters wanted to end the influence of the two Directors most closely associated with the neo-Jacobins, Gohier and Moulin, whose promotion had symbolised the Directory's lurch to the left the previous year, and they were prepared to stage a coup in order to do so. The re-emergence of Jacobinism as a credible political force frightened many in the centre as well as on the right of the political spectrum, as Madame de Staël recognised, when she wrote, 'It was not the external reverses suffered by France that produced the fatal attraction to Bonaparte in 1799, but rather the fear inspired by the Jacobins inside the country which worked so powerfully in his favour. The Jacobins had few resources at their disposal and their reappearance was no more than a spectre which stirred in the ashes; but it was sufficient to revive the panic they had generated in the past.' As a consequence, the French nation 'threw itself into the arms of Bonaparte, simply to escape from a phantom'.[15]

The plotters needed to be sure that they had military support before they launched their conspiracy. They could not risk facing the collective strength of the army, and they therefore had to win over to their side a general who commanded the respect of other officers. Some of those who would have been considered the more obvious candidates, notably Lazare Hoche, were dead; and Joubert, the man on whom they placed the greatest faith in the months before Brumaire, was killed in battle in 1799. Moreau and Pichegru were considered; Macdonald was approached, but refused. It was only then that the plotters turned to Bonaparte, the choice as much the effect of chance and circumstance as of purposeful planning.[16]

In this regard the timing of his return proved crucial, since it suddenly made available a general with whom some of them enjoyed good relations and who, behind a staunchly republican façade, was known to be a man of order on whom they could depend. His part in what came to be known as the insurrection of 18 Brumaire (9 November 1799) was intended to be quite specific: to provide military muscle in the streets of Paris and, if needed, in the two chambers of government. Indeed, on the morning of the coup Napoleon's entourage was almost entirely military. It consisted of troops from every regiment in Paris, many of them veterans of the Italian Campaign, as well as forty adjutants of the Paris division of the National Guard.[17] Their involvement was vital to the plot's success, since they would impose emergency measures in Paris during and immediately after the coup, and so help to initiate the new regime. At that point – it was naively believed by some – Bonaparte would stand aside and the politicians would assume power. But those who thought that Bonaparte was nothing more than a military man were soon to be disillusioned. His control of the army meant that power was his to retain or relinquish as he chose; and from the moment the coup was launched he was in no doubt as to who would really be in command.[18] The much-anticipated battle for influence between Bonaparte and Sieyès never took place: the former revolutionary general imposed his will on those around him, and impressed with his dynamism and energy.

Napoleon played mercilessly on his popularity during the two days of the coup, assuming an active role in both the constitutional manoeuvres of 9 November and the military uprising the following day. The gift for publicity that he had demonstrated in Italy and in Egypt did not desert him. He had the walls of Paris plastered with posters singing his praises, and urging the implementation of his solutions to what was now openly seen as a political crisis; solutions involving the resignation of four of the five Directors and leaving a gaping void at the heart of the polity. At the same time his brother Lucien, who had been elected to the Cinq-Cents the previous year and was at the time of the coup its president, provided further ammunition by distributing a pamphlet in Paris warning of a supposed Jacobin plot against the Directory and of the dangers of anarchy.[19]

To resolve this crisis Napoleon proposed a stronger and more compact executive, three consuls in place of five directors, but nothing that implied any weakening of republican principle. The plan was rapidly enacted, and the new constitutional arrangements put in place. On 9 November the assemblies were transferred out of Paris to the relative safety of Saint-Cloud, and Bonaparte was appointed commander of the army in the capital. The following day he was in Saint-Cloud, where he addressed the two assemblies, ordering the dissolution of the Directory and the creation of a provisional consulate. On 11 November the provisional Consulate met and a new government was formed. A new constitution, prepared in advance by Daunou, was adopted on 12 November, which established the Consulate in its definitive form.[20] This had all been accomplished in four days.

Napoleon was very careful to do nothing that would alienate republican opinion. He went out of his way to win support for the coup in the ranks of the army and the National Guard, two notably republican institutions, and presented the ousting of the Directors as a necessary measure to sweep away corruption and protect the founding principles of the Republic. Indeed, in a proclamation issued

on 12 November, he and the other consuls went so far as to call on
the French people to take an oath of loyalty to 'the Republic, one
and indivisible, founded on the principles of equality, liberty, and
representative government'.[21] Although he was allied to men of a
conservative bent, or so the argument went, there was no reason
for republicans to fear the new regime. He, Bonaparte, was strongly
committed to the republican ideal and the coup was carried out in
a mood of constitutional propriety. A few disagreed publicly and
violently; Bernadotte in particular broke with Bonaparte over
Brumaire and fled from the capital, threatening to return with troops
at his back.[22] But he did not carry out his threat, and most Frenchmen
seemed to go along with the change of government; if there were
some outbursts of protest from the more radical clubs, they were
quickly silenced, and the Consulate was installed without a drop of
blood being spilt – a rare achievement in France's republican history.

Even Paris, so ready in the recent past to meet political protest
with violence, remained singularly calm. Indeed, the salient mood
would appear to have been one of unconcern and public indiffer-
ence, mingled with an ill-disguised hope that the new regime would
bring the political and commercial stability that could deliver
economic prosperity. Above all, the people wanted peace, and the
presence among the Consuls of the all-conquering general
contributed, somewhat perversely, to their confidence. To the Paris
masses, Napoleon was a hero, a conqueror, the protector of the
Republic and, above all, someone who, by delivering a rapid victory,
could bring the peace treaty they craved.[23] The many messages of
support from local authorities in the provinces provided some
comfort to the new regime. 'The echoes of the Alps redouble our
applause,' gushed the departmental authorities in Gap, while other

authorities greeted the Consulate as an effective defence against royalist reaction.[24] But these endorsements cannot be read as evidence of real enthusiasm; since the early years of the Revolution, mayors and local officials had learned that it was wise to be cautious, and many, like Elbeuf in Normandy, ensured their own survival by congratulating the organisers of every victorious coup and siding with the leaders of every incoming government.[25] Over the previous ten years Frenchmen had seen too many false dawns, too many constitutions and supposed guarantees, too many governments welcomed on one day only to be jettisoned the next. They were thus unlikely to suspend entirely a degree of well-tried scepticism.[26]

The lack of widespread opposition can also be explained by the tactful way in which the new regime presented itself to the people. Continuity was emphasised, as was the essential republicanism of the Consulate, a republicanism which others had put at risk. The *Conseil des Anciens* had provided that continuity by accepting a move to Saint-Cloud, away from the turbulence of the Paris populace, and this move had been presented to them as one that would help guarantee constitutional government. The *Conseil des Cinq-Cents* had been less compliant, requiring an impassioned speech from Lucien Bonaparte and the threat of military intervention before even a rump of deputies voted for the provisional Consulate, but their stubbornness could be blamed on dangerous neo-Jacobin elements who sought anarchy and the destruction of the state. In the tense hours that followed, propaganda was everything. The Brumairians presented themselves as responsible men, anxious to avoid violence and disruption. If the institutions guaranteed under the previous constitution had been dissolved, and dissolved by force, was there anything to suggest that this was more radical than other coups of the Directorial period? The Directors themselves had either resigned or were now forced to resign – in Gohier's case after being held against his will in the Luxembourg Palace for forty-eight hours. The deputies of the lower house were unceremoniously driven out of their meeting hall by Bonaparte's troops, and the rump of the deputies obediently voted for the dissolution of the Directory itself.

But the government that replaced them was not so different in kind. A provisional Consulate of three was not so different from its five-man predecessor, and its membership – Bonaparte, Sieyès and Roger-Ducos, two of them former Directors – did not of itself spread alarm in the country. And the Consulate seemed to promise many of the same goals that the Directory had been trying to deliver for the previous four years, to make France's parliamentary system work in permanently testing circumstances. The longer-term aims of the Brumairians were left unclear – always a wise tactic in moments of crisis – and the language they used did nothing to dispel this ambiguity. Bonaparte in particular showed great diplomacy and tact. So, for example, where Sieyès advocated a pre-emptive strike against some of the most prominent Jacobins as a measure of state security, he opposed it, eager both to distance himself publicly from Sieyès and to maintain a germ of consensus.[27] The Consulate had to appeal to more than a narrow ideological constituency if it was to win public support.

The previous government, declared Fouché in the days following, was the victim of its own shortcomings. It had been vacillating and ineffective, he said, 'too weak to maintain the glory of the Republic against outside enemies or to guarantee the rights of citizens against domestic factions'.[28] This alone provided justification for regime change and, at least in the short run, the majority of the population seemed willing to accept his assessment. Bonaparte told the deputies on 19 November that the republic no longer had a government at all; to save it required intervention, and intervention backed by force.

The Consuls hammered home the same point in their proclamation two days later. 'The Constitution of the Year III,' they insisted, 'was dying. It could neither guarantee your rights nor assure its own existence. Repeated assaults were robbing it of the people's respect.'[29] They were determined not to repeat this mistake. Under the Constitution of Year VIII which followed, France was given two legislative chambers: a Tribunate with one hundred deputies aged at least twenty-five, and a Legislative Body with three hundred members aged at least thirty. These age restrictions were imposed to ensure responsibility and avoid the intemperate passions of youth, though – given the limited powers that were extended to the assemblies – they might seem to have been scarcely necessary. For neither the Tribunate nor the Legislature was directly elected by the population; they were nominated by the Senate, the third element established by the constitution: it was composed of sixty notables – career politicians, generals, admirals, scientists and magistrates – largely chosen by Sieyès. Through the Senate he had hoped to create an element of constructive opposition, and hence offer sufficient protection against tyranny.[30] But the Senate was a deeply conservative body, and the authority given to the three chambers was strictly limited. In particular, they had no power to introduce legislation, or even to propose amendments, rights that were reserved to the First Consul and the Council of State. The Tribunate might debate laws that were presented to it and offer its opinion to the Legislative Body, which would discuss that recommendation in its turn.

The Legislature was to meet annually for this purpose, its session lasting for no more than four months.[31] Cynics talked of tyranny; certainly, by any measure, it was scarcely a recipe for a robust parliamentary system.

Not everybody was impressed by the new institutional framework, especially in those areas where Jacobin clubs had been reinstated or where the threat of a royalist revival seemed imminent. Here the anti-Jacobin tone of the Consulate did nothing to reassure local people, and there were widely held fears that the Consuls' real aim was to subvert the Republic and its values. The first days of the new regime had to be carefully handled, and it was in those same first days that Bonaparte eclipsed the other Consuls and imposed his will on the polity. A number of the addresses that were sent to Paris were surprisingly critical of the regime, expressing their unease about the safeguards for democracy. Some initially refused to publish the decree of 19 Brumaire setting up the provisional Consulate, and one eastern department, the Jura, went as far as to denounce Napoleon as a 'usurper' who rode roughshod over essential civil rights guaranteed by the Assemblies of the 1790s.[32]

Once in power, the Consuls did everything they possibly could to ensure that the errors of the Directors would not be repeated and that the authority of the state commanded the respect of all. To this end they sought the support of those powerful interest groups on whom stability would depend, in particular the social elites and the army. The support of the army was, as Bonaparte recognised better than most, critical to the success of the project, and establishing the loyalty of other generals was the essential first step in securing public acceptance of the regime. He realised that there would be jealousies and broken ambitions among the high command, jealousies accentuated by his own elevation, and he knew that he could not simply attack them head-on. Instead he sought to secure the loyalty of the army to his person by responding to some of the long-standing grievances of the troops: invoking the promise of better pay and pensions, raising the question of a further distribution of land to serving soldiers, and taking more severe measures against deserters and those who shirked their military duties. There was to be increased surveillance of the conduct of soldiers, too; more rapid military justice, and tighter discipline. Behind these measures was a determination to raise the morale and public image of the army, to reward bravery and inculcate a sense of honour and professionalism. It would bring its reward on the battlefield in a new surge against the Coalition powers. And of course there was a political purpose, too. 'In cafés and on public thoroughfares,' states Jean-Paul Bertaud, 'the First Consul paid army veterans so that they could combat the activity of the Jacobins inside the army and act as publicists for General Bonaparte'.[33]

Army officers enjoyed new influence and prestige during the Consulate, but it was not a military regime, nor yet can it be charged with militarism, since civil authorities remained firmly in charge of political decision making. The army, under the Consulate, and the Empire that followed it, was there to carry out orders and enforce policy; it was an arm of the state, and army leaders were actively discouraged from holding political views of their own. The aim was to make the army more professional and less ideologically driven than in the more radical moments of the 1790s. Government remained in the hands of politicians, not soldiers. Its legitimacy was grounded in law and one of the Consuls' first priorities was to establish that legitimacy through a new constitution.

This was quickly achieved: the constitution was short – the document consisted of ninety-five clauses where its predecessor had had nearly four hundred – and it took less than seven weeks to prepare. Gone was any reference to the rights of man, which was a constant feature of all the constitutions of the revolutionary years. The new document placed a strong emphasis on the powers of the executive at the expense of the legislative body, the objections of constitutional lawyers like Sieyès being curtly swept aside. Voting for the Legislature was to be indirect: adult males would vote for communal lists of men eligible to stand, who, in turn, would choose some of their number to sit at departmental and then at national level. This produced a list of some five to six thousand men who were eligible for election. It was a system that avoided any risk of turbulent electoral meetings and guaranteed a stable electorate.[34] But in practice the new legislative counted for little; its primary function was to demonstrate the legitimacy of the new regime. Power passed from the legislature to an executive of three Consuls, whom Sieyès had the honour of naming, though in reality the choice was Bonaparte's; of the three, only the First Consul exerted real power, retaining direct control over most aspects of French foreign and domestic policy, including matters of diplomacy and war. In these tasks the First Consul was to be assisted by a Council of State. The Second and Third Consuls both had had a revolutionary past – the republican deputy Jean-Jacques Cambacérès and the moderate royalist Charles-François Lebrun – but theirs was to be a consultative role: their function was to advise, not to govern. The First Consul, of course, was Napoleon Bonaparte, who identified the institutions of the state so unequivocally with himself and his rule that the Consulate has even been described by some scholars as a step back from republicanism towards monarchical government.[35] Guaranteeing stability was always a more important objective than spreading democracy.

The new constitution was approved by plebiscite, a form of electoral consultation that appealed to Napoleon because it averted electoral disorder and exaggerated the appearance of popular consensus. The Consuls were eager to demonstrate the popularity of the new Constitution in order to enhance their legitimacy, and, though only one in four of those eligible chose to vote, the authorities quite openly inflated the number to demonstrate that the new order was more popular than either the Jacobin regime or the Directory. They placed great emphasis on the very small number of votes cast against the Constitution, an outcome that can occasion little surprise given that voting was not secret, and was done by individual ballot. It would have taken a brave man, or a foolhardy one, to express his opposition to the regime so openly. It was far easier to abstain, or to stay away, which they did, in their millions.[36] But that was not what the French people were told by their new rulers. Turnout was low: no more than about twenty per cent of the electorate endorsed the constitution, but Lucien Bonaparte published very different figures to suggest that the regime had been welcomed by six million voters. It was a lie, but a very effective one, which persuaded many Frenchmen that their government ruled with popular support. [37]

This would be the first sign among many that the First Consul had little interest in the niceties of democratic government. He was concerned to take effective action against perceived enemies and opponents, and proved to be contemptuous of established interest groups. He was also a staunch defender of property rights, which endeared him to men of substance, while his mastery of propaganda helped ensure that he enjoyed a good press in Paris – though here he took no chances, closing down opposition journals and limiting the number of newspapers published in the capital to only eight. (At the height of the Revolution they had been numbered in hundreds). At the same time he increased censorship, and control of the Paris book trade; and he showed little tolerance towards those who broke the law. In particular he turned the power of the state against banditry, condemning the high rates of crime and violence that characterised the French countryside and were endemic in many parts of the Midi. In the last months of the eighteenth century police patrols were stepped up, gendarmes sent into dissident villages, and military patrols established to round up brigands and army deserters. In an attempt to root out resistance in the badlands of the Rhône valley, Bonaparte gave special powers to General Férino to combine national guardsmen with units of the regular army to form 'flying columns' against outlaw bands. He authorised them to execute any brigands who fell into their hands, and set up a Special Military Tribunal at Avignon – one of thirty-two that were created in metropolitan France and across Belgium, Piedmont and the Rhineland[38] – where those arrested could be given military justice, without the benefit of a jury. Férino did not stamp out violence and banditry; and his excesses may have added to the government's unpopularity in the lawless South-east. But his ruthless approach to the problem and his disregard for judicial procedures demonstrated the Consulate's determination to impose order at almost any cost. In 1801 alone, extraordinary military commissions were responsible for two hundred and three death sentences, and within a few years even the most feared royalist brigands in the region had been rounded up and guillotined. Napoleon was unconcerned by the violence that this policy involved. Security and order had been restored, and these were his paramount considerations. [39]

Paramount, too, was the successful pursuit of a war in Italy and Germany, which the Directory had been in danger of losing and where the French armies seemed to have lost the initiative that had provided Bonaparte with his greatest triumphs in the months leading to Campo Formio. The First Consul was desperate for an emphatic victory that would re-establish his authority in Europe and allow him to appear to his own people as a man of peace. He succeeded in getting his victory when he encountered the Austrian army on the plain of the Po at Marengo, but in unusual circumstances, since it was one of the few battles where he allowed himself to be outnumbered and the enemy to attack. There is no doubting that he was lucky, and that for a time he ran a serious risk of defeat. In the end, he owed victory to the timely arrival of reinforcements and the bravery of younger generals like Desaix and Kellermann rather than to his own tactical awareness.

The Battle of Marengo cannot be seen as a triumph of battlefield manoeuvres. Nonetheless, it turned the war with Austria in France's favour, especially since Moreau followed up with victory at Hohenlinden in southern Germany, which had the Austrians suing for peace. That peace was duly signed, first with Austria, then with Britain, in the treaties of Lunéville and Amiens, in 1801 and 1802 respectively. The battle quickly became a central element in the Napoleonic myth, one perpetuated in David's painting of the General crossing the Alps on his white charger. But Napoleon's own version of the Battle of Marengo remains largely fictional. David Chandler, in common with other modern historians of the battle, sees things rather differently, and claims that 'the real attritional nature of the struggle, the fact that few plans survived the first minutes of battle, the parts played by sheer good luck and inspired subordinates in achieving victory, and, above all, the grave errors of Napoleon's judgement – these features were carefully hidden beneath successive layers of myth'.[40]

For the present, however, the First Consul had delivered the peace that so many Frenchmen craved, the longest period of peace that would be achieved in all the years up to Waterloo. In truth it was a fragile structure, leaving neither side satisfied, and it was always likely that the continent would again be plunged into war. But it did provide an important breathing space, to Napoleon as much as to his most persistent adversaries, Austria and Britain, and this allowed him to concentrate on a series of domestic reforms which, together, constituted the basis for the Napoleonic state. Policing, as we have seen, was part of it, the rooting out of lawlessness and internal dissent by a ruthless display of law enforcement. But it was only one element in a process by which Napoleon sought to turn the often rebellious citizens of the Directory into obedient and cooperative *administrés*, men and women who would be acquiescent in carrying out their legal obligations and fulfilling their responsibilities to the state. To this end he built on the achievements of the revolutionary years, the financial, administrative and judicial reforms that had gone before. But whereas the revolutionaries had felt bound by the principle of election, the accountability of public authorities to local people in towns, districts and departments across France, the First Consul was more concerned with efficiency and the smooth running of an administrative machine. And where the men of 1793 had often been forced to pass emergency measures to deal with short-term crises, adding new laws to traditional legal codes that they inherited from the Old Regime, Napoleon sought a more ambitious, more permanent, more rational reform of the law. The revolutionaries had not had the time or space even to dream of codifying the entire legal system, creating a common law code for all. Napoleon, on the other hand, dreamed in these terms, and he had both the personal authority and the bureaucratic means to carry it out.

Central to Bonaparte's concept of efficiency was the idea that, as citizens, men had obligations, and that these could not be evaded. These obligations were quite separate from ideological commitment; they were the duties that the state had the right to expect all its citizens to perform, regardless of politics, and were imposed upon them accordingly. The payment of taxes, service on juries, military requisitions and conscription – above all, conscription – the state could impose of right. These impositions were the price the individual must pay for membership of the political community. Administrators, prosecutors, judges and public officials must be loyal to the state because of the nature of their office, not because they believed in the state's precepts; in short, they were servants of the government, bureaucrats in the modern sense of the term. This change did not originate with the Consulate; the Directory had already begun to steer France in this direction and to rely on civil servants rather than on militant *sans-culottes* or Jacobin idealists to carry out its policies.[41]

Napoleon, however, took this principle further, building on what the Revolution had achieved, yet unafraid to incorporate elements of practice borrowed from the Old Regime where these seemed to serve him best. Thus he retained the principle of direct taxation which the revolutionaries had introduced, but supplemented it by less progressive indirect taxes of the kind that had been levied in the eighteenth century. He reformed the secondary school system to train an educated elite for the new regime, introducing *lycées* in major cities and centralising the curriculum through the new University of France. And he took the system of local government which the Revolution had created in 1790 – the system of departments, districts and municipalities that essentially remains intact to this day – and reformed it to make it more clearly answerable to central government.

The principle of election was played down, and the new office of prefect created to ensure that provincial governance reflected the wishes of Paris, not pressures from local people. A decree of 1800 replaced elected representatives in the departments with co-opted members, whose function was then reduced from administration to simple deliberation. Some have seen the institution of the prefect as a return to the Old Regime's royal intendants, but the new system – where the sub-prefects were chosen locally so as to have inside knowledge of the department, whereas the prefect always came from outside, bringing the objectivity which that guaranteed – was a much more effective tool of centralisation. The institution lay at the heart of the Napoleonic system. As Nicholas Richardson writes, 'Authoritarian and highly centralised, the prefectoral corps was a typically Napoleonic innovation: indeed, if government was to mean not only Paris but the provinces, it was the essential innovation.'[42] Napoleon applied the prefectoral system to the sister republics created under the Directory, and in the years that followed to further territories that France came to occupy across Europe.

Administrative and judicial reforms went hand in hand as the First Consul sought to codify the rights and obligations of citizenship. Perhaps the greatest single initiative of the Consular period – and certainly the one of which Bonaparte himself was most proud – was the Civil Code, which was the principal legal reform of the Consulate, though it only came into law in March 1804. Napoleon was not the first to dream of codifying the laws of the new Republic, or of bringing some coherence to the mass of Roman and common law, constitutional law and statute law which the First Republic had amassed. As early as 1792 a commission of jurists – on which Bonaparte's future allies, Cambacérès and Merlin de Douai, were already prominent – had been established to codify civil laws, and there had been repeated attempts, right up to Brumaire, to bring order to the legal code. Once in power, the First Consul appointed a committee of four legal luminaries to draft a comprehensive code of laws, a draft of which was produced within four months. It was stalled, however, by discussions in the Tribunate, delays which angered Bonaparte and led him to purge its membership, before the Code was finally passed into law.[43]

Hereafter, the Code would be central to everything that Napoleon did, and would be imposed on all peoples who were integrated into his Empire. It was a substantial achievement: it confirmed property rights, announced the disappearance of the feudal aristocracy, and placed great value on the family and on the interests of the state. It also adopted the social principles of 1789, such as individual liberty, equality before the law and the secularisation of the polity. That in turn explains the immediate impact it made, both in France and beyond its frontiers. For Georges Lefebvre, it was a landmark moment; it 'swept through Europe as the symbol of the

Revolution, and heralded, wherever it was introduced, the fundamental laws of modern society'.[44]

Behind the First Consul's reforms lay a double objective – the desire to control and administer effectively, and the ambition to unify the people behind him and thus end some of the ideological splits that had dogged the revolutionary years. In 1800 rebellion broke out again in the Vendée, and his response was telling – a decisive military intervention to suppress the rising and a refusal to tolerate armed rebellion, combined with his desire to end any further threat of religious schism. He recognised that the Revolution's attempts to curb the Catholic Church had helped to mobilise the deeply religious West against its policies and had been one of the primary causes of rebellion. This was a political, not a spiritual, decision, and the Concordat which he signed with Rome was at heart a political treaty, delivering peace with Rome while bestowing the government of the French Church on a carefully selected administrative elite of bishops and archbishops, responsible for clerical recruitment, pastoral oversight, administration, and clerical finances.[45]

Bonaparte himself gave little hint of religious belief; his eternal soul was not in danger, and he could afford to regard the Church, and indeed the Papacy, as pieces on his political chessboard. But his political instincts told him that there was much to gain from reconciliation with Rome, and Pius VII appeared gratifyingly willing to make concessions to regain for the Church the richest country in Catholic Christendom. When agreement was finally announced, after eight hard months of negotiations, Pius achieved his most important aim: Catholicism was recognised as 'the religion of the great majority of the French people', and French Catholics could again worship freely. But the Pope paid a high price. The number of bishoprics and parishes was severely reduced, and the bishops who had embraced counter-revolution were left out in the cold while some of those who had sworn the oath to the Civil Constitution were retained. Above all, Bonaparte enjoyed the loyalty of this new clergy, a loyalty he would exploit brutally in the years ahead. Royalists were at a stroke deprived of their most powerful ideological support, while anti-clericals – still a large majority of the French population – were appeased. Besides, Napoleon could now count on support from the Papacy in those Catholic territories that France annexed or occupied.[46]

In his domestic reforms Bonaparte could present himself as a moderniser, as the one man capable of giving France a new and stable polity that would deliver good laws and institutional stability at home, and earn esteem abroad. Those who had emigrated or fled from France during the Revolution were pardoned and allowed to return – on condition, of course, that they now swore loyalty to the new order; those who continued to plot and campaign for a royalist restoration could expect, and received, little mercy. Consular France was a meritocracy, where men could make their fortunes and be richly rewarded, but where the highest honours were reserved for service to the state. It was in this spirit that, in 1802, the First Consul instituted the Legion of Honour for those who had provided the most meritorious service or who had distinguished themselves in the pursuit of national objectives. The award could be made equally to civilians and soldiers, though in practice it is true that most of the first recipients were army officers, and that most of the adjudged merit took the form of military valour. To that degree it can be seen that the *Légion d'Honneur* built upon the earlier award of the *armes de récompense* to men serving in the armies of the

Directory, or the *armes d'honneur* which the Consuls themselves established in 1800. The real difference lay in its prestige: the Legion of Honour was instantly recognised as the most important acknowledgement of merit in any field, whereas the other orders that Napoleon would create subsequently, like the *Couronne de Fer*, commanded far less prestige and passed into almost instant oblivion.[48] These things mattered to Bonaparte. He believed that men could be lured and inspired by such symbols of esteem, and saw them as necessary if the France of the Revolution was to be nudged towards stability and order.

There was one policy of these years, however, which marred his reputation as a moderniser and seemed to pull France back to its pre-revolutionary past. In 1801, after years of war and insurrection, the black leader and former slave Toussaint Louverture seized control in the French West Indian colony of Saint-Domingue, known today as Haiti, and promulgated a new constitution in defiance of the French. Many of the French planters on the island fled, either back to France or to the United States – Philadephia or New Orleans – or to other sugar islands in the Caribbean where they could establish new plantations, notably Cuba, where the slave economy continued to flourish across much of the nineteenth century. The question Napoleon faced was how to respond to an insurrection that threatened to destroy France's most valuable colonial possession and to leave Britain with an unchallengeable position in the Caribbean. He planned a new trans-Atlantic strategy that would allow France to regain something of her former power in the region, and in 1802 he mounted an expedition to recapture the island for France.

He ordered a sizeable fleet and around nineteen thousand soldiers to the Caribbean, with instructions to impose French rule on the colony, using whatever force was needed, capture Toussaint and the other Haitian leaders, and to bring them back as prisoners. He also let himself be persuaded by the powerful colonial lobby that this was an opportunity to restore both slavery and the Atlantic slave trade, both of which had been abolished eight years earlier by the Convention.[48] It proved a misguided decision. His troops were decimated, both by fever and in battle against the former slaves, while the threat to restore slavery spread havoc and disorder across the French Antilles. Toussaint was duly captured and taken back to France to die, but little else was achieved. The French cause was lost on the island until, on 1 January 1804, Jacques Dessalines published a declaration of independence that abolished the French name and brought into being the world's first black republic, Haiti.[49] In neighbouring Guadeloupe, where France *did* restore order, slavery was reinstituted in 1802, but any French dream of a new conquest of Haiti was doomed to fail as Bonaparte turned his back, not just on the Caribbean but on the whole of the American hemisphere. The sale of Louisiana to the United States was the logical next step, one that not only avoided a new war in America but helped to disguise the extent of France's failure in the sugar islands.[50] It represented, however, something of a *volte-face* for Napoleonic foreign policy, a quick and radical change of direction that took even the American negotiators by surprise. The sale brought France some eighty million francs and left Napoleon to focus his ambitions on the European continent.[51]

The years from 1799 to 1803 were critical for Napoleon. It was in those years that he laid down the broad lines of policy which he would pursue, both at home and abroad. In spite of continued royalist agitation, he entrenched his authority over domestic politics, and in 1802 another plebiscite confirmed him as First Consul for life, a change that proved one step too far for some of the more committed republicans. They were also critical years for Napoleon personally: he was reunited with Josephine and at last seemed to find some stability and fulfilment in his relationship with her. In Egypt it had seemed that his expressions of affection were unrequited and that Josephine was a free spirit who could not be reined in. But his fortunes in love changed dramatically after his return to France and his rise to political power in Paris. Josephine, who had thrown herself with such abandon into the high life of Directorial Paris, and whose affair with Hippolyte Charles had been the stuff of gossip in all the salons of the capital, now lived a more retiring – though far from chaste – existence. She was deeply in debt, however, in part due to the three hundred and twenty-five thousand francs she had lavished on the château of Malmaison, near Saint-Germain-en-Laye, a debt she tried desperately to hide from her husband. But at least she seemed pleased to see him, was at his side during the events of Brumaire, and showed suitable alarm at the supposed attempt on his life at the time of the coup, an event, in the very chamber of the legislature, which was probably invented, like other attempts on deputies' lives in the years since Robespierre's fall.[52] They were apart again, of course, during Napoleon's enforced absence with the army; but after Marengo, when he returned to Paris they lived in apparent harmony, first in the Luxembourg palace, then at Malmaison.

Napoleon's secretary, Bourrienne, paints an idyllic picture of this period of his master's life, lived in tasteful surroundings, with a wife with whom he was clearly deeply in love. He lavished attention on the chateau, buying art works and ordering rare plants to pander to Josephine's tastes. He even bought around five thousand acres of surrounding farmland and improved the estate. 'Except on the field of battle', wrote Bourrienne, 'I never saw Bonaparte as happy as he was at Malmaison.'[53] Of course, it would not last. As Josephine became aware of her infertility and realised that this must put the future of their marriage at risk, she began suffering deep attacks of depression. For Napoleon this was an enchanted period in time, but those close to him realised that even as he cavorted with his family on the lawns, the storm clouds were already gathering.

7

From Consulate to Empire

Though much of Napoleon's reforming agenda as First Consul had its roots in the French Revolution, with his administrative and judicial reforms extending and codifying laws passed during the previous decade, his conception of personal liberty was strictly circumscribed. Throughout the Consulate his concern to protect the authority and the interests of the state was maintained, and there was an unmistakably authoritarian streak in his approach to government and in his response to any hint of opposition. The First Consul might speak the language of a republican; but when he found himself challenged he frequently betrayed the instincts of a dictator, silencing opponents and concentrating power on the small body of men whom he felt he could trust. He had little patience with libertarian notions, even those expressed by his friends and allies; and if the Consulate was a period marked by important measures of judicial, educational and religious reform, it would also be remembered as a regime that drastically eroded the civil liberties which had been granted in 1789 by the National Assembly.

The behaviour of the First Consul and his collaborators contributed significantly to that erosion in censoring the print media, extending the powers of the police, and making liberal use of preventive detention to contain opponents of the regime.[1] These measures made a mockery of their claims to act as defenders of 'public liberty', and help to explain the increasingly frequent portrayal of Bonaparte in Britain and other European countries as a usurper and a tyrant. They must also cast doubt on his claims to be a republican who was carrying forward the legacy of the French Revolution. British writers emphasised his supposed excesses of cruelty, citing his behaviour at Jaffa where he allegedly ordered the poisoning of his own plague-ridden troops to prevent them from falling into enemy hands.[2] He was routinely compared to Cromwell, to William the Conqueror, or to those 'great bad men' of Antiquity, Alexander and Caesar. The sheer difficulty they found in placing Napoleon in any single political category left pamphlet-eers searching for exotic ways to explain his contradictions. In a pamphlet of 1802 he was intermittently described as a 'monster'; while for the *Morning Post* in 1803 he was simply 'an unclassifiable being', slippery, elusive and enigmatic.[3]

He certainly loved power, and showed little taste for delegating it to others. He had no patience with long, drawn-out discussions, or with debating the merits of individual measures or heeding the oscillations of public opinion. The Tribunate attracted particular scorn as a time-wasting talking shop, and Napoleon's contempt was increased by the inclusion in its membership of a number of former Jacobins who were ready to defend the legislative gains of the Revolution.[4] In place of the legislators, he turned to a small circle of trusted counsellors in whose hands he concentrated wealth and power, and who became loyal spokesmen for his policies. Several of those who would become the most powerful political figures of the Empire emerged to prominence under the Consulate, proving their usefulness to Bonaparte and helping maintain some pretence of pluralism in the decision-making process. They also symbolised the continuities that bound the Consulate to the revolution that preceded it, since, almost by definition, those who rose to a position of power in 1800 had served in one or other of the revolutionary administrations. Napoleon would appear to have cared little about their past affiliations as long as they offered him unswerving loyalty and brought their legal and administrative skills to the service of his regime. And there was plenty of talent to be tapped. The generation that had governed France under the Revolution was both highly talented and more mature; and individual careers, like his own, reflected the sudden explosion of opportunity that had come in 1789.

Three examples will suffice to indicate the range of their experience. Napoleon's right-hand man, Cambacérès, was chosen for his undoubted qualities as a cautious and punctilious administrator. A lawyer from Montpellier, he had been elected to the National Convention in 1792 and went on to support each successive phase of the Revolution as a highly competent member of committees and a moderate but loyal republican. Cambacérès first supported the Girondin administration, then, when the Girondins were overthrown, he accepted their downfall and the Jacobin seizure of power.[5] Talleyrand, who had charge of foreign affairs, was far less transparent. A nephew of the Archbishop of Reims, he had spent the months of the Jacobin Terror in exile in London, returning after Robespierre's fall to take over the foreign ministry in 1797. It was in this capacity that he had first met General Bonaparte, with whom he corresponded at length in Italy and whose career he had helped to advance; he was among the conspirators at Brumaire, and Bonaparte rewarded him richly.[6] Talleyrand could certainly not have been more different from the staunchly Jacobin Joseph Fouché, to whom Bonaparte entrusted overall control of policing. Fouché had enjoyed a reputation for being a ferocious terrorist, both in the Convention and on mission to Lyon in 1793, but had then helped to overthrow Robespierre and had been Minister of Police under the Directory. As a former Oratorian, educated for the priesthood, he reserved a particular dislike for the Catholic hierarchy and was happy to help the First Consul forge a largely secular state.

Looking back on a long career, the future Duke of Otranto displayed no humility in listing his many achievements. During the Revolution, he would remind readers of his memoirs, he had been 'solely indebted for the honours and power with which he was invested, and, in short, for his distinguished fortune, to his own prudence and abilities'. Under Bonaparte, Fouché would go on to enjoy a dazzling political career as 'an ambassador, three times a minister, a senator, a duke, and one of the principal directors of state affairs'.[7] He was among the few in the inner circle who counselled caution at key moments, attempting to dissuade Napoleon from getting too deeply involved in Spain in 1808, from further antagonising the British in 1810, or from launching his expedition against Russia in 1812.[8] He commanded respect for his political wisdom, but he was an opportunist who did not invite trust. Napoleon knew what he was doing in investing authority in Fouché: he was a man whose pride he could exploit for his own ends.

It is instructive to linger on Joseph Fouché, not because he brought a sinister or vengeful style to politics – he appears to have been suave and urbane, and to have led a blameless private life as a good family man with his wife and four children in an apartment on the rue du Bac[9] – but rather because of the crucial role he gave to policing in Napoleonic France. He extended the manpower at the disposal of the police, especially in Paris, and supplemented them with a network of secret agents, informers and police spies who kept him informed at the first sign of disaffection or public disorder. They were drawn from across society: men of wealth and substance – when these could be induced to inform – but also a variety of people of humble stock: pedlars and hairdressers, valets and servants, bartenders and prostitutes, on whom police pressure could be brought to bear.[10] Fouché's methods earned him notoriety in the eyes of liberals and defenders of the rights of individual citizens. His spies were given official status within the police force, and from being, initially, private policemen paid for out of special funds, they were subsequently given the rank of inspector and paid by the state or by the city authority. They were authorised to shadow suspects, open private mail, and collect witness statements from passers-by; in short, they collected information on those they pursued, passing it to the ministry to be entered in the systematic and detailed filing system which Fouché constructed. These files were not just on criminals and insurgents, but on spies and ministers, radicals and royalists, army officers, state officials, even, it was alleged, on Napoleon himself.[11]

It is unsurprising that Fouché made so many enemies, not least among rivals for power like Cambacérès and members of the Bonaparte clan, who, with the sole exception of Josephine, regarded him with a certain revulsion; his relations with Lucien Bonaparte, who as Minister of the Interior ran his own spy network, were especially strained.[12] But Napoleon's repressive apparatus did not stop with the police. The Consulate was also the period when he made greatest use of military courts and special tribunals in a bid to crush brigandage and impose summary justice without recourse to a jury. In 1801 special tribunals were created in twenty-seven departments, largely in the badlands of the South and the West; another nine came to be added over the following two years, until they covered more than a third of the country.[13]

Napoleon's measures to control the population and curb opposition did not pass without criticism and he needed to justify them – not least to the political class. He was conscious of the dangers of political insurrection, of the possibility of a renewed outbreak of royalist intrigue in the West, of neo-Jacobin intrigues in the capital. Recent attempted coups – Fructidor, even Brumaire itself – showed how vulnerable the government could still be to factional plots and undercover manoeuvres. But it was difficult to justify what many saw as repressive laws on the basis of mere speculation. Then, quite dramatically, the First Consul was himself the victim of an act of terrorism that killed at least eight people and injured over twenty when a huge bomb exploded after his carriage passed along the Rue Saint-Nicaise in Paris on Christmas Eve, 1800. Bonaparte was travelling to the Opera, his coach escorted by a company of mounted troops, when his way was partly blocked by a seed-merchant's cart. The coachman did not hesitate, but continued at his usual gallop around the obstruction, a decision which almost certainly saved the First Consul's life and rescued the Consulate from constitutional crisis. Napoleon impressed those around him by pretending that all was calm and going ahead to the performance. But there was no denying the seriousness of what had happened. The regime was confronted by a breakdown in security and the possibility that it might now face a series of assassination attempts.

The 'infernal machine' inspired the government to unleash a new wave of repressive measures as Napoleon turned his anger against the neo-Jacobins, ordering the closure of their remaining clubs and pressing for their prosecution. Fouché's position, too, was undermined, both because he had failed to unearth the plot in time and on account of his own Jacobin connections. In the event, patient police work and Fouché's files would exonerate the Jacobins and the Left from any responsibility in the bombing, which was the work of embittered royalists. The perpetrators were duly tried and executed. But the consequence of the 'infernal machine' was far more deep-seated. It allowed the First Consul to justify new measures to protect public order, including a full-frontal assault on the remaining neo-Jacobin activists who, though they had committed no crime under the Consulate, were deemed to constitute a future threat to the regime. One hundred and thirty of them were arrested and deported without trial in an unprecedented show of police power.[14]

The affair of the Rue Saint-Nicaise was ultimately remembered more for its legacy than for the damage it did at the time. It demonstrated that the First Consul did not hesitate to turn the law against those he perceived as his opponents, just as he was prepared to ride roughshod over legal niceties when it suited him to do so. The failed assassination attempt merely provided him with the justification he needed. It also played to his authoritarian nature, since the deportation decree was an act of absolute power – and an undisguised abuse of that power – that was clear to all. It also had more far-reaching implications for society at large, contributing to a more authoritarian atmosphere in the Tribunate and the Council of State, where it discouraged open discussion and silenced criticism of the regime. Perhaps because his victims were Jacobins, associated in the public eye with the blood-letting of the Terror, their victimisation may have caused less of an outcry abroad. But it was a significant moment in Bonaparte's political evolution, the first time that he had acted in defiance of the law, and an act of vengeful spite against those who had dared to challenge his authority. The timid response of the deputies only proved to him that he had got away with it, a lesson which he was not slow to take to heart. The Consulate became more and more personalised, 'a democracy', in the words of one of its champions, Cabanis, 'purged of all its disadvantages'.[15]

Other plots followed. After the uncloaking of the royalists responsible for the Christmas Eve bomb, Fouché and the new Prefect of Police for Paris, Louis Dubois, concentrated their investigations on right-wing groups, royalists, Breton rebels (*chouans*), and others whose aim was to destroy the republican regime and restore the monarchy. There were, as always, constant rumours of conspiracy, the majority of them said to be planned from London or funded by the British government's lavish secret service funds. These had been used throughout the revolutionary period to finance military and diplomatic missions against France, including the ill-fated expedition to Quiberon under the Directory. During the truce following Amiens, Henry Addington had sought to extend the secret service campaign, stirring up royalist discontent and offering succour to any dissident generals who could be persuaded to topple Bonaparte's government from the inside.[16] The most threatening outcome was the so-called 'Grand Conspiracy' of 1803, in which the King's brother, the Comte d'Artois, was complicit, and which Britain financed to the tune of around a million francs. The Royal Navy also smuggled the conspiracy's leaders, the dissident General Pichegru and the royalist Georges Cadoudal, across the English Channel to the French coast.

But at that point the conspiracy lost momentum. Following the bomb attack on Napoleon's life, the French police were active in hunting down *chouans*, a number of whom were arrested in Paris in October 1803. They were hauled before a military commission and sentenced to death, but one of them, to save his skin, made a confession that implicated Cadoudal, with whom, he said, he had landed from a British ship at Dieppe five months earlier. The net was closing, especially once the police were given further names, among them those of two French generals, Moreau as well as Pichegru. The conspiracy, it seemed, was gaining force by the day, and it was only the sharp wits of the Paris police and the willingness of others to inform on their leaders that came to Bonaparte's aid. He showed little mercy to those who were found guilty. Moreau, who denied any involvement, may have escaped with a two-year sentence, but he was the exception. Georges Cadoudal, Armand de Polignac, the Marquis de Rivière, with seventeen of their accomplices and several other conspirators, were sentenced to death. As for Pichegru, he was found dead in his cell, the victim, in the words of the police report, of 'self-inflicted strangulation', no doubt his way of escaping the clutches of the executioner.[17]

In demanding the punishment of the conspirators, Napoleon was unyielding, but it could be argued that he was not unjust: they *had* plotted his overthrow and conspired with a hostile power, so that their sentences did not seem incommensurate. During his interrogation, Cadoudal had not concealed the purpose of the conspiracy: he made it clear that he had planned to use force against Napoleon, adding that his ambition was 'to put a Bourbon in place of the First Consul', and identifying the Bourbon in question as 'Louis, Xavier Stanislas, formerly known as Monsieur, recognised by us as Louis

XVIII'.[18] There could be no ambiguity, but the exposure of the conspiracy and the seriousness of the royalist threat raised further questions to which the First Consul demanded answers. Cadoudal had indicated to the police that he had been alone in Paris, lying low until it was time to attack, since 'I was only to attack the First Consul once a French prince had arrived in Paris, and he is not yet there.' But who was this mysterious 'prince'? It was a question that consumed Bonaparte, as it did his investigators.

The Duc d'Artois himself was ruled out because he was in exile in England; and suspicion fell on the young Duc d'Enghien, the son of the Prince de Condé who had commanded the émigré army. There was little evidence to support the charge that d'Enghien was an active conspirator – little more, indeed, than vague statements of admiration from a number of condemned rebels and known royalists. One of the final acts of the Consulate, and among its least honourable, was to arrange for him to be kidnapped from Etten-heim, in the neutral territory of the Duchy of Baden, and brought back to France to face trumped-up charges of conspiracy and treason. There was no evidence that he had had any role in the conspiracies of the previous year; but he was an emblematic figure for the counter-revolution, a Bourbon-Condé on his father's side, descended from Louis XIV's greatest field commander, and on his mother's from Philippe d'Orléans, who had served as regent during Louis XV's minority. Among the Duke's direct ancestors he could count Henri IV, and news of his birth in 1772 had been announced immediately to the King at Versailles.[19] The condemnation of this man was widely seen across Europe as an act of blatant injustice, devised to show the world that even the most powerful family connections now counted for nothing.

From the very beginning, the First Consul took a personal interest in the affair, reading countless despatches and sending detailed instructions about the measures to be taken. To Réal, whom he charged with the investigation of the Pichegru conspiracy, he even listed the questions which he wanted the investigators to put to their prisoner. All pointed to his involvement in treasonable activity. He was to be asked whether he had borne arms against his country; if he was in receipt of payment from the English; if he knew of payments by the English to émigrés camped along the Rhine; and whether he had proposed to raise a legion of troops by encouraging desertion among the soldiers of the Republic. There were other questions, too, in Bonaparte's catechism, about the letters the Duke had sent and received, and about his contacts with known conspirators, all suggestive of his involvement in a conspiracy against the regime.[20] Bonaparte knew his man: for the Duke was notoriously impolitic, consigning too many of his thoughts to paper, dreaming of seizing Alsace and invading France from the east. He was known abroad, too, and some of his correspondence had even been quoted in the British press.[21] Finding evidence of his counter-revolutionary sentiments, or of the awe in which he was held in royalist circles, would not be difficult, and by the time he appeared before a hastily assembled military commission, d'Enghien was already doomed.

The young prince was executed by firing squad at the military fortress of Vincennes, to the east of Paris, and almost immediately he was immortalised in romantic legend. For Chateaubriand the execution did not only offer proof of Napoleon's cruelty, or of his despotic nature. It spread a glacial fear, he wrote in *Mémoires d'outre-tombe*, fear of a return to the reign of Robespierre. 'Paris thought it was seeing again one of those days that only happen once, the day of Louis XVI's execution.'²² Napoleon, of course, saw things differently. On Saint Helena he would justify his decision on the basis of national emergency and natural law, and would try to blame those who had plotted his assassination for what he seemed to admit was an act of vengeance. 'A great nation had placed me at its head,' he explained. 'Almost all of Europe had accepted this choice; my blood, after all, was not made of mud; it was time to show that it was the equal of theirs.'²³

Napoleon's critics argued that the d'Enghien affair was not just a momentary aberration, but proof of the degradation of public accountability during the Consulate, the dangerous concentration of power in the hands of one man. Indeed, there is ample evidence that the character of the regime had changed since the days after Brumaire, with the First Consul becoming less answerable to the public, and the checks and balances of Sieyès' original constitution less respected. The state might still be republican in form, but the move to personal power was unmistakable. From the very beginning some had harboured doubts about the Consulate, perceiving its potential to turn into a dictatorship; and the replacement of the original candidates for Second and Third Consul with Caulaincourt and Lebrun, known moderates and men favourable to Napoleon, confirmed the suspicion that the only voice that really counted was Bonaparte's. Besides, the constitution gave him unprecedented authority: he was authorised to appoint the members of the legislative bodies as well as government ministers, ambassadors, and army and naval officers.²⁴ Thibaudeau, one of the most astute of his critics, recognised how far this was an assault on the principle of representative government. Since the coup of 18 Brumaire, he wrote in a note to the First Consul, 'things have come to the point where no free constitution is possible unless you specifically want it.' And if Napoleon were to disappear from the scene, what would remain of the brave new world they had built? 'Nothing', he replied. 'Nothing of the Revolution, of liberty, of the glory of the nation, of your own glory, nothing other than bitter memories and lacerations.'[25]

Because executive authority was strong and political factionalism discouraged, the First Consul could leave Paris with relative equanimity when he went on campaign. But he clearly still wanted more recognition, more stability, more power; and in 1802, following his military triumphs and the signing of peace, the moment seemed ripe for some expression of the nation's gratitude. What followed is deeply instructive about Napoleon's political ambition. The Senate, eager to please him and anxious not to lose his services, voted to extend his term of office by a further ten years, which would have kept him in office till 1820. But this did not suffice; some suggest that the First Consul even found the offer insulting. What is certain is that Cambacérès, doubtless reading Napoleon's wishes, persuaded the Senate to withdraw its offer and, instead, to put to the people in a plebiscite the proposition that Bonaparte be made First Consul for life, the reward which he really sought. Obediently they did so, and obediently – and publicly, for there was nothing secret about the ballot – the electorate voted. The result, Cambacérès reported, was a resounding triumph. Of the 3,577,259 Frenchmen who cast their vote, 3,568,885 voted for the life consulate.

For good measure, the Senate added expressions of affection and deference. In proclaiming Napoleon Bonaparte First Consul for life, they declared that they wished to express 'the confidence, love and admiration of the French people'; and, without any apparent sense of irony, decreed that 'a statue of peace, holding in one hand the laurels of victory, in the other the Senate's decree, will bear witness to posterity of the gratitude of the Nation'.[26] But we need not be deceived. Voting in plebiscites during the Consulate and the Empire was conducted in public, and fear played its part in harvesting votes for the regime. Soldiers' votes also helped to boost the appearance of enthusiasm for Napoleon, while lists of voters were drawn up by prefects and sub-prefects, conscious of the need to produce figures that sustained his authority. Recent research has demonstrated that the figures were systematically manipulated, that the declared result of the plebiscite on the Constitution of the Year VIII was simply wrong, and that in some departments polling was kept open for additional days until enough people had been dragooned into voting.[27]

There were other changes, too, in the new constitution of Year X, all reinforcing Napoleon's executive authority: the number of deputies in the Tribunate was cut and its freedom of action reduced; and the First Consul could now sign treaties without legislative ratification and exercise the prerogative of mercy. Most controversially of all, he was given the right to name his successor and thus, potentially, to found a dynasty – though, at this stage, the law did not rule the post hereditary.[28] For many republicans, however, this was a step too far, a step that unmistakably pointed in the direction of monarchy and represented a betrayal of the values they had fought for throughout the previous decade. Thibaudeau, in his note for the First Consul, stated tersely that the executive appeared to be arming itself at the expense of public liberties. 'The word stability is the order of the day; I am astonished that it is not replaced by eternity.'[29]

Napoleon paid little heed to such fears, accepting the new powers conferred on him and offering his thanks to the senators. The language of his reply on 3 August 1802 is gracious, and seemingly consistent with the ideal of the Republic. 'The life of a citizen', he began, 'belongs to his country. The French people wish that mine be entirely devoted to it. I obey its will. In giving me a new pledge, a permanent pledge of its confidence, it imposes on me the duty of consolidating its system of laws on well-founded institutions. By my efforts and your cooperation, Citizen Senators, and with the assistance of all the authorities, with the confidence and will of this immense people, the liberty, equality and prosperity of France will be sheltered from the caprice of fate and the uncertainty of the future'.[30] There was little in his words to frighten his listeners, or imply monarchical ambitions.

There was, though, more than a suggestion of the regal about these new powers, whatever the language in which they were couched. The boy from Ajaccio had already taken a large step towards the throne, and contemporaries noted that the First Consul surrounded himself with much of the panoply of a monarch. There is little doubt that he enjoyed the pomp and luxury of office. His taste for lavish display had first aroused comment during the Italian campaign, when he sometimes seemed to act less like a republican general than a ruler in his own right, insisting on an elaborate etiquette that was redolent of court ceremonial. When he stayed at the Palazzo Serbelloni in Milan, the poet Antoine Arnault compared his drawing room to the foyer of the Paris Opera, and observed that 'never did a military headquarters look more like a court'.[31] At the castle of Mombello in 1797, Miot de Melito observed that he held court like a king, received diplomats and ambassadors like a king, and even dined in public like a king, drawing an adoring gaze to his person. As a consequence, remarks Philip Dwyer, 'Italians who came to catch a glimpse of the conqueror of Italy were allowed into the galleries to watch while he ate in a remarkable public display of the self reminiscent of Louis XIV's performances at Versailles'.[32] This taste for display and his concern for the niceties of etiquette continued to mark his public appearances – his excursions in to Paris, his presence at lavish dinners at the Tuileries – during the Consulate. The household, whether at Josephine's palace at Malmaison, or at Saint-Cloud, where the Consulate had been inaugurated, was increasingly likened to a pre-revolutionary royal court.[33]

Rather in the manner of a monarch, Bonaparte showed a consistent concern to further the interests of his family and, even as First Consul, appeared to give thought to hereditary succession. His family remained important to him – not just the nuclear family that might one day produce an heir, but also the wider Bonaparte clan, while his mother, Letizia, was still frequently consulted by her son. The older brothers, Joseph and Lucien, had been among his supporters at Brumaire, and they continued to play a significant part in the politics of the Consulate. Joseph had been named Commissioner of War for the Army of Italy, a highly lucrative post that enabled him to accrue a substantial fortune and establish valuable literary and artistic contacts which he put at the service of the regime. Lucien, whose relations with Napoleon were always uncertain, was briefly rewarded for his loyalty with the post of Minister of the Interior, but after a row with his brother he found himself dismissed from his position and despatched as ambassador to Madrid.[34] Nor did Lucien ingratiate himself with Napoleon when in 1800 he authorised the publication of Louis de Fontanes' heavily ambiguous pamphlet offering what he termed a *Parallel between Caesar, Cromwell, Monk and Bonaparte*, a comparison repudiated by the First Consul in spite of Fontanes' conclusion that, of the four, only he could be classed a true hero.[35]

The comparison itself was, in many people's eyes, a damning one, since to most Frenchmen Cromwell was a tyrant and usurper, and not the guarantor of English liberties,[36] and Napoleon viewed the publication with distaste, seeing it as further evidence of Lucien's unreliability. Lucien did not seem unduly perturbed, and made it clear that while he was happy to work with his brother in government, he baulked at serving under him. It is doubtless not without significance that under the Empire three of Napoleon's four brothers would be rewarded with kingdoms to rule (Joseph in Naples, Louis in Holland, and Jerome in Westphalia); only Lucien was given nothing. Napoleon was only too ready to berate him for what he deemed to be frivolity, a lack of the seriousness that his membership of the Consular first family demanded. Increasingly, he saw such failings as a reflection upon – if not a direct insult to – his own standing in the eyes of the nation.

The promotion of his brothers to positions of authority in the state, and later to the status of kings in their own right, was a flagrant instance of nepotism which demonstrated just how far he was prepared to go to further the interests of his family. But that does not mean that his brothers were without talent, or ill-suited to the high offices bestowed upon them. The problem did not lie in their reluctance to accept responsibility, nor yet in their abilities as rulers. Joseph made a decent job of two well-nigh impossible missions in Naples and Spain, while Louis could claim the remarkable achievement, for an outsider imposed on the Dutch people against their will, of protecting their interests, at times in defiance of the instructions he received from Paris. Rather, the problem lay with Napoleon, who wanted to control them, to manage their governance, and to impose policies and economic obligations on them that would almost certainly have led to their rejection by the nations they ruled. It was soon clear that Napoleon expected his brothers to reward him with their undivided loyalty. But, like Lucien, they soon followed their own instincts. They were not prepared to be mere puppets of the Emperor.

Louis turned out to have quite a talent for kingship, despite the fact that the timing and circumstances of his appointment as King of Holland did nothing to endear him to the Dutch. In the four years he was allowed to remain on the throne – before Napoleon had him removed in 1810, angry that Louis had done nothing to stop the widespread smuggling that was letting British goods enter the continent – he established a reputation as a conciliator, doing what he could to stamp out political factionalism and demonstrate that he was prepared to stand up for Dutch interests. He did not completely succeed, of course: Holland remained at peace during these years, and there were no national crusades that would have allowed him to emerge as a Dutch national hero and thus win the affection of the people. In any case, the Dutch were not accustomed to being ruled by kings, not kings with real powers and authority. But it would be harsh to adjudge his reign a total failure, since it took place against the backdrop of a much larger, pan-European war, conditions that made it impossible for him to oppose his brother's wishes. Domestically he had real achievements to his credit. He simplified the polity, improved educational provision, strengthened and modernised the state. These were significant steps in a country where power was largely decentralised and decisions left to provinces and to commercial elites. Of course people grumbled, but if there was some popular resistance to taxes and conscription during his reign, there was no general insurrection. And the Dutch in the nineteenth century looked back on Louis' reign without a lasting sense of grievance.[37]

Joseph, whose gentle nature and genuine commitment to many of the ideals of the Revolution irritated the First Consul – he confessed to hating the war and seeking happiness in nature – found himself continually at loggerheads with his bellicose brother, for whom the major role of a king was to extract men and money for the French war effort.[38] Their differences became clear in 1802, when Napoleon had offered to place Joseph at the head of the newly created Cisalpine Republic. It was true, Joseph is quoted as saying, that he had been offered the post, 'but at the same time he wanted to chain me to it, and – knowing my brother as perfectly as I do, knowing how heavily his yoke can weigh one down – I felt, as a man who has always preferred the obscurity of private life to the role of a political puppet, obliged to turn it down. I asked him, though, to tell me what his conditions would be had I accepted . . . I insisted that Piedmont be reunited to the Italian republic, that I be given freedom to re-establish the principal fortresses, and that he withdraw French troops from the territory, and especially General Murat'.[39] Joseph might be mild-mannered, but he was not spineless.

This personalisation of politics lies at the root of the move away from republican traditions and towards the declaration of the Empire in 1804. Linked to it was Napoleon's desire for an heir, his insistence that the regime be perpetuated, and his frustration, which he made little attempt to conceal, that Josephine had not succeeded in bearing him a son. The decree granting him the Life Consulate was clearly a turning point, with the months that followed marked by a discernible emasculation of the republican symbolism and public ceremonial on which the Directory had been so insistent. Instead, public festivals became more martial in tone, celebrating victories in battle and the return of triumphant armies from war, rather than the rights of citizens or the fall of the Bastille. Cambacérès observed the alarm expressed by a number of prefects who were convinced that even the National Day of 14 July might be sacrificed, and republican opinion outraged.[40] The list of festivals celebrated in one provincial city, Nantes, gives substance to these fears. The republican themes appear to have been deliberately played down in favour of the military and the person of Bonaparte. In 1801 there were public celebrations of the proclamation of peace, both on land and at sea; in 1802 a festival to celebrate the elevation of Napoleon to the Life Consulate; in 1804 festivities to mark the uncovering of the conspiracy against his life.[41] The emphasis on his victories and his person was redolent of the expressions of thanksgiving that were routinely authorised by the Bourbon monarchy, or even the public celebrations that had been part of the sustained campaign more than a century earlier to establish the authority of Louis XIV.[42]

The Senate took steps to encourage the move to a hereditary system, sending the First Consul loyal addresses and urging him to complete his political project. Some of the senators held monarchist views, and many were advocates of a conservative social order which lent itself easily to the hereditary principle. Among them, too, were men who had seen service under the Directory; Talleyrand belonged to this persuasion; so, vociferously, did Regnaud de Saint-Jean d'Angély, who announced with satisfaction that 'The Senate has presented an address to the First Consul, finishing with the request for a high court for the nation and for institutions that could consolidate his work, so that, having repaired the damage from the past, he might now guarantee the future.'[43] Those pushing for change included some of his most trusted advisers, and not all of them can be dismissed as toadying sycophants.

If Bonaparte harboured personal ambitions to be a dynastic ruler, he was given plenty of encouragement by those around him, and by the winter of 1803–04 the moment seemed ripe. The truce in the war had allowed him to regroup, his army was preparing to attack Britain, and the plots against his person had been destroyed. Within France he appeared to enjoy unparalleled popularity. The only question must be whether he did indeed harbour these ambitions: whether his coronation as emperor was carefully planned in advance. The answer must surely be yes. The obsessive detail of his political interventions, the increasingly authoritarian nature of the regime, the diminution of the powers left to elected deputies, the apparent contempt for public opinion and the vote of the life consulate: all contribute to a coherent picture of a man who, impatient with the niceties of constitutional government, was moving perceptibly to a more personal, more monarchical style of rule. Bonaparte consistently denied this, of course, and even in exile he continued to maintain that he had been following no clear plan and had no ambitions to overthrow the Republic. 'During the Consulate', he insisted on Saint Helena, 'my true friends and most enthusiastic champions would ask me, with the best of intentions and for their own guidance, where I was heading. I always answered that I had not the least idea.'[44] The fact that he argued in this way does not, of course, mean that it was true.

The imperial constitution was established in May 1804, apparently in response to popular demand from around the country. In the Tribunate, speaker after speaker hailed the 'hero' Bonaparte and cited empire as a device to secure his power rather than as a betrayal of the Republic. Indeed, even as they conferred the imperial title on Napoleon, they seemed illogically loath to let go of their republican identity. 'The government of the Republic,' asserted the rather confused words of the law, 'is entrusted to an emperor, who takes the title "Emperor of the French".' The creation of the Empire was entirely personal, a seamless transference of authority that was a reward to one man: 'Napoleon Bonaparte, currently First Consul of the Republic, has become Emperor of the French.' And unlike the Life Consulate, the imperial title was hereditary, rather as the thrones of kings were hereditary.

The second clause of the decree established dynastic succession: 'The imperial dignity is hereditary in the direct, natural, legitimate lineage of Napoleon Bonaparte, from male to male, by order of primogeniture.'[45] In fact, for as long as he himself remained childless, his natural heirs were his brothers, though one by one he disinherited them for their waywardness, their unsuitable marriages, or their disobedience, till the decree named 'Louis Bonaparte and his descendants' as successors to 'the imperial dignity'. To Louis' dismay it then clouded the issue by leaving open another option, that Napoleon might choose his successor by adoption. 'Napoleon Bonaparte may adopt the sons or grandsons of his brothers, providing that they have reached the age of eighteen years and that he himself has no male children of his own at the time of adoption.'[46] The law was supple enough to be adapted to Napoleon's whims and preferences.

Surprisingly, the promise of a Bonaparte dynasty caused less trouble with the electorate than it did inside the family. Men who had previously declared their loyalty to the Republic swallowed this contradiction with apparent ease. Only Carnot, the former Jacobin who, as War Minster, had delivered the victories of 1793 and 1794, had the courage to speak out against the measure and decry the Empire as a betrayal of republican principles. As Thierry Lentz notes, the new constitution was verbally sanitised. There is no hint that sovereignty rests in the French people, a phrase that had become something of a mantra for the revolutionaries; and any words with a strongly republican connotation, like 'nation' and 'people', are no longer part of the lexicon.[47] The imperial title and the principle of heredity were put to the people in a plebiscite in June. However, as we have already noted, since votes were open and Napoleon controlled both the police and the media, it would be rash to think of this as a meaningful form of public consultation. The result confirmed this impression, with only 2569 voters recording their opposition. The Republic was allowed to die with barely a whimper.

The coronation ceremony that followed in December in Notre-Dame was lavish and sumptuous, heavy with the symbolism of state authority and personal power. It had many of the trappings of a royal coronation except that, unlike the Bourbons who were traditionally crowned in Reims, Napoleon chose Paris, at the heart of the nation. He was quite prepared to break with tradition here, for it was not to the Bourbons that he looked for precedent but further back in time, to Charlemagne and the Holy Roman Empire, a thread of continuity which he saw as a source of legitimacy.

The décor was solemn, and the costumes of the Emperor and Empress suitably lavish.[48] Their robes were designed to recall the antique splendour of imperial Rome as well as to produce a sense of awe among onlookers. Napoleon was attired in the imperial mantle of crimson velvet, lavishly decorated with the golden bees that were his insignia; while Josephine wore a heavily embroidered robe in matching colours, its train carried by five imperial princesses, including Josephine's daughter and Napoleon's three sisters.[49] The procession entered Notre-Dame through a temporary portico, specially enlarged for the occasion and constructed in wood, cardboard and stucco in a neo-Gothic style to complement the cathedral's architecture and conceal damage done to the building during the anti-clerical excesses of the Revolution.[50] In Marshal Marmont's words, it was impossible to conceive of any scene 'more majestic or more imposing'. Nothing, he claimed, was lacking from the ceremony. 'The glory of arms, the triumph of civilisation, and the interest of humanity, all contributed to its magnificence and its adornment.'[51]

Following the Concordat, the Catholic Church, too, was present in all its pomp, to give its blessing to the Emperor. The fact that the Pope himself attended made a deep impression on onlookers, since it was a rare honour for a pope to attend a coronation, still less to travel out of the Vatican to do so. Charlemagne himself had had to go to Rome in 800 to be crowned; yet here, before their eyes, was Pius VII, passing through Paris at the head of a cortège of carriages glowing with the bright clerical robes of archbishops and cardinals – a sight many had believed unthinkable during the anticlerical fervour of the Revolution.[52]

The Pontiff's presence was a diplomatic triumph for Napoleon, the result of months of hard negotiation and, at times, brutal threats. It was a moment heavy with symbolic power, its political message carefully tailored to its intended audiences. Internally, it was conceived of as a gesture of reconciliation. For France's millions of Catholics, and for the rebel departments of the west, it demonstrated papal approval for the new regime and conferred the blessing of the Church on the person of the Emperor. For foreign rulers, especially those of Catholic Europe, it was calculated to offer a degree of legitimacy to a regime that remained, in their eyes, founded on a regicide. But it did not convey any spirit of submission or allegiance. Just as the Concordat had been a political agreement, drawn up between two unequal partners, in which the state's interest was paramount, so the coronation ceremony was a symbolic affirmation that power was now Napoleon's. Famously, he did not allow the Pope to place the crown on his head; the Church's role in the ceremony was restricted to that of blessing the Imperial couple. Napoleon refused both Confession and Holy Communion for himself, and kept Pius waiting for a whole hour in the church before he and Josephine arrived for the ceremony. Nor did he kneel before the altar in Notre-Dame. That would have implied acceptance of the authority of the Church, which he had no wish to acknowledge.[53]

Throughout Pius' extended stay in Paris – he did not leave his assigned quarters at the Tuileries until April 1805 – Napoleon treated his guest with a studied lack of respect, constantly reminding him that he, not the Papacy, now commanded temporal authority, and that temporal power always took precedence. In truth, Pius managed to extract few concessions from his host on the matters which he considered important, most notably the continued employment of ex-constitutional bishops and revolutionary laws on secular marriage and divorce.[54] Napoleon was careful to give little away, for his view of the world remained fundamentally irreligious. He was a son of the Enlightenment, a man forged in the spirit of the Revolution, and in his coronation oath he went out of his way to confirm many of the gains of the Revolution. He swore on the Gospel 'to maintain the integrity of the territory of the Republic; to respect and to impose respect for the laws of the Concordat and the freedom of religious worship; to respect and impose respect for the equality of rights, for political and civil liberty, for the irreversibility of the sales of national lands; to raise taxes and impose duties only in accordance with the law; to maintain the institution of the Legion of Honour, and to govern to advance the interests, the happiness and the glory of the French people'.[55] Nowhere among his priorities was there any special status for the Church of Rome.

For all this, the steps he was beginning to take made many ask themselves where Napoleon's real aims lay. Had he really turned his back on the founding principles of the French Revolution in the pursuit of personal glory and dynastic ambition? Back in 1799, in a proclamation to the French people, the three Consuls had recommended their new constitution, claiming that it was 'founded on the true principles of representative government, on the sacred rights of property, equality and liberty'. They had concluded with the highly ambiguous claim that 'the Revolution is established upon the principles which began it. It is ended'.[56] Historians have long discussed the meaning of these seemingly portentous words. Did they imply that their purpose was to overturn the Revolution and revert to a more stable, more authoritarian regime? Or did they see the Revolution as being complete, its gains acquired, allowing France to end its long years of turmoil and disruption? Their ambiguity allowed many of those present to be persuaded, once more, to go along with measures with which they profoundly disagreed or of which they were deeply suspicious.

For one deputy, however, the meaning of the new powers bestowed on Napoleon and of the monarchical grandeur of the coronation ceremony was clear. Lazare Carnot had known Napoleon long enough to feel that he understood his ambitions, and they were not for the Republic. Addressing his colleagues in the Tribunate on 1 May 1804, Carnot expressed the fears that many of them must surely have felt. They had, he reminded them, witnessed the creation of a host of institutions, one after the other, that were quite obviously 'monarchical' in spirit, but on each occasion they had been reassured that they had been devised to protect liberty. And now, he declaimed, 'we are being called upon to pronounce on the formal proposition to restore the system of monarchy and to confer the hereditary imperial title on the First Consul'. For a republican like himself this was one step too far. While carefully expressing no desire to return to a world of political parties and factions, he had had enough; he preferred to go into political exile rather than serve the Empire. 'At the time, I voted against the life consulate; and in the same way I shall vote against the re-establishment of monarchy, as I believe my position as a member of the Tribunate obliges me to do.' He added a note of perceptive regret as he surveyed the way in which the revolutionary decade had disintegrated. The previous dynasty, he reminded his listeners, had lasted for eight hundred years. Now a new one was being born. His main regret was that 'we have not been able to establish the republican regime among us, however hard we have tried in a succession of more or less democratic forms'.[57] With these words the former Minister of War cast his vote against the imperial constitution and brought down the curtain on a remarkable political career.

8

Quest for Glory

The peace signed at Amiens in the spring of 1802 was always fragile, and within a year Napoleon was once more at war with the country that he identified as his most determined and most dangerous enemy, Great Britain. There was little surprise when the peace was broken. Both governments recognised that nothing substantial had been resolved in the treaty, and that it had been a truce in hostilities rather than a resolution of differences. The British, in particular, were resentful that they had gained so little from their efforts. Colonies that had been taken by both sides were handed back, while France was left as the predominant land power in Western Europe, complementing the power of Russia in the east and effectively excluding Britain from influence on the continent. The French still controlled the states to their east, from Holland and Belgium to the plains of Lombardy and northern Italy. Austria had been weakened, perhaps terminally. Through the Family Compact they also had a defensive alliance with the Spanish throne. Napoleon could well feel fairly satisfied with his work, for, as Thierry Lentz notes, he had exceeded the most optimistic war aims and had realised the traditional foreign policy objectives of the kings of France.[1]

Amiens, like the sister treaty which Napoleon signed with the Austrians at Lunéville, gave both sides a much-needed breathing space. France and Britain had been exhausted by war, both were in need of some economic rebuilding, and both clearly derived benefits from months of prosperity and good harvests. The Consulate even found the resources to develop the economy and expand the country's industrial base, returning to a level of prosperity to which the French people had become unaccustomed. At the same time few doubted that the two governments were preparing for a renewal of hostilities. New ships were laid down, and large orders placed in iron foundries and arsenals. Yet peace was barely given a chance to flourish before Britain declared war in May 1803, having already responded to the growing tension in the spring of that year by calling out the militia to raise men for home defence.[2] The French quickly retaliated by sending troops into George III's other state, Hanover, and ordering the arrest of the substantial numbers of British nationals who had taken advantage of the truce to visit France, many of them as tourists curious to view at first hand the results of the French Revolution. Why, it may be asked, did France and Britain return to the battlefield so precipitately, and at a time when the other continental powers remained, however uncertainly, at peace? The two neighbours, who had so regularly lined up on opposing sides across the eighteenth century, found it impossible, it seemed, to sustain the idea of peace.

For some historians the answer to this question is self-evident: Napoleon's restless nature made it impossible for him to renounce war, while France's military economy cried out for further campaigns, further territorial gains, and further conquests.

This view is especially held in Britain – the target of so much of

Napoleon's spleen – where the 'Black Legend', representing Bonaparte as a callous warmonger willing to send countless thousands
of men to their deaths in the single-minded pursuit of his military
ambitions, has proved particularly persistent. Indeed, persistent to
the extent that some are inclined to discount his periodic attempts
at diplomacy and attribute all the blame for the wars to him, and
him alone.[3] To Paul Schroeder, for instance, Napoleon's peace
manoeuvres were all about gaining advantage, 'tactics of division
and manipulation', and had little to do with establishing a lasting
peace. 'The British went to war,' Schroeder argues with a satisfying
finality, 'simply because they could not stand being further challenged and humiliated by Bonaparte; France went to war because
Bonaparte could not stop doing it.'[4]

The terms of Amiens were themselves part of that 'humiliation';
for peace to hold, Napoleon would have had to make concessions,
and that went against many of his most basic instincts. Yet it was
Britain that declared war, Britain that formally violated the treaty,
and Britain which, during the months of the truce, interpreted
Napoleon's every move as an act of provocation. French troops were
still stationed in 'sister republics' in Holland and Switzerland, and
in Italy where the Cisalpine Republic was restructured, Piedmont
and Elba were annexed, and Parma was invaded after the death of
its duke – all initiatives which Britain denounced as contrary to the
spirit of the treaty. And that was only in Europe. Throughout the
Arab world, from Algiers and Tripoli to Damascus and Muscat,
French agents were busily trying to seal pacts with native leaders,
and Decaen sailed for India in 1803 with sufficient staff to establish
sepoy regiments in French service.[5] Britain was understandably fearful
of French ambitions in India, and in response refused to honour

its own obligation under the treaty to return Malta to the Knights of St John, a refusal which Napoleon seized upon as a telling instance of British bad faith.[6] Each side regarded the other with distrust and sought to make the greatest propaganda gains at the other's expense.

So how responsible was Napoleon for the renewal of the hostilities in 1803? It is very tempting to follow the example of the British press and British caricaturists of these years in labelling him as a warmonger and a usurper who put the security of Europe at risk. Certainly, Napoleon had made no secret of his expansionist ambitions, both in Europe and overseas, and had boasted of his willingness to shed the blood of his troops in pursuit of them. But war was for him a means to an end rather than an end in itself. His ambition was to create a Europe united under French hegemony, liberated from feudalism and absolutism by his armies, a Europe stretching from the Atlantic to the Urals with at its core the old Carolingian heartland of Lotharingia, that sliver of Central Europe stretching from the Rhineland across the Alps into northern Italy. Napoleon had not forgotten the lessons of the Enlightenment, nor turned his back on the humanism of the Revolution. He had steeped himself in classical authors and in European history, had studied the rise and fall of great empires, and did not hesitate to talk of himself as the new Charlemagne, a lawgiver and administrator bringing benefits to his people as much as he was a soldier and hero on the battlefield. For his coronation, indeed, he had replicas made of Charlemagne's crown and sword when the Austrians refused to release the originals. The symbolism surely could not have been more transparent.[7]

There was another matter that pushed Napoleon towards a resumption of war with Britain, however, and that was his particular animosity towards the British and his desire to remove all vestiges of their influence from the European mainland. This persistent hatred could not but inflame the already strained relations between the two countries and, some feel, gave the new British Prime Minister, Henry Addington, little alternative but to go back to war. He also had done nothing to encourage trade between Britain and France, whose commercial advantage he resented and correctly identified as the major reason for her strength in war. For British merchants this was a key issue; they had hoped, at the very least, to force France to accept a free trade treaty along the lines of the Eden Treaty of 1786, which would have given their manufactures entry into France's protected markets. These grievances had cut little ice with the First Consul, however. Napoleon never ceased to be a military man at heart; he understood the culture of the military and sought military solutions to international problems. His temperament remained that of a general on the battlefield, impatient for results and victories; impulsive at times, and with a tendency to anger that grew more pronounced with time.

But such personal characteristics alone do not explain the resumption of hostilities; nor was France alone guilty of stirring up the embers of war. The other European powers, Britain included, had shown themselves to be aggressive in their own foreign policy objectives, whether in opposing French ambitions, in exploiting the weakness of the Austrian Empire, or in expanding their commercial and colonial empires at one another's expense. The French wars were not France's alone; they were European and world wars, expanding across whole continents, to which David Bell and others have applied the twentieth-century descriptor of 'total war'.[8] And because of their character as national wars, these conflicts became closely entwined with wider processes of political and cultural nation-building across Europe.[9]

But in August 1804 these wider considerations were far from Napoleon's mind. The newly crowned Emperor had once again turned his attention to his favoured target, a military invasion of Britain – the same mission that had been undermined by storms during the years of the Directory. He rightly recognised that Britain was his most single-minded and persistent enemy, and he saw that France's continental interests were constantly blocked by British intransigence. And so, as in 1798, he dreamed of sending his army across the Channel to disembark on the beaches of Kent; though he would find that, as in 1798, that dream was again thwarted by the presence of the Royal Navy, with its bases at Portsmouth and Chatham. While the timing was not ideal for Britain, which had taken advantage of the truce to undertake a significant ship-building programme, there is no doubt that the French navy was in much worse shape, split among a number of dockyards along the Atlantic and the Mediterranean, and effectively restricted to port by the deployment of British squadrons. The French were shown to be impotent: over half their navy was still in the Caribbean, and what remained of the battle fleet was unable to offer any resistance; indeed, the British warships that blockaded Brest took two French ships as prizes.[10]

The problems were magnified, however, by Napoleon's unbridled optimism, and his willingness to be diverted into other adventures – against Jamaica, for example, and other British islands in the West Indies. The real threat posed to Britain was tiny; yet the militia was put on standby, fortifications around the south coast were strengthened, and newspapers and print shops resounded to a cacophony of invasion scares. London enjoyed a new form of propaganda, the invasion squib, which poured scorn on the French, showing their ships blown off course by storms or sinking sedately into the mud of the Thames, or John Bull hurling defiance from atop the cliffs of Dover.[11] At the same time the British government pumped additional funds into anti-French propaganda, including savage personal attacks on Napoleon's character. In 1803 they also helped to fund the vicious French-language press of right-wing *émigré* journalists like Regnier and Peltier, buying up bulk subscriptions and encouraging the expansion of the *émigré* press across Europe.[12] Pro-French journalists, on the other hand, were expelled under the provisions of the Alien Act, which Napoleon viewed as further evidence of British hypocrisy and malevolence.[13]

But Napoleon's military manoeuvres did not disintegrate into farce, as his British opponents liked to claim. It is true that he was forced to abandon his invasion plans in the face of British naval superiority, but he did take the opportunity to display his military might to the world. He assembled an army of around eighty thousand men – the *Armée des Côtes de l'Océan*, successor to the Army of England which the Directory had decreed in 1797 at the time of an earlier invasion plan – at the huge military camp which he set up at Boulogne, looking out over the Channel towards England. The spectacle of the Camp de Boulogne took its place in the mythology of Imperial France, and acted as a stark warning to the rest of Europe. For there, in August 1804, at a ceremony to distribute eagles to his legions and the coveted Legion of Honour to his officers, Napoleon held the most dazzling military festival of his entire reign. He decorated two thousand new members of the Legion, all but a dozen of them soldiers, in a timely reminder of the central importance of military values, of the place of honour and glory in war in the new polity, and in the society of the Empire.[14]

At the same time, the truce gave Napoleon, at his headquarters at Pont-de-Briques, the breathing space he needed to plan his next move. These months saw the genesis of the key military institution of the Napoleonic years, the Grande Armée which would soon march eastwards and take the war once again to the heart of Central Europe.[15]

For a time Napoleon also succeeded in seizing the diplomatic initiative to leave Britain isolated from the European mainland, an important step since Britain could never achieve her foreign policy objectives unaided. For Pitt and Addington the defeat of France was always the most urgent concern, the single cause to which everything must be subordinated; but the powers of Central and Eastern Europe, fresh from their struggles over the partition of Poland, saw things very differently. Their attention was not glued to a supposed French threat or blinded by the spectre of Napoleon, nor was fear of imminent French invasion their primary driving force. Prussia and Austria vied for predominance in Germany, and were fearful of any expansionist ambitions by Russia towards the west and south. As a result none of the three major states of the region, Austria, Prussia and Russia, was willing to concentrate on helping Britain against Napoleon when they had more pressing anxieties closer to home. Besides, they had no reason to trust Britain's own motives in resuming the war against France. Like the maritime powers on the continent, they shared a suspicion of Britain's commercial and colonial ambitions, and feared that London was prepared to shed their blood in war so as to secure a monopoly position in the Americas and India. In the eyes of many continental powers, Britain blatantly mixed military and commercial ambitions and used war, ruthlessly and selfishly, to further her own economic goals. They needed to be persuaded that they had an interest in supporting Britain's cause.

Russia, in particular, harboured deep doubts about Britain's commercial ambitions. In 1801, following the death of Catherine the Great, she adopted a new commercial policy, forming a Baltic Armed Neutrality to oppose Britain's claim in the North. This served Napoleon's interests well, as it both opened up points of tension between Britain and her potential allies and placed British diplomacy at a disadvantage when she tried – as she did between 1803 and 1805 – to construct a new coalition against France. The French, of course, played upon such tensions, often with consummate skill: France offered rewards and inducements to other states in the form of blocks of territory she had conquered, or raised fears of British maritime predominance in what Michael Duffy has identified as a 'skilful game of divide and rule'.[16]

The war effectively resumed in May 1803, when the British Privy Council ordered the implementation of naval warfare against France and authorised the detention of French commercial vessels. But Britain was alone and vulnerable; the British government had to work hard between 1803 and 1805 to attract allies and establish a Third Coalition to pursue war on land as well as at sea. They had one argument in their favour that had not previously been available to them: the fact that France could no longer realistically present herself as an idealistic or revolutionary polity that could hope to attract sympathy from liberals across Europe or ignite rebellion in Britain itself. Napoleon was now unambiguously a conqueror, France a country with imperial ambitions; and Britain played on the fears of European rulers that what they were witnessing was the emergence of a new and more dangerous version of Louis XIV.[17] There was some justice in this claim, especially as Napoleon could now call on Spain, and on the European states he had invaded, to provide additional forces to help oil his military machine. As was customary, the debate was not conducted exclusively by means of argument and propaganda. London was ready to pay substantial sums to buy the support of the allies Britain needed, though the negotiations with Russia, Prussia and Austria proved protracted and often acrimonious. When 1805 dawned, there was still no agreement and thus no formal alliance against France.

The Third Coalition that was eventually signed later that year owed less to British gold than to Napoleon's bellicose behaviour. In April, Britain and Russia signed an agreement that committed Russia to war unless the French adhered to the terms of Amiens and Lunéville. Shortly afterwards, Austria was moved to join them after Napoleon had arbitrarily annexed the Italian city states of Genoa, Parma and Piacenza and had seized control of Lucca. His coronation as Emperor in 1804 had alerted some to his pretensions but, for Austria and many in Central Europe, it was his second coronation in March 1805, as King of Italy, that provoked the greater outrage. Held in Milan, that coronation bristled with imperial imagery, linking Napoleon – in the popular imagination – to the Holy Roman Empire of Charlemagne. But it was also a ceremony directed specifically at the Italians. To this end he had himself crowned with the historic iron crown of the Lombards, the crown that had been worn in Lombardy by every Holy Roman Emperor since Frederick Barbarossa.[18] The symbolism was not lost on the Austrians, who took pride in the thousand-year history of the Holy Roman Empire, however much its effective authority had faded with the years. In the following year, after Napoleon's victories at

Ulm and Austerlitz, the Holy Roman Empire would be expunged from the map.[19]

In all there were five partners in the Third Coalition – Austria, Britain, Russia, Naples and Sweden – but it soon became apparent that not all had the same priorities. Several of the Allies laid down conditions for their entry into the war. The Swedes would not move unless the Prussians did so, while the Russians held back part of their army for use in the Balkans – which weakened both the Coalition's resolve and its readiness for battle.[20] In the meantime Napoleon was still planning to lure the Royal Navy away from the English Channel in order to leave his army free to invade. The ruse, of course, failed, with the French fleet defeated twice by its British rival, first in a relatively minor engagement off Cape Finisterre in July, then, decisively, by Horatio Nelson at Trafalgar in October. The impact of Trafalgar proved crucial in several different ways. Internally, it helped to undo some of the damage done to naval strength by Lord St Vincent's misguided reform of naval administration, reversing a process of attrition which had jeopardised Britain's naval superiority over France. The battle, it should be noted, did not destroy French sea power or end the threat to Britain's maritime supply routes, but it left the Royal Navy with effective command of the seas and enhanced Britain's economic superiority without the need for further victories. Or as the leading naval historian of the period sees it, Trafalgar 'restored what we might call the normal mechanism of British sea power, which secured home defence, protected trade and opened strategic possibilities all over the world outside Europe'. Napoleon, on the other hand, was unquestionably weakened. Trafalgar exposed France to naval attack, removed possibilities for trade and wealth generation, and restricted her ambitions outside the European sphere.[21]

Napoleon was also compelled to change his military priorities and to abandon dreams of invading Britain. Instead, as the Austrian army moved against neighbouring Bavaria, he was forced to turn eastwards, transferring around two hundred and ten thousand men at dramatic speed from their camp at Boulogne to positions in Central Europe. The Allies mounted offensives against him in Hanover, Lombardy, and on the Danube, which was where Napoleon himself concentrated his forces, while Murat and Lannes grouped their forces in the Black Forest, and Gouvion Saint-Cyr staged a diversion against Naples.[22] His army was well prepared, with around two hundred thousand troops organised under seven seasoned commanders. Camped at Pfaffenhofen before engaging the main Austrian force, Napoleon reminded his men of the forced marches they had undergone, the sacrifices they had made, and the plans they had had to postpone. Without the intervention of the Austrian army they would now be in London, he insisted, and reminded them that 'tomorrow you are fighting against the allies of England'. He called on them to inflict a great defeat, a total annihilation of the enemy, for which posterity would forever remember them — words of inspiration which, as always, he addressed directly to the soldiers.[23]

The events of the following day amply justified his confidence. In a series of attacks from the north, south and west, the French army surrounded the Austrians at Ulm, cutting their supply lines to Vienna and their contact with their Russian allies. They forced the unfortunate Austrian commander, General Mack, to surrender with twenty-six thousand men, without firing a shot. Further disasters followed. Archduke Ferdinand, escaping towards Bohemia, was cut off and defeated by Murat, while a further six thousand Austrians surrendered to Soult in Memningen. Only the fifteen thousand troops who fled towards Kempten managed to escape capture.[24] Having destroyed the main Austrian force north of the Alps, Napoleon took the capital, Vienna, before turning against the advancing Russians. Ulm had been a spectacular strategic victory, a triumph of planning that inflicted defeat and humiliation in equal proportion. But it did not end the campaign. The Austrians quickly regrouped, the Russians received reinforcements, and the Allies, boosted by their numerical superiority, counter-attacked. Grouped around Olmutz, to the north-east of Vienna, the joint Austrian and Russian army numbered some ninety thousand men. Napoleon risked finding his army over-exposed.

The battle that followed, at Austerlitz, is judged by many to be the greatest of Napoleon's military career. This time he was outnumbered, with only seventy-five thousand men lined up against the ninety thousand of Austria and Russia. His victory cannot be put down to good fortune – although he enjoyed an element of that – but to overall military superiority in battle. He took some inspired tactical decisions, showed superior battlefield deployment, had excellent corps commanders, and a well-honed corps system which he used to telling effect. The battlefield, just south of the town of Brünn (what is today Brno), had been selected by his opponents, who sought to turn the French right flank and cut them off from the main road to Vienna, which they saw as vital to French supply and communication.

But Napoleon, despite his smaller numbers, took advantage of speed of manoeuvre and deployed his men against specific units of the enemy, effectively cutting them off from the main body of their army to drive home his advantage. Around the villages of Telnitz and Sokolnitz the French marked one of their most remarkable victories, when some six thousand six hundred French troops held up the advance of nearly forty thousand Austrians, pinning them down and giving Napoleon the chance, as the sun rose and dispelled the morning mist, to attack the only high point on the battlefield, the plateau of Pratzen. By eleven in the morning Soult's troops were masters of the plateau, defended with the cavalry of the Imperial Guard, which Napoleon had kept back for the purpose. Meanwhile, other units scattered the Russian army, driving them into the muddy terrain to the south of the battlefield. From that moment the battle was won. In the words of the French military historian Jacques Garnier, 'The remainder of the battle was no more than a pursuit. The Russians retreated through the frozen lakes to the south of the battlefield. The ice broke, the gun carriages got stuck in the mud, and men drowned.'[25]

While Napoleon may indeed have contributed to his victory by deceiving the Russian leaders into thinking that he planned to withdraw, this was a battle won by tactical acumen, not by deception; by quick thinking on the spur of the moment as much as by any grand advance planning. Just as he had done at Toulon and in Italy during the Wars of the Directory, at Austerlitz he proved his virtuosity as a military commander, something which his detractors would never be able to deny him.[26] It was also a decisive moment in the war, ensuring that Prussia did not send reinforcements and effectively ending the Third Coalition. The Treaty of Pressburg which followed allowed Napoleon to consolidate his position in Central Europe, most especially in Germany, where he took advantage of Austria's humiliation to distribute largesse to his new allies, Bavaria, Baden and Württemberg, and bind them more closely to the Napoleonic system.

Two rulers, in Bavaria and Württemberg, became kings, with Napoleon, not the Holy Roman Emperor, now guaranteeing their freedoms. Outside Germany the Treaty stripped Austria of territory in Italy, the Tyrol and Dalmatia, preparing the way for further restructuring in the following months. In 1806 Napoleon grouped a number of Rhineland states into a loose Confederation of the Rhine, again under his protection; while the extent of his control over Italy was enhanced by the invasion of Naples, also in 1806. With the extinction of the Holy Roman Empire in the same year, his dominance of Western and Central Europe seemed total, and his foreign policy objectives might appear to have been achieved.[27]

Oddly, perhaps, the settlement was undermined less by Napoleon's ambition than by Prussia's impatience and sense of betrayal. In the course of his reconfiguration of Germany, Napoleon had offered Hanover to Britain as a goodwill gesture in return for peace, but Prussia also had claims to Hanover and resented having her interests ignored. Just as important was the reading of the international situation by the Prussian king, Frederick William. He had no wish to be relegated to the status of a French puppet-state, and, having reached an agreement with Russia and Britain, entered into a Fourth Coalition against Napoleon in 1806. Then, in October, he took the surprising initiative of declaring war on France at a time when his army was still in a poor state and he had received no commitments from his new allies. It proved a fateful blunder. Prussia was left to fight alone against France and suffered an overwhelming defeat in the linked battles of Jena and Auerstedt, due largely to deficient organisation and mediocre leadership. Recent scholarship suggests that the Prussian army was essentially sound, whatever the shortcomings in its training and preparation. There was no shame implied in being beaten by a formidable opponent. What was really humiliating was the collapse that followed as the French drove across Prussia, rounding up what remained of the army and forcing the surrender of towns and fortresses, leaving Napoleon ensconced in Berlin and master of all he surveyed. The defeat on the battlefield had turned into a rout because of the chaos of the days that followed, and the alarming demoralisation of both the soldiers and the civilian population.[28]

Jena destroyed the Prussian army, but it did not end the war. Frederick William and the remnants of his army fell back into Poland where they joined up with the Tsar, and it was there, in February 1807, that Napoleon, in pursuit, engaged them once more at Eylau. It was a bloody and relentless battle, fought in a biting February blizzard by around seventy thousand men on each side. It was also, in spite of Napoleon's attempts to claim it as a French victory, a grim stalemate. The French army sustained the highest losses of any battle in the war to that date – a reminder that glory in the mud-drenched fields of an eastern European winter could only be bought at a price. The soldiers who had fought and suffered at Eylau knew this too well to be deceived, and Napoleon's military Bulletins, routinely so upbeat and triumphant, suddenly took on a more sombre tone. 'After the Battle of Eylau,' remarked the 64th bulletin on 2 March, 'the Emperor passed several hours each day upon the battlefield, a horrible spectacle, but which duty rendered necessary. It required great labour to bury all the dead.' The Bulletin, almost inevitably, placed the greatest emphasis on the Russian losses, and on Napoleon's show of compassion. 'Forty-eight hours after the battle, there were still upwards of 5,000 wounded Russians whom we had not been able to carry off. Brandy and bread were carried to them, and they were successively conveyed to the hospital.'[29] But the words could barely conceal the shock and depression that had hit the French, too, at the scale of deaths and injuries.

If Eylau was presented as a victory, it could only be a Pyrrhic victory, won at the cost of countless French lives. When the painter Antoine-Jean Gros consigned it to canvas, he outraged some in the Academy by showing the unmentionable in the very foreground of his work: the contorted corpses of dead soldiers, piled high before the eyes of the Emperor.[30] It was an image that could not fail to shock, or to cause offence. The same harrowing image is repeated in the eye-witness accounts of the battle in the letters and memoirs of soldiers who lived through that day. One of Napoleon's surgeons-in-chief, Baron Percy, does not conceal the gloom he felt when he surveyed the scene. 'At the back of the cemetery, towards the plain, blood had flowed in terrible quantities; it was the blood of the Russians. Around the church, in the town, in the courtyards, houses, everywhere you saw only bodies and dead horses; carriages pass over them; the artillery wagons mow them down, crushing their limbs and their skulls.'[31] For the victors as much as the vanquished, the battle left a memory of loss and overwhelming sadness.

But a much greater victory lay beyond. Napoleon moved rapidly, seizing the cities of Danzig and Königsberg before engaging the Russians at Friedland on 14 June, where he split the Russian army in two and inflicted twenty thousand casualties. Following this defeat, the Tsar felt he had no choice but to negotiate. The two Emperors met at Tilsit, on a raft on the River Niemen, where they divided the continent into two spheres of influence, one French, the other Russian. Tilsit marked the zenith of Napoleon's power, and he savoured the moment, displaying his military strength to a bemused Europe. For once he did not impose harsh peace terms on a defeated enemy, preferring to flatter Alexander I and win his support for a future struggle against Britain. In return he accepted Russian expansion along the Danube and in Finland, while extending French influence in the region through a new Duchy of Warsaw. In contrast, Prussia suffered badly at Tilsit, being stripped of almost half its territory and forced to pay a heavy indemnity to the Emperor. After the humiliation of Jena, Prussia found its Great Power status seriously undermined. Napoleon's diplomatic ambitions were now clear, and they impinged on German Central Europe, an area which Prussia regarded as her hemisphere. Having imposed his will on Austria the previous year, he had now defeated Prussia and established his authority in the north-east of the continent. To drive the point home, he went on in the autumn of 1807 to occupy Swedish Pomerania.[32]

There remained, of course, in Napoleon's eyes, one obstacle to his domination of the continent: Britain, whose commercial strength continued to pose a threat to his military ambitions and whose machinations he saw behind every act of treachery. Britain, he declared in 1806, had sought 'to excite Prussia against France, to push the Emperor and France to the end'. And what was the outcome? 'She has conducted Prussia to her ruin, procured the greatest glory for the Emperor and the greatest power to France.' He went on to warn that France might declare England in a state of Continental blockade, asking 'is it with blood that the English hoped to feed their commerce and revive their industry?'[33] After Trafalgar and the defeats inflicted on France and Spain at sea, the British navy looked to make gains elsewhere in Europe and in the colonies, turning its guns on a variety of targets from Copenhagen to Istanbul and Cape Town in an attempt to expand its commercial and colonial dominance. Then, from May 1806, Britain used her naval strength more directly against French trade and prosperity, imposing by a series of Orders in Council a blockade on the European coastline from the Elbe in the east to the Atlantic in the west, and threatening to place a stranglehold on French commerce and shipping.

Napoleon's response – the establishment of the Continental System – was immediate: first in the Berlin Decree in 1806, then at Tilsit and in the Milan Decree of November 1807, he sought to close the whole continent of Europe to British goods in the hope that this would stifle Britain's trade and force her to sue for peace. The Berlin Decree declared the British Isles to be under blockade, and forbade all trade and communication with them; it also provided Napoleon with a justification for imprisoning any British citizens, whether merchants, ships' captains or simple tourists, who strayed on to the European continent. The Milan Decree turned the screw further by placing restrictions on neutral shipping. Any ship which put in to a British port was thenceforth considered to be stripped of its nationality and subject to seizure, as was any ship that complied with the British demand that it be searched by the Royal Navy.[34] It was a grand design to win the war with Britain by destroying her economy and turning the mercantile community, which was so powerful in the House of Commons, against Britain's war policy.

The Continental System also had important domestic implications. With France already cut off from many overseas and colonial markets, Napoleon sought to create a wider domestic European market that France could control and dominate by keeping British goods out. Customs posts were built along the frontier of this greater

Europe – three hundred customs men were posted along the banks of the Elbe alone in 1806.[35] This was more than a trade ban; it was a complex system of economic warfare designed to deny Britain access to neutral shipping, and hence to her markets, and thus to destroy the greatest mercantile economy of the day. And it did bring benefits to certain commercial and industrial sectors in France, which enjoyed a level of protection from cheaper British products that they had not seen since the Eden Treaty in 1786. Geoffrey Ellis explains how, in Alsace for example, the Continental System established a new *entrepôt* trade with Germany and encouraged new industrial enterprises, among the biggest of them in Mulhouse. It created what he terms 'a French Continental market design' that worked to the benefit of French manufacturers and traders. And he shows that it was far more than a blockade and more of an economic strategy, with 'the Blockade decrees, the rough treatment of would-be neutrals, the proclamation of the closed market (*marché réservé*) in Italy, and the series of preferential trade treaties with client states' all helping to ensure that, for French manufactures and for the industrial areas of the north and east, the benefits would be real and permanent.[36] Napoleon's willingness to support industrial innovation and to fund technological change helped ensure that the economic impact was often favourable to those in the manufacturing sector, and that textile towns were among those that prospered most under the Empire.

But the success of the strategy must be qualified. If the Alsatian economy expanded, it was in part due to fraudulent trade and widespread smuggling, backdoor methods by which Frenchmen profited from the blockade. And, as in many eastern and northern areas of France, expansion was closely tied to the military market's huge demand for armaments and textiles.[37] In other sectors the restrictions on trade caused great misery, especially in such port cities as Marseille, Nantes and Bordeaux, along the Mediterranean and Atlantic coasts. The Atlantic ports in particular, once so prosperous on the back of the wine trade, colonial produce and Caribbean slavery, had already seen their economies undermined in the 1790s by the Haitian revolution, and now slipped into a seemingly terminal decline.[38] Yet in 1806 the idea of waging economic warfare against Britain, a country more dependent than any other on its trade and commercial links with the world, did not seem absurd so long as French strategists continued to believe that they could use the blockade to destroy Britain's political will to pursue the war. That they failed was partly due to the inherent strength of the British economy, but also to France's inability to enforce its decrees on an often unwilling population. National frontiers proved porous, with smuggling and contraband undermining the power of the law and resulting in such breaches of the blockade that the Continental System was undermined from within.[39]

In 1807 Napoleon can justifiably be seen at the peak of his success, with Tilsit the crowning moment. He had destroyed the military power of the great German states, Austria and Prussia, to the point where his empire stretched across half of Europe – far beyond the most fertile imaginings of Louis XIV, who thought only of natural frontiers along the Rhine. Yet he still was dissatisfied, using the Russian alliance to buy time rather than achieve a lasting peace, and determined, to the point of obsession, to defeat France's perpetual enemy, Britain. In retrospect, the Continental System must be seen as a strategic error, a measure that ran counter to the interests of local communities, that aroused resistance, and that led to further measures of police repression across Europe. It was a crudely exploitative system that served to bully and alienate Napoleon's allies, and it failed in its main objective of bringing Britain to her knees. By 1807 even Charles James Fox, who had been the most consistent of British politicians in his opposition to the war, accepted that Napoleon must be defeated if peace was to be achieved. In rejecting a Russian offer of mediation in 1807, the British Foreign Secretary, George Canning, made it clear that in his government's eyes the problem was Napoleon himself, since his excessive power and his overweening ambition excluded the possibility of securing a lasting settlement.

Canning explained this position in a private letter to the diplomat Lord Granville in October. 'Could any peace settle Europe now,' he asked rhetorically, 'in a condition in which it could remain? Unquestionably not. But it would sanction and settle some dozen of green and tottering usurpations; and leave Bonaparte to begin anew.' Peace, in other words, in the conditions of 1807, could serve only the interests of the French, and for that reason it had to be resisted. 'Our interest is that *till* there can be a final settlement that shall last, everything should remain as unsettled as possible: that no usurper should feel sure of acknowledgement; no people confident of their new masters; no kingdom sure of its existence; no spoliator secure of his spoil; and even the plundered not acquiescent in their losses.'[40] War, in other words, had to go on, for any ultimate peace demanded it. And war did go on, relentlessly. Indeed, it was war that would determine the history of the remaining years of Napoleon's reign.

9

A Vision of Civil Society

The history of Napoleonic Europe is too often presented as little more than the history of military conquest: the submission of a continent to one man's all-consuming dream. Of course it is true that the needs of war were paramount in Napoleon's France. The war effort indubitably distorted the economy and imposed a huge burden on the population in the form of conscription and requisition, while the French army enjoyed greater prestige and prominence than at any time since the reign of Louis XIV. Generals were rewarded with the baton of marshals; marshals with titles, wealth and lands; and the majority of those awarded the Legion of Honour during the First Empire were serving soldiers, especially officers. The pomp and elegance of military uniforms, the use of military bands and martial music, and the increased military presence in state ceremonial were all symptomatic of the growing power of the army. If Napoleon was to achieve his goals, he depended on his army to deliver them, and he would never forget his debt to the generals and marshals who supported him. They would be richly rewarded, and military values attained a new prominence in French society: the glory of war was seen as the supreme good.[1]

Some have suggested that Napoleon's debt to the army was still greater, that the very legitimacy of the Empire derived from the military victories which sustained it and which had the effect of concentrating authority so unambiguously in the person of the Emperor. On Saint Helena, replying to a question from Las Cases about the personal character of the regime, Napoleon virtually conceded this point. 'That situation was not of my choice,' he replied. 'It was not my fault.' He maintained that it was the consequence of the circumstances of the time, and that the legitimacy of his rule depended on his continuing to win battles, and with them glory: 'I was the key to a completely new building,' he said, 'and one with such shallow foundations! If it was to endure it was reliant on each and every one of my battles.'[2]

Though Napoleon's Empire was the product of war, and the Emperor himself was often absent on campaign, spending months at a time on horseback, his vision of Empire remained stubbornly that of a civil society. He did not appoint army officers to ministries of state, though some, Duroc and Sébastiani among them, were entrusted with diplomatic missions; and it was observed, not always approvingly, that Napoleon appointed several of his generals to embassies around Europe (Brune to Constantinople, Lannes to Lisbon, Andréossy to London).[3] But there the army's political influence stopped; officers were not given political control, and the army as an institution was kept firmly answerable to the civil authorities. Despite its overarching military ambitions, therefore, it is misleading to indict Napoleon's regime for militarism, since the army was never allowed to exercise power autonomously. Indeed, it is more accurate to see the Empire as an exercise in state-building, in institutional reform and modernisation – a process that would leave behind monuments to administrative efficiency which many in the nineteenth century would seek to emulate. Napoleon saw himself as a moderniser, and his impatience with old structures and privileges – shown most notably, perhaps, in his willingness to challenge the Papacy and tear down what remained of the Holy Roman Empire – is a symptom of his modernising zeal. Like many of his ideas, it had its roots in the revolutionary period, when first the Jacobins then the Directory had pursued a policy of conquest, imposing administrative and judicial reforms on the countries they invaded, and recreating them as new departments of France or sister republics allied to Paris. The French, they preached, brought liberty – new freedoms – to the peoples of Europe.

Few at the time, with the notable exception of Maximilien Robespierre,[4] had expressed any doubts about the wisdom of this policy, and they had shown little understanding to those who preferred to resist the imposition of liberty at the point of a French soldier's bayonet. It was only too easy to equate opposition with counter-revolution, banditry, or religious obscurantism, and to seek to quell such opposition with military force. In this respect the Empire merely carried on the policy of its predecessors, though with greater efficiency and ruthlessness. The Imperial regime swept aside such rebellions as it encountered and imposed French-style institutions on the peoples it conquered. It was not, of course, perfect, certainly not everywhere, and it left pockets of resistance that would never be broken. And the institutions that were put in place had ceased, as John Davis has noted in the case of Italy, to offer any true reflection of the 'egalitarian aspirations of the Revolution'. Instead they were 'instruments of administration' that served to strengthen the powers of the state, with the consequence that 'what had remained only aspiration in even the most powerful of the eighteenth-century monarchies' was finally given substance in the service of Napoleon.[5] Serving the state had been transformed into the highest of political ideals.

State service implied loyalty above any deep ideological commitment. Napoleon went out of his way to declare himself a pragmatic leader who took advantage of such circumstance as presented itself, and who acted opportunistically in matters of diplomacy just as he did on the battlefield. He did not, he boasted to Dalberg, the newly appointed ruler of the Confederation of the Rhine, in 1806, work in accordance with pre-conceived systems or inflexible plans: 'I seize events and push them as far as they will go.'[6] Like many of Napoleon's flash judgments, this is perhaps too facile, but it is clear that in foreign policy matters he did act instinctively, at times impetuously, to press home his advantage or to avenge a perceived slight. There was no single blueprint of Empire in his mind, no staged plan that he stuck to coherently from the moment he came to power. The early years, however, can most plausibly be presented as part of a consistent strategy that built on the expansion of French power under the Directory and Consulate. Italy was already an established sphere of influence into which it seemed logical to expand further; then he turned to Germany, establishing a bridgehead through his alliances with Bavaria, Baden and Württemberg. The defeat of Prussia and the peace signed with the Russians at Tilsit allowed him to harbour much grander ambitions, and from this moment Napoleon could dream of a new Carolingian empire with Paris at its heart. A new Europe 'of federated states, or a true French empire' was to be created, he declared.[7] With the destruction of Prussia's military power at Jena, all the pieces seemed to be in place for the realisation of his dream; yet within months he was being diverted by other short-term goals or passing irritations.

The later years of the Empire came to be dominated by attempts to implement the Continental System against Britain and by long and costly invasions, first of the Iberian Peninsula, then of Alexander I's Russia. Imperial policy had become prey to over-arching ambition and to Napoleon's own rash and opportunistic decision-making.

The Empire evolved over time. Part of it, the so-called 'French Empire', was organised as departments of France, lands annexed by conquest that were sucked into a greater France which, by 1812, extended to one hundred and thirty departments and forty-four million inhabitants. The French departments were largely concentrated in the territories adjoining France herself – the Low Countries, Germany and northern Italy – and they were administered exactly like other parts of France. Much more inchoate and far flung was the 'Grand Empire', a series of independent kingdoms and electorates more loosely tied to France, which incorporated a further forty million people. These territories were generally ruled by a local prince who had agreed to cooperate with Napoleon, often in return for honours and titles, or, increasingly, by a member of the Bonaparte family. There was little sign of consistency, even within a single region. In 1802, for instance, Napoleon had set up the Republic of Italy in Milan with himself as president and the Milanese patrician Melzi d'Eril, a moderniser like himself, as his vice-president. But after he became Emperor, he abruptly transformed the Republic into the Kingdom of Italy, to which he progressively added various conquered territories – the Veneto and Istria in 1806, the Marche in 1808, South Tyrol in 1810. In one sense it made little difference, in so far as whatever their titular status, they were still client states, supplying soldiers for the French army and providing for the upkeep of troops stationed on their territory.[8]

Across Germany there was no common template, though the loyalty of local rulers was often richly rewarded. Napoleon presented himself as the Protector of the various Rhineland territories thrown together into the Confederation of the Rhine; elsewhere he elevated Bavaria and Württemberg to the status of kingdoms, soon followed by Saxony and Westphalia; and Karl Friedrich of Baden saw his lands quadruple in size and was raised to the status of Grand Duke.[9] Other states found themselves favoured in a different way, receiving as king a member of the Bonaparte family: Napoleon's brother Louis was crowned King of Holland, Jerome was made King of Westphalia, and Joseph became the King of Naples. Even these arrangements could be of short duration. In 1808 Joseph was moved to the even more troublesome throne of Spain. In 1810 Louis, distrusted by his elder brother for being too sympathetic to his subjects and seeking to harmonise his rule with the wishes of the Dutch people, was simply removed. Only four years after it was established, the Kingdom of Holland abruptly ceased to exist and the Netherlands were annexed to France.[10] All pretence of independence was abandoned.

To administer the Empire Napoleon needed trusted collaborators, men who would serve him unswervingly. What mattered was their loyalty, both to his person and to the Empire, and he gave his trust as easily to men of the Right as of the Left, as much to aristocrats and returned émigrés as to former Jacobins and terrorists of the Year II. He was concerned that men of all political colours could find something with which to identify in the imperial order, qualities which they could embrace. Thus the Right would find something of the stability of monarchy, and perceived in its strong executive powers and its lack of concern for elected bodies and popular opinion the kind of authority which they craved. The former second and third consuls, Cambacérès and Lebrun, both recognised in the political culture of the Empire something redolent of the old monarchy, something that Catholics and conservatives might find deeply reassuring. Lebrun believed that he was witnessing the dawn of an 'imperial monarchy'; Cambacérès noted succinctly that 'everything is taking us back to the former order of things'.[11] The fact that the Empire had made peace with the Vatican and allowed, even welcomed, the return of aristocrats who had fled France during the Revolution helped to consolidate the sense that the revolutionary years were finally over and that men were no longer judged by their political pasts.

Republicans, too, had little difficulty in serving an Emperor whom they identified with at least some of the ideals of the defunct Republic, a man with a republican past who was committed to a culture of service and meritocracy. That was the beguiling ambiguity of Napoleon's regime, the nature of its relationship to the Revolution that had made way for it. Théophile Berlier was among the republicans of all hues who allowed themselves to be persuaded that they could find a new political home in the First Empire, since 'in the heart of an old and monarchical Europe, the best France could reasonably hope for definitively was a representative government under a new dynasty, whose power would be limited by liberal institutions'.[12] And Regnaud de St-Jean d'Angély, who would be among Napoleon's more loyal supporters, agreed, though he had not always sided with the Jacobins in the 1790s and was identified with the more liberal wing of republican thought. He insisted that civil liberties were best served by the imposition of a hereditary empire, which could help to guarantee the gains his generation had made from 1789, gains which he defined as 'individual liberty, religious freedom, the inviolability of property, the irrevocability of the sale of the *biens nationaux*, the political equality that opens all positions to all citizens, the civic equality which assures that all citizens are judged according to the same laws, and the approval of these laws and of the annual levels of taxation by a national representation'.[13] These, he argued, had not been diluted by the demise of the Republic.

Not all agreed; even some who had served Bonaparte while he was First Consul found the abandonment of republican institutions too much to bear and, like Carnot, preferred to step back into the political wilderness.[14] But they were a minority. Most republicans did agree to serve the Empire, some arguing, with Fouché, that it would be 'absurd on the part of the men of the Revolution to compromise everything in order to defend our principles, while we had nothing further to do but enjoy the reality'.[15] Napoleon in their eyes remained a standard bearer for the Revolution and its ideals. Their past support for egalitarian principles was not held against them, any more than was their involvement in voting for the execution of Louis XVI (which the Bourbons would never forgive, even after the Restoration of Louis XVIII). Regicides, indeed, played a significant role in the Empire: Sieyès as a senator, Fouché a government minister and chief of police, David in the role of court painter, Lakanal given the task he had always relished of reorganising the education system, and Cambacérès himself as *archichancelier* and the second most powerful man in the Empire.[16] Many of them were first-class officials and loyal administrators, and they were assured

Napoleon's support provided that they were single-minded in serving the new order. Their collaboration ensured that the new regime had an abundance of talent at its disposal and experience of government on which to draw, which the Emperor did not hesitate to use.

The ministers and dignitaries of the Empire were the outward symbols of the new meritocracy – men drawn from widely differing backgrounds but each with the relevant experience to occupy the great offices of state. A few examples will suffice.[17] Talleyrand, in charge of foreign affairs until 1807, had already been Foreign Minister under the Directory; before 1789 he was the Bishop of Autun and had served as Agent-General of the Clergy of France. Maret, who held the foreign ministry between 1811 and 1813, was a lawyer, attorney at the Parlement of Dijon before the Revolution, then a deputy to the Estates-General in 1789. Portalis, entrusted with the delicate portfolio for Ecclesiastical Affairs, also came from a legal and political background, an attorney at the Parlement of Aix-en-Provence in the Old Regime who had helped to draft the Civil Code. The Ministry of War, unsurprisingly, went to men with army experience. Among them were Alexandre Berthier, who had served in America under Rochambeau, remained in the army during the Revolution, and became chief of staff to Bonaparte in Italy and Egypt; and Henri Clarke, who had been an officer in the old line army during the 1780s and was Private Secretary to Napoleon after 1802.

Such links were seen as signs of a deep, personal loyalty to the Emperor, and some went a long way back. René Savary, Fouché's successor as Minister of Police in 1810, had been aide-de-camp to the future Emperor in Italy after Marengo. Navy and the Colonies, again unsurprisingly, was given to an experienced naval officer, Denis Decrès, who had first joined the navy at the age of eighteen, risen to the rank of captain under the Revolution, and then been cashiered in 1793 because of his noble origins. It was Decrès' subsequent action in Malta and the Nile that won Napoleon's favour.[18] Napoleon's appreciation of a man's past record did not, however, depend on his social origins, and if Decrès belonged to the Old Regime nobility, other ministers came from the humblest of origins. Of his Ministers of the Interior, for instance, Jean-Antoine Chaptal was the son of a peasant family in the Lozère, while Emmanuel Cretet's family were shopkeepers in a small town near Grenoble. This did nothing to hinder Cretet's career under the Empire. He served in turn as Governor of the Bank of France and, from 1807 to 1809, as Minister of the Interior. He would end his life ennobled, as the Comte de Champmol.

By appealing to all men of good will, regardless of their social origins or their political pasts, Napoleon hoped to establish the Empire on a solid foundation, providing it with efficient leadership and appealing to a broad swathe of the French public. He also sought to secure the support of the landed interest and to help develop a new capitalist class in France.[19] Here, Napoleon was continuing the policy he had initiated during the Consulate, offering the promise of internal order and stability and, with it, an end to the bitter faction fighting that political ideology generated. He preferred, like De Gaulle in the twentieth century, to play down specific ideological commitments, and sought to rally the population to his person. After the bitter schisms of the revolutionary years there were attractions in this seemingly open approach, with its promise to bring an end to internal divisions and the kind of revenge killing that had fractured the South during the previous decade. But there were also dangers in this approach, most notably that the Empire would be judged an unsatisfactory, unsustainable compromise between the warring parties. Cambacérès expressed this succinctly in his memoirs. On the one side were the many Frenchmen who had not entirely lost their affection for their former kings, and to whom Bonaparte would always be an impostor. 'A number of them adhered with alacrity to the re-establishment of the throne, but they will not understand that it could be occupied by anyone other than the present head of the House of Bourbon.' For committed republicans, Cambacérès believed, the Empire offered an equally unsatisfactory outcome, since 'the project to restore heredity in government and to start a new dynasty' would not suit any of them. And, he warned Napoleon presciently, 'I fear that it will deprive you of friends, and especially of support in the general public.'[20]

Cambacérès' pessimism about the Empire's durability proved ill-founded, and most former republicans dutifully fell into line, accepting that the Consulate had run its course and that Napoleon would take care to safeguard the gains they had made from the Revolution. Indeed, it can plausibly be argued that the Empire retained enough of the policy that it inherited from the Republic to satisfy all but the most fiercely ideological, and even that Napoleon, for all his craving after respectability and dynastic legitimacy, had remained loyal to the most crucial of the beliefs of his youth. Napoleon had a marked authoritarian streak, of course. His preference for control and efficiency left little place for local accountability and was translated into a marked distrust of elections. But these traits were not born with the Empire; they had been evident since the beginning of the Consulate and the constitutional reforms of 1800. The institution of the prefect and the vast authority given to the Ministry of the Interior were proof, if proof was needed, that this was a regime where authority emanated from the centre, and not from local electors. The prefect was an agent of central power, inviting comparison with the *intendant* under the Bourbon monarchy.[21] Under the Empire France moved further away from the liberal individualism of the early Revolution, imposing controls and censorship, extending the outreach of the police, and restoring constraints on the operation of the free market. By 1810, for instance, only four newspapers had licences to publish in Paris;[22] while the city's book trade was subjected to new controls and regular surveillance. Indeed, the newly established General Direction of the Book Trade set out to monitor 'not only every printer, publisher and bookseller in the entire Empire, but also every piece of printed matter'.[23]

This was not a liberal regime – but it was not anti-revolutionary, either: Napoleon's most significant programmes of reform, to education, the Church and the justice system, had a solid foundation in the achievements of the previous decade. He saw little reason to change the institutional structures – the departments and districts, communes and cantons, courts and tribunals he had inherited from the Revolution, and where he innovated it was generally to increase their authority and their professional expertise. There was little here that former republicans could reasonably object to. The France they had so carefully forged in 1790 and 1791 was scrupulously retained, and there was no suggestion of a return to the Old Regime. Napoleon was an authoritarian, but he was no reactionary, and many beyond the frontiers of France identified his regime with progressive and enlightened values.

Two areas of policy in particular were suggestive of the continuing influence of revolutionary values. One was education, where

Napoleon expanded on the ideas which the Revolution had preached but never found the resource to implement. He envisaged an imperial education system, monitored by the new University of France, in which state-run *lycées* provided secondary education to the gifted while a level of public instruction was made available to all. But the costs of war took priority and, like the revolutionaries, the Empire soon found that it did not have the money to provide a school in every parish. As a consequence, free primary education would not be offered to all for another half-century. Greater attention was given to the *lycées*, which the government saw as vital in training an educated elite; though even here, budget cuts meant that fees had to be imposed which made them the preserve of families with money. As for the University – founded in 1806 and implemented in 1808 – it was given a monopoly in the award of degrees throughout the Empire; a single secular institution, it would, through intensive instruction, contribute to the process of nation-building. The University was divided into twenty-six academies, with the lofty mission of spreading enlightenment throughout Europe but also the duty to train new generations in the skills needed to run government. Education policy should not be seen uniquely in terms of spreading liberal values. It was also devised in the service of the state.[24]

The other policy, and in Napoleon's eyes the more important, was the codification of the law, a huge task in which he took a personal interest over four years until the Civil Code was finally decreed in 1807. Again he had inherited unfinished business from the revolutionaries, who had ripped away the old codes based on Roman or custom law, abolished feudal law, removed clerical jurisdiction in moral matters, consecrated certain principles in constitutional law, and passed an impressive number of decrees and statutes. The result, though, was considerable confusion, especially over land ownership and the laws of inheritance, and Napoleon, with his customary concern for order, determined to resolve it in a single legal code. At the heart of the code was the idea of property as an individual right, to be enjoyed free of any feudal obligations. Noble privilege was everywhere abolished, but he also swept away some of the more egalitarian legal reforms of the revolutionary years, upholding the authority of husbands over wives, parents over children.

Marriage law, too, was revised to guarantee the man's right to administer property in marriage, and though divorce was maintained as a secular institution – as the revolutionaries had decreed in 1792 – the law now demanded a clear demonstration of mutual consent, or evidence of ill-treatment, adultery or a criminal conviction. This led to plummeting divorce rates, depriving women of the escape route that had been opened up to them by the Revolution. Illegitimate children were stripped of any property rights. The Empire was an ordered society where the rights of property-owners and of the heads of families had priority. In this sense the Code had educational significance, too, presenting a template for the kind of ordered, strictly hierarchical society that Napoleon favoured.[25] It defined the individual's relationship with the state, and would be a central feature of imperial administration in all the countries France annexed during the Napoleonic Wars. Wherever the French went, the Code necessarily followed.

In his administrative appointments in the territories France invaded, Napoleon looked for professionalism and good judgment above all else – the key attributes, as he saw it, of modern civil administration. At the very top, of course, he might have little choice:

princes and electors had to be won over to work for the imperial project, and the reward of a title or a kingdom seemed a small price to pay if it bought their loyalty and maintained administrative continuity. Where no such solution presented itself, as in Naples, Holland or Spain, a member of the Bonaparte clan would be sent in to rule over a conquered people. Though in these instances family interest was clearly in play, even Napoleon's brothers had to prove their efficiency and defer to the Emperor's will if they were to avoid his contempt and risk having their authority overruled. He had no hesitation, as we have seen, in undermining his brother Louis in Holland in 1810, when his failure to enact the Continental System led the Emperor to annex his kingdom and, quite arbitrarily, to abolish Louis' position as monarch.[26] More generally he looked to men of some standing in their local society: men of a certain wealth who would be capable of distinguishing public service from family interest and self-aggrandisement – a distinction that was sometimes difficult to maintain in the corrupt political culture of southern Europe and the Mediterranean.

In other words, Napoleon sought men of substance, akin to the British or American notion of independence, with a degree of wealth and ease that could make for a disinterested servant of the state. This, as much as any innate social conservatism, was what led him to search out the *notables* in each department, to compose lists of the six hundred households that paid most tax, or to bestow titles and honours on his most trusted collaborators. It also led to a greater rigour in the choice of administrative personnel; he replaced early empiricism with a targeted training programme for future prefects and sub-prefects, magistrates and judges, a programme that was made available to the sons of the new elite. With the aim of channelling the brightest among them into key administrative roles, he created auditors to the Council of State in 1803, and within ten years a quarter of the prefects had started in this role. The scheme proved attractive as a channel of advancement for the new social elite, the 'masses of granite' who would rally to the Empire across France and beyond, for those 'sons, sons-in-law and nephews of ministers, senators, state councillors, generals, prefects' who would attach their star to the fate of the Empire.[27] It would contribute significantly to building the imperial administrative elite.

Only such men, Napoleon believed, could see things with an objective eye; and they alone – civilised Europeans working for a secular state in a post-Enlightenment culture, men who, like himself, had lived through and assimilated the values of the French Revolution – could hope to govern with objectivity, submerging personal interest in the greater good that was the interest of the Empire. They did not have to be French as long as they understood the values that made the French the great imperial nation they had become; and in those parts of Europe (generally those in the north and the west, closest to France) where men of standing could be found, willing and able to assume the key administrative roles, the government of the country would be entrusted to them. Elsewhere, in places where these qualities were deemed deficient, French administrators were drafted in. Criminal justice, tax collection and army recruitment were much too important to be consigned to men whose loyalties or probity were suspect. Yet these were exactly the issues most likely to cause popular anger and even to incite rebellion.

In many parts of Europe the French taxed relentlessly, extracting the wealth and grain which the inhabitants produced in order to raise soldiers and feed their armies. The demand for conscripts was even more divisive, turning family against family, rich against poor, and uniting whole communities in their opposition to the state. Across Napoleonic Europe, deserters and draft-dodgers defied the authorities, seeking protection from local people, joining armed gangs, and attacking the gendarmes and agents of the state who were sent to act against them.[28] Law enforcement and policing fuelled popular resentments, especially in mountainous regions of southern Europe like the Alps, the Apennines and the Dolomites, where feelings of autonomy were strong and traditions of banditry ingrained. Nowhere was this resentment more damaging than in the furthest outposts of Empire – the Illyrian provinces and Dalmatia.[29]

Part of the problem from the French point of view was that in such regions, which had traditionally been poorly policed and loosely administered, imperial agents were often resented as intruders, impinging on local customs and imposing unwelcome regulation. In southern Europe in particular, many parts had lain outside the control of any form of state police, while tax collectors and customs officers were rarely seen in rural areas. The greater efficiency and longer outreach of the Napoleonic state meant that gendarmes and troops were used to do jobs that had previously been left undone; taxes were now collected, smuggling rings broken, requisitions imposed, draft-evaders and their protectors rounded up. To local people these innovations smacked less of good government than of foreign interference in local matters where the state had no business to meddle. Similarly, having armies billeted on local villagers was seen not as a source of welcome protection from bandits and robbers, but rather as a harsh imposition that was widely resented. Soldiers stole and looted, since the imperial armies customarily travelled light and depended on requisitioning and foraging if they were to feed their men and horses. Their presence was often actively detested to the point that, in many areas, peasants hid their grain and their animals and refused to sell them food. The fact that the soldiers were foreign could fan the embers of nationalism; but it was their presence that gave offence and drove many villagers to take to smuggling or side with bandits, brigands and partisans from their own community.

It did not help the Empire's civilising mission when its demands were perceived as unethical or its agents condemned as bullies. It merely united the people, especially those in rural areas, against the demands of outsiders, against what was presented to them as modernisation. This was true even where there were no ideological differences on which the opposition could play. Where there was, as in deeply Catholic regions where the French tried to impose secular civic values, the Empire could easily be seen as the Antichrist. In much of Italy, for instance, traditional piety was not extinguished, and religion gave those who opposed Napoleon a sense of occupying the moral high ground which they exploited to the full. Here, the conflict was seen in broader terms as one 'between the concept of society that emerged from the French Revolution, as nurtured by the Napoleonic regime, and the Catholic religion', or, as Michael Broers aptly terms it, a 'war against God'.[30] That was one conflict Napoleon could not hope to win.

Napoleon was not overly concerned that his policies left many Europeans feeling as though they had been colonised by the Empire. Once a country was annexed or occupied, the French suddenly had a very different mission. It was no longer a conquered foreign state, but part of an organic whole, subject to the same laws and administrative dictates as France. The French were no longer mere

The Bonaparte family home in Ajaccio: painting by Fontenay, 1849. © *akg-images / Laurent Lecat*

The Bridge of Arcole, scene of a legendary victory, 1796; by Baron Louis-Albert-Guillain Gros.
© *The Art Archive / Musée du Château de Versailles / Gianni Dagli Orti*

Bonaparte at the Bridge of Arcole: Antoine-Jean Gros, 1801. © *Corbis*

The Victor of Italy: an unfinished portrait by David, 1797. © *The Art Archive / Musée du Château de Versailles / Gianni Dagli Orti*

The Lure of the Orient: the Battle of Aboukir as seen by Lejeune. © *The Art Archive / Musée du Château de Versailles / Gianni Dagli Orti*

BATAILLE DES PYRAMIDES.

The Battle of the Pyramids: a 19th century popular print. © *The Art Archive / Musée Carnavalet Paris / Gianni Dagli Orti*

The Imperial Moment: Napoleon's Coronation as recorded by David. © *The Art Archive / Musée du Louvre Paris / Gianni Dagli Orti*

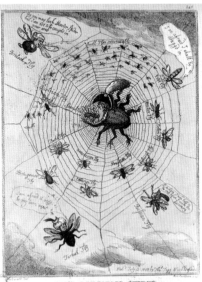

THE CORSICAN SPIDER, IN HIS WEB!

The Corsican Spider in His Web: a caricature by Thomas Rowlandson. © *Guildhall Library, City of London / The Bridgeman Art Library*

Fighting for the Dunghill: James Gillray's Vision of 1798. © *Courtesy of the Warden and Scholars of New College, Oxford / The Bridgeman Art Library*

Consolidating Christianity: a satirical 19th century broadsheet. © *Roger-Viollet / Topfoto*

Maria Walewska, Napoleon's Polish mistress: a portrait by Robert Lefevre. © *akg-images / Erich Lessing*

Napoleon in his study at
the Tuileries: a study by
David, 1811. © *The Gallery
Collection/Corbis*

The Passage of the Bérésina:
the miseries of the Moscow
Campaign. © *The Art Archive /
Musée Carnavalet Paris / Gianni
Dagli Orti*

Above: Longwood House on Saint Helena: where Napoleon spent his captivity. © *Kent Kobersteen / National Geographic Society / Corbis*

Left: Geranium Valley: imagining Napoleon's final resting-place on Saint Helena. © *The Art Archive / Napoleonic Museum Rome / Gianni Dagli Orti*

Below left: Napoleon talking to a soldier: a romantic representation by Hippolyte Bellangé. © *Brooklyn Museum / Corbis*

Opposite top: Apotheosis, after Horace Vernet: a favoured theme of 19th century artists. © *The Art Archive / Museo Glauco Lombardi Parma / Gianni Dagli Orti*

Opposite middle: Napoleon working in the Longwood Garden: mid-19th century by Olivier Pichat. © *Stefano Bianchetti / Corbis*

Opposite bottom: Transferring the Ashes to the Invalides: lithograph by Napoléon Thomas, 1840. © *The Art Archive / Marc Charmet*

Napoleon and the cinema:
Abel Gance in 1927.
© *SGF / Gaumont / The*
Kobal Collection

Napoleon and the cinema:
Sacha Guitry in 1955. © *Les Films*
C.L.M. / Album / akg-images

occupiers; they had to establish a sustainable imperial rule.[31] This involved more than force: it involved persuasion, an inculcation of French values, and a change in the relationship between the centre and the local powerbrokers. It exaggerated the contrast between those countries like Holland, northern Italy and large parts of Germany that had little trouble embracing imperial institutions, and those, further east and south, where the elites proved unreceptive and popular resistance was widespread. Europe divided into an inner and an outer empire, as the French were very well aware. In the former, local lawyers and landowners – some with radical ideas, many deeply conservative – collaborated readily with them to provide strong justice and administration; the latter offered little cooperation, and was always prey to rebellion and counter-revolution.[32]

The exception in eastern Central Europe was the Grand Duchy of Warsaw, established between 1807 and 1813, where, after the miseries of the Partition between Austria, Prussia and Russia, Napoleon could hope to be seen as a liberator and appeal to Polish national aspirations. The Grand Duchy enjoyed little freedom; it was a satellite state, incorporated in the Continental System and allowed diplomatic relations only with France. But there were compensations. The administration was run by Poles, the Duchy raised its own regiments, and the official language was Polish. Besides, the Polish nobility had a long-standing sympathy for French ideas and French culture. This was one corner of Europe where Napoleon's arrival was guaranteed to be greeted with a degree of sympathy.[33] But it must be seen as an exception, and further French expansion after 1807, in Spain and Portugal at one end of Europe and into Russia at the other, only served to underline how fragile their hold over the outer empire really was. Popular resistance could so easily spill over into guerrilla fighting, and peasant anger into a full-blown people's war.

More sobering was the reception given to the French in Naples, where they had sought to exploit the weakness of the Bourbon monarchy. Napoleon had reason for some optimism because the French invasions under the Revolution had been widely welcomed by the country's liberal elite, even though the undisguised anti-clericalism of the French soldiers had antagonised large swathes of this intensely Catholic society. Napoleon himself was scornful of the Neapolitan Bourbons. He proclaimed after Austerlitz that the dynasty had simply 'ceased to reign' and sent an army of forty thousand men to dethrone them in response to what he saw as their 'treacherous' support for his opponents. The territories around them he treated as political pawns, turning the Grand Duchy of Tuscany into an independent kingdom, then summarily annexing it; and in 1808 he occupied Rome and took the Pope prisoner, the second pope to be seized by Napoleon in a decade. Meanwhile, in 1806, he had given the Neapolitan throne to his brother Joseph Bonaparte; then, when Joseph was moved to Spain, Naples passed to Napoleon's brother-in-law, Joachim Murat. The Emperor clearly saw strategic importance in Naples, and was prepared to impose his rule whatever the cost in public hostility. It mattered to him in terms of his control of the northern Mediterranean, and also played an important part in enforcing the Continental System. Murat was given a heavy legislative programme to implement, including a new land tax and a new organic law that would spread the burden of taxation more equally and bring justice to all, part of what Napoleon tried to sell to the Neapolitans as his modernising mission.

But the Emperor well knew that these reforms ran counter to much of Neapolitan tradition as well as to the interests of powerful families in the city. His administrators, many themselves Neapolitans, were thwarted or forced to resign by the force of public outrage, and magistrates refused to enforce the new laws. Government proved impossible to enact: taxes went uncollected and conscripts faded into the landscape, while proposed reforms to the Church and public education had to be abandoned. By the end of the war, the state's finances were in ruins and public anger against the French boiled over, with the central bureaucratic model of government which they had introduced widely held to blame for the country's failures. There was little sympathy for the French, and little that they had legislated on survived the regime's collapse. It is surely indicative of their anger that Joachim Murat, alone of the rulers installed by Napoleon across his Empire, should have been executed by the people over whom he ruled.[34]

10

The Reinvention of Monarchy

One of the secrets of imperial success lay in the Janus-like quality of the Empire and of the values which Napoleon sought to nurture. He never renounced the principles of the revolutionary years; indeed, in his insistence on the rule of law and implementation of the Code, or his view of the state as an essentially secular entity free of ecclesiastical interference, he showed a determination to stick by those aspects of the First Republic which he identified with an ordered, modern society. To some, indeed, he remained a republican, albeit a republican who was wedded to ideas of order and authority. Where he rejected the revolutionary model was in its belief that Frenchmen were endowed with rights rather than obligations, that citizenship implied a necessary involvement in the processes of government.

If there were still parliamentary institutions and periodic elections under the Empire, they were but a pale reflection of the massive changes to political culture that had followed after 1789. Of the two houses, the Tribunate lasted only until 1807 before it was condemned to extinction, probably because it had failed to secure the obedience of the legislators. And the Legislative Assembly itself had a limited role, with the combined sessions of 1809 and 1810 lasting for no more than four months.[1] Local government, too, saw its autonomy reduced; it was made more answerable to the ministries in Paris, reporting up through the sub-prefect and prefect to the Minister of the Interior, while the judicial system was firmly directed by the Minister of Justice. At every level the Empire emphasised authority and obedience, the maintenance and, if necessary, the imposition, of order. The Emperor showed little interest in accountability downwards to the local community or the local electorate. For him these were practices which had become dangerously exaggerated, luxuries with which he could dispense.

Electoral accountability, which the revolutionaries had insisted on at every level of administration, was dramatically cut back. The electorate was reduced, along with the number of elected officials; and for many years the electoral process ceased to operate on a regular basis. Napoleon's own preference, when it was necessary for the people to be consulted on an issue of constitutional importance, was for a plebiscite rather than an election. There were four plebiscites in all during the successive Napoleonic regimes, all to ratify proposed constitutional change: two were held before 1804 (on the constitution of the Consulate in 1800 and the subsequent establishment of the Life Consulate in 1802), a third in 1804 to endorse the proclamation of the Empire, then nothing till a vote on the supplementary constitution (or *Acte additionnel*) in 1815. On all four occasions there were no cantonal assemblies or collective votes, as there had been in the 1790s. Those taking part signed a register individually to indicate their agreement or disagreement; some added a few sentences to qualify their opinion; but, significantly, very few dared to express dissent.[2] As an exercise in consultation the process was clearly flawed.

Yet it allowed Napoleon to claim that he was annexing part of the revolutionary heritage by associating the people in his constitutional reforms, while ensuring that their opinions remained muted and controlled in the executive interest.[3] Consultation had its place in the Empire, but only as long as it could be carefully managed. Yet Napoleon did not discard it entirely. He did nothing to remove the ambiguity about his commitment to republican ideals or to his own revolutionary past, an ambiguity that had been evident since his acceptance of the Life Consulate in 1802, and which had re-emerged amid the symbolic splendour of the imperial coronation in 1804. He was still ready to present himself as the people's emperor when circumstances demanded it.

His progressive adoption of the trappings of monarchy was, however, obvious for all to see. He clearly enjoyed the pomp and ceremonial that came with his imperial status and was conscious of the political gains they conferred. After the creation of the Empire, Napoleonic propaganda changed subtly, no longer focusing solely on his person or his claim to public consideration, but insisting on the dignity of the imperial office and on the standing that it gave France in international affairs. Above all, he sought to establish his legitimacy in the eyes of the international community, a legitimacy that was proclaimed but still had to be put to the test. The imperial coronation ceremony, with its sumptuous costumes and carefully choreographed movement, had been intended as a moment of theatre to impress all Europe with an image of state power. The Emperor and Empress were surrounded by their retinue and by the great officers of state, and the Pope, in turn, by the bishops and archbishops of the Catholic Church. But the coronation was a French affair, where the Emperor was surrounded by the political and legal elite of France: the Senate, the Council of State, the Legislative Body, the Tribunate, the various civil and criminal courts of the land.[4]

The Pope was the only foreign leader to attend. There were no kings or queens, no heads of other European states, many of whom continued to regard the French emperor as a parvenu, an upstart who had no legitimate claim to the throne. In the years ahead Napoleon was only too conscious of their contempt, and of the need to gain their recognition. He knew that to establish his Empire on a sound footing he first had to establish his legitimacy among the crowned heads of Europe, and this he set out to achieve as a matter of the highest priority. He might hope to win the approval of the French people by appealing to his republican roots, but these would do little to win over Europe's traditionalists. First in Paris, then later in Milan, he used the symbolism of the coronation ceremony to establish a different sort of legitimacy, that of a hereditary monarch.[5]

By imitating established monarchies while adopting his own style of monarchy, Napoleon was not merely playing to his own fantasies: he was laying claim to the power that traditionally belonged to kings whom he increasingly summoned up as his ancestors in office.[6] He could not, of course, appeal directly to the Bourbon line in France, or in any way invite comparison between his power and theirs; the last Bourbon, Louis XVI, had ended his life in defeat and humiliation, dethroned by the revolutionaries to become the most prestigious of the guillotine's sixteen thousand victims. Napoleon was well aware that the French people could be fickle in their loyalties, not least to kings; he had watched as the Paris crowd had overturned the equestrian statues of past monarchs in their city's squares, and he was equally well aware that in the future he might enjoy no more flattering a fate.

But some of the great European monarchs were a different proposition, especially the mighty Carolingian emperors whose power had extended beyond any one kingdom to embrace a multinational empire. In them, Napoleon found worthy points of comparison that would help to cement his own reputation. In his speeches and his correspondence he openly appealed to the memory of Charlemagne, himself adopting the insignia of the old Frankish kings and conjuring up images of a new Holy Roman Empire stretching proudly across Europe. It was with the aim of reinforcing the parallels between his reign and Charlemagne's that he made an official visit in the first months of his Empire – in October 1804 – to Aix-la-Chapelle, now the German city of Aachen, to visit Charlemagne's tomb and venerate the medieval emperor's memory. It was a moment pregnant with the symbolism of power and filled with propagandist intent.[7]

If Napoleon went to Aachen to lay claim to Charlemagne's succession, he made the point more forcefully in the following year when, just six months after his imperial coronation in Paris, he had himself crowned a second time, as King of Italy, in Milan. This was more than empty ceremonial, the presentation of Napoleon and Josephine to the Italian nation: the consequence of this coronation was to dissolve the Italian republic which the French had established and replace it with a monarchy in March 1805 – a move that followed the exclusion of Austria from Lombardy and helped clear the way for Napoleon's major reconstruction of Italy.[8]

The Emperor did not intend to rule Italy in person. Despite the insistence of various Italian rulers that he should do so, on the grounds that he was of Italian stock and at home in the Italian language, he took care to brush such claims aside and showed little desire to concentrate his energies on Italy. He divided his time between the affairs of state in Paris and his many absences on campaign; the day-to-day business of government in Italy he gave into the hands of his viceroy in Milan, Josephine's son, Eugène de Beauharnais. But that does not mean that the coronation ceremony lacked purpose. On the contrary, Napoleon took great care to leave a strong impression on the Italians, surrounding himself once again with symbols and artefacts that linked him in the popular imagination to the Carolingians. Once more he was laying claim to historical antecedents that provided him with popular legitimacy: the Iron Crown, kept in the treasury of the cathedral at Monza, was regarded with awe and veneration by the people of Lombardy.[9] Napoleon would show that he was deeply conscious of the dignity that was bestowed on him, and after 1805 the official documents of the Empire would refer to him by the dual title of 'Emperor and King'.

Yet though he took care to present himself abroad as a legitimate monarch, it is not clear how much he really respected kingship as an institution. Kings might have heredity on their side and be bolstered by legitimate succession, but in the final analysis imperial power rested upon the army and on efficient administration, and Napoleon had by 1807 demonstrated that he was more powerful, more to be feared and obeyed, than any monarch. Across the continent, indeed, he made and unmade kings, seemingly at will. Legitimacy seemed to count for little in this chess game; pieces, including his brothers, were moved around the board at Napoleon's will. Local rulers found themselves promoted to the royal title at the whim of the Emperor, as a reward for their reliability and loyalty or as part of his strategy for administering Central Europe. In Bavaria, for instance, Napoleon elevated Max-Joseph, who had been Elector since 1789, to King from January 1806. At the same time the elector of Württemberg, Frederick II, was also given a kingdom, and before the end of the year a similar reward was heaped on the Elector of Saxony, now crowned King Frederick Augustus I.[10] Royal titles, it seemed, came cheaply; the title that really mattered was Napoleon's alone. Kings were not supposed to wield sovereign authority, and their kingdoms would remain client states, providing supplies and conscripts for the Emperor's army, at least until French power began to crumble around 1813 and the German rulers were presented with the challenge of the Wars of Liberation. The Bavarian king had little loyalty to the Empire, and was happy to change sides when his national and dynastic interest demanded it. Some, however, were less astute, most notably Frederick Augustus, who failed to jump ship in time and paid for his continued allegiance to Napoleon by losing three-fifths of his territory at the Congress of Vienna.[11]

For the Emperor – as for all the royal courts of Europe – gaining legitimacy meant also maintaining a lifestyle that he equated with monarchy: a level of grandeur to impress the other crowned rulers and their retinues. Though Napoleon himself, unavoidably, spent much of his time on campaign, he and Josephine nevertheless lavished considerable attention on their various imperial residences – at the Tuileries in Paris; at Saint-Cloud, an elegant chateau overlooking the Seine which Napoleon had used as his consular residence and on which he had spent some three million francs between 1801 and 1803,[12] later at Fontainebleau, which Napoleon sought to convert into a second country home; and at Malmaison to the west of the capital, which the couple had bought jointly in the late 1790s and which Josephine came to regard as her home. Compared to Versailles, of course, these properties may seem modest, but modesty was not Napoleon's style. In 1804 it was already being observed that at Saint-Cloud 'everything was assuming the appearance of a sovereign court': the lavish music, the public mass on Sundays, the audiences which Napoleon granted in the gallery after the service – all 'recalled the vanities of Versailles'.[13]

The houses were used to stage elaborate state ceremonials, dinners and receptions that grew more lavish with the years. And across Europe were dotted the many palaces reserved for members of the Bonaparte family. From his experience of the Austrian and Bavarian courts, Napoleon learned the importance of pomp and luxury, and he aimed to create in Paris a court of his own that would outshine all others. Nothing was left to chance. The Emperor employed a huge staff to ensure that everything ran like clockwork, and the rules governing etiquette were of exemplary precision, especially the etiquette surrounding formal meals, since eating was at the very heart of court life. 'When their Majesties eat in public, the Grand Chamberlain proffers a basin for the Emperor to wash his hands; the Grand Equerry offers him his armchair; the Grand Master of the Palace takes a napkin and presents it to His Majesty. The Empress's First Prefect, the First Equerry and the First Chamberlain perform the same functions for Her Majesty. The Grand Almoner goes to the front of the table, blesses the meal, and retires.'[14] It all seems a world away from the puritanical, rather Spartan mores of the Jacobin Republic.

In the organisation of court life the Empress Josephine was a key figure, the two coronation ceremonies having pressed her into the spotlight and given her a taste for public life. She longed to assume an even more central role, feeling mortified to be left behind in France when her husband went on campaign, and several times pleaded with him in vain to be allowed to accompany the army.

From time to time, we are told, he would relent and agree to her accompanying him on the first stage of his journey, where she would hold an informal court in cities like Mainz or Munich. But beyond that it was made clear that she was not welcome: the war zone, in Napoleon's eyes, was a man's world where she had no place, and so she returned to her domestic stage. On the way, of course, she was caught up in an unavoidable round of official receptions in the towns and cities that she passed through; she could never return wholly to the life of a private citizen. But with Napoleon away, she did have time on her hands; and during the long months of war she filled her days adorning and embellishing her palace at Malmaison and interesting herself in the lives of her family – Hortense, married to Napoleon's brother Louis, and her son Eugene, now ensconced in Milan.[15] At times she seemed lonely, bored, and even slightly disaffected.

The war consumed long periods of Napoleon's life as he criss-crossed Europe, and Josephine was left behind for months on end, sometimes in garrison towns behind the war zone, but more often in the private space of Malmaison. When she was away from Paris she at least had a role to play, and she continued to play it. In Strasbourg, for instance, she hosted a busy round of receptions, balls, concerts and operas, where the various German princes could pay homage to the power of imperial France. Here, as elsewhere in France, she was received as Empress in her own right, with full military honours: officers presented arms and the artillery fired welcoming salvos. According to one biographer, she enjoyed the bustle of court life in such cities, surrounding herself with courtiers and equerries, and spending freely on 'plants for her garden at Malmaison, animals for her zoo, art objects and bric-a-brac'.[16] The menagerie was her special creation, and its fame spread to the point where ships returning from exotic lands would bring a present for the Empress: thus the cargoes of two ships arriving in Le Havre in June 1803 included 'an antelope, a gnu, a zebra, a falcon, five parrots, various other tropical birds, and seventeen assorted tortoises'.[17]

But she remained discontented. Her letters make it clear how much she missed her husband, how much she wanted to travel with him and resented what she saw as her enforced isolation. In reply, Napoleon proved a regular correspondent, sending her a succession of letters outlining the progress of his military campaigns and avowing his love for her. By 1806, as the war dragged on, Josephine remained dissatisfied, and became more and more insistent that she wanted to accompany him on campaign. But Napoleon was having none of it: the army quarters were miserable, he was constantly on the move, and the towns in the lee of the army were unsuitable places to receive her. 'I received your letters in a miserable barn', he wrote from Pultusk on 31 December 1806, 'amid mud and high winds, and with straw for bedding. Tomorrow I shall be in Warsaw. I think everything is over for this year. The army will go into its winter quarters.' He then discouraged her from going to Cassel, where the ruler had just been deposed, and urged her to try Darmstadt instead.[18] A few days later he virtually ordered her to return to Paris. 'Go to the Tuileries,' he commanded her on 7 January, 'hold receptions and carry on the same life to which you were accustomed when I was there; such is my will.'[19] On the following day, responding to yet another plea from Josephine, he spelt out his wishes. 'I had begged you to return to Paris. The season is too inclement, the roads unsafe and detestable, the distances too great for me to permit you to come hither, where my affairs detain me. It would take you at least a month to come. You would arrive ill; by that time it might perhaps be necessary to start back again; it would therefore be folly.'[20] His tone was businesslike, at moments even peremptory. Though he continually declared his love for his wife, he preferred to keep her at arm's length in wartime, so that he could pursue the war and concentrate on military strategy.

It was soon evident that Napoleon had other good reasons for keeping Josephine at bay, and that the love he professed for her, and which was surely genuine and often passionate in the first years of their marriage, was beginning to fade. Back in the 1790s, indeed, it had been Napoleon who continually avowed his love while Josephine's capricious ways and easy morals had attracted a whiff of scandal. There were, of course, many women in his life, too, including a series of passing affairs that had begun in Egypt, and may in part be explained as a protest at the stories he heard of Josephine's repeated infidelity back in Paris. However, conjecture is perhaps of little help here. Already in 1799 their marriage had seemed precarious. That it lasted another ten years spoke volumes about their desire to persevere in a union that remained stubbornly childless, and showed that Josephine was prepared to reform her somewhat profligate lifestyle. With the Consulate came the need for greater restraint, and Josephine duly obliged. As Emperor and Empress they would be even more in the public eye, and even more careful to appease opinion. Their original marriage, in true revolutionary style, had been a secular affair, conducted in front of the mayor; now a hastily devised religious marriage ceremony took place in 1804 in the private chapel at the Tuileries, which established the legality of their union in the eyes of Rome and of Catholic Europe.

But the marriage was now facing new problems, exacerbated by Napoleon's lengthy absences and the stream of rumours assailing Josephine about the new women in her husband's life. Most were no more than passing affairs, with little long-term consequence, though a fleeting dalliance with Eléanore de la Plaigne presented the Emperor with a son late in 1806. But in Poland, at a state ball thrown by the French Foreign Minister, Talleyrand, something more significant happened: Napoleon met a woman with whom he fell passionately in love, the beautiful and sensitive Polish countess, Maria Walewska. This would not be something that would last a mere matter of a few hours or a few days: indeed, theirs would become one of the most famous romances of the century, a love story made for Hollywood and duly filmed in 1937 as *Marie Walewska* (also known as *Conquest*), starring Greta Garbo and Charles Boyer. Maria Walewska, escorted by her brother and with the full knowledge and connivance of her husband, drove out of Warsaw on a snowy April morning in 1807 to join Napoleon at his winter quarters in Osterode in East Prussia.[21]

The Countess's brother would later claim that she saw this as a patriotic mission, her duty as a Polish aristocrat, and we can only assume that her husband agreed, though it is more probable that she was dazzled by the Emperor and his record of military glory. Whatever the explanation, Maria would never return to her husband, and she later had a son by Napoleon, Alexander Walewski, who would go on to have a highly distinguished military and political career. In 1851 he was appointed French ambassador to London, and in that capacity would represent his country at the Duke of Wellington's funeral; he would also, not without a certain irony, present the Court of St James with the credentials of France's new regime, the Second Empire.[22] Nor did Maria disappear from

Napoleon's life. She was accepted into the Bonaparte clan, and in 1815 she would sail to Elba to visit him in exile.[23]

Maria could provide the Emperor with a son, but her position meant that she could not provide him with an heir – the heir he needed if he was to prepare a dynastic succession, which by 1806 had become a major issue for Napoleon and his advisers. At the age of thirty-seven he still lacked a legitimate heir, had little reason to put trust in his brothers, and was no longer attracted by the notion of an 'adoptive succession' which he had contemplated at the time of his coronation. His close advisers made it clear that they, too, felt there was a pressing need for an heir if the regime was to be established on solid foundations. Nor should that heir be a mere commoner; that would do nothing to impress or appease the crowned heads of Europe. What Napoleon needed was a family connection with one of the great European dynastic families. If he was to be treated as their equal, he had to behave like them, and in their world marriage was not about love and spontaneity; it was closely planned to form powerful political and family alliances. That, in the opinion of such ministers as Fouché and Talleyrand, could mean only one thing: that Napoleon must seek the hand of a royal princess, preferably from either Russia or Austria, in order to secure his throne. Failure to do so would endanger the future of the Empire. Or, as Fouché indiscreetly expressed it to Josephine in 1807, the welfare of France demanded that she should seek a divorce. It was not a question of emotions; it was an issue of politics, of *Realpolitik*.

As rumours circulated about the Emperor's intentions – the Austrian ambassador, Metternich, passed these on to Vienna, and tongues wagged across Europe – Josephine felt depressed and resentful at what she imagined to be the machinations of Napoleon's brothers, whom she had long seen as her enemies. Yet months passed without the situation being in any way clarified, and the marriage was not finally annulled until January 1810. Josephine had little choice but to agree; she was forty-six, and accepted that she could no longer have children. She was compensated by being allowed to keep the title of Empress-Queen, and was given Malmaison in full ownership and the Elysée Palace as her Paris residence. The government also voted her an annual pension of two million francs, to which Napoleon added a third million to support her lifestyle and help pay off her considerable debts.[24]

With the embarrassment of Josephine conveniently removed – the Catholic authorities in Paris had obligingly confirmed the annulment in record time – Napoleon was free to weigh up the diplomatic advantages of a marriage alliance with either Russia or Austria. In fact, his mind was already made up, and both his advisers and his family declared that their preference lay with Austria, in the person of eighteen-year-old Marie Louise, daughter of the Austrian Emperor Francis I. In March 1810 they were married by proxy in the Augustine Church in Vienna without Napoleon even meeting his bride. She then left for Paris, where, after an initial meeting in the Forest of Compiègne, they married for a second time on 2 April, in a religious service following a civil ceremony the previous day. Again, the Catholic Church proved astonishingly cooperative, with Fesch, a fellow Corsican and close collaborator of Napoleon's, there to officiate. Within three months the Emperor had obtained a divorce and found a new bride from the oldest monarchy in Europe. It was a symbolic moment, one that defined the transformation of the regime from a republic founded on revolution and regicide into an empire legitimised by heredity and dynastic succession. Or, as one historian has elegantly expressed it, it was the moment when the *enfants de la patrie* of the 1790s mingled their blood with that of the oldest monarchy in Europe and believed that they could 'transform themselves from being regicides to fathering kings'.[25] A son of the Revolution agreed to marry the niece of Marie-Antoinette, and, perhaps even more astonishingly, he was accepted, however reluctantly, into the royal family of Austria.[26] If Napoleon had intended to stupefy Europe, he surely succeeded. And within a year he had fulfilled another ambition: in March 1811, Marie Louise provided Napoleon with a son and heir.

The marriage ceremony and the formal celebrations that framed it show just how far Napoleon had moved away from his republican roots. The civil ceremony was held in the Gallery of Apollo at Saint-Cloud, the palace beautifully illuminated for the occasion, before the imperial party left for Paris. The religious service then followed in the Chapel of the Tuileries, copying in every detail the wording used for the last royal marriage held in France, between Louis XVI and Marie-Antoinette back in 1770.[27] It was a lavish and dignified affair: the imperial procession swept into Paris amidst a vast crowd, entering the Tuileries gardens through a specially erected triumphal arch and a temporary colonnade, and after the marriage they received the delegations that came to congratulate them in the throne room of the palace.

All Paris was bedecked with flags and public buildings floodlit to mark the occasion; and with an eye to popular reaction, care was taken that this should also be a popular festival, which ordinary Parisians could join in and admire. There were fireworks along the banks of the Seine, displays of horsemanship, games and dancing on the Champs-Elysées, a military procession and military music.

On the Champ de Mars a hot-air balloon carrying Madame Blan-chard rose into the sky against the backdrop of the École Militaire. Napoleon, as was his wont, aimed not just to impress onlookers with the solemnity of the occasion, but also to provide spectacle and amusement. Indeed, it was a characteristic of Napoleonic festi-vals that they deliberately incorporated elements of the spectacular and fantastic, and understood the propaganda value of fun. In this they stood in stark contrast to the more prosaic, staidly educative festivals that had been staged by the revolutionaries; there was a modern, flamboyant element in them that aimed to set the public pulse racing. The Emperor's advisers and designers made sure that the day of his marriage to Marie Louise was one that all Paris would remember with pleasure; and the detail of the celebrations was lovingly recorded by the artist Louis-Pierre Baltard.[28]

Festivals were part of an armoury of propagandist devices to which Napoleon turned to project both his own image and that of his Empire. He used what he knew of the history of past regimes, from Ancient Rome to the court of Louis XIV, to see how others before him had exploited pomp and symbolism to burnish their image and impose their authority. If the public persona of Louis XIV was a 'fabrication', the result of a deliberate campaign of expo-sure and self-advertisement,[29] so, too, was that of the Emperor; and the increasing grandeur of his court and the public glorification of his victories in battle were intended to add both to his own repu-tation and to the lustre of his regime. In his earlier life he had sought to present himself as a hero, to captivate the imagination of the French people through his valour and his military exploits; now the emphasis changed to stress his serious devotion to the cause of the Empire and his role as saviour of his people. He assumed the traditional monarchical role of law-giver and dispenser of justice, who had helped preserve the hard-won rights of the people while bringing stability and security to the whole of Europe. Sometimes, perhaps, he took the process too far, as when, in 1806, a new saint, Saint Napoleon, was introduced into the Catholic calendar, his saint's day, 15 August, conveniently timed to coincide with both the Emperor's birthday and the festival of Assumption, a major holiday in the Christian year. The aim was clear enough: to draw attention to Napoleon's achievements – and it is no accident that he was presented as a warrior-saint, the victor of Jena and Austerlitz – and to mark the return of Catholic worship to lands secularised by the Jacobin Republic. But the festival was given a muted reception. Most Catholics seem to have remained unimpressed, finding the whole notion of Saint Napoleon mildly ridiculous, and continued to mark Assumption traditionally, as the feast of the Virgin.[30]

For Napoleon himself the image appeared anything but ridiculous; indeed, in his proclamations and his use of language he cemented the idea that he was all-powerful, omniscient, a man capable of seeing clearly where others got lost in a fog of confusion. The magnificence of public festivals and the love of sumptuous parades all served a single purpose, that of reinforcing his authority. There was something godly about the way in which he was spoken of and represented, an aloofness that isolated him and kept him apart from his people.[31]

This image was reinforced by the statesmanlike portraits and classical busts produced by the leading artists of the day, all of which served to identify the Emperor as someone with special abilities and unchallenged power, presenting him in turn as a military hero, a far-sighted law-giver, and a patron of the arts. Image, it seemed, was everything, an aspect of his reign in which Napoleon, like the Sun King before him, took a personal interest. As he had in the 1790s, he visited the Paris salons and took an active part in choosing prize themes for the Academy. He was a patron of artists and sculptors, and turned to the leading portraitists and history painters of the day to present his image and hence further to legitimate his power. Gros, Ingres, David and Géricault were among those he commissioned to paint canvases in his honour, whether triumphal battlefield scenes of Jena and Austerlitz, images of care and compassion like Gros' famous 1804 picture showing him tending the plague victims in Jaffa, or those wholly imagined scenes that appealed to the romantic imagination, like that by David showing him as First Consul crossing the Alps on a romantic white charger. Was this propaganda? As David O'Brien points out, the government did make some attempt to gauge public opinion, but this 'does not alter the basic fact that under the new regime official painting sought to shape, rather than respond to, popular sentiments'. Under the Bourbons, official art had increasingly tried to respond to the art criticism generated by the Salon, whereas Napoleon was less interested in interaction, and a strict regime of censorship severely limited the influence of popular sentiment.[32] Artists struggled to fulfil commissions while still maintaining a degree of autonomy from the state; they knew that history painting that appeared too deferential attracted little critical interest. Some admitted to feeling frustrated that their talent was being undermined. As the painter Girodet wrote, 'We are all enlisted now, even if we don't wear the uniform.'[33]

Napoleon was well served by his artists, some of whom, such as David, took the short step from serving the Revolution to becoming the official court painter of the Empire. His canvas *Le*

Sacre, for example, completed in 1808, did not just impress by its size or its cast of hundreds; it exuded the glory and majesty that Napoleon was so eager to project. Military painters, too, were careful to focus the onlooker's eye on the glamour and dash of the Emperor, always prominently deployed in his signature greatcoat and *tricorne* hat. He was the hero who threw himself and his men into battle, the strategist who planned every detail of the engagement and out-thought the opposition. The emphasis on war and empire-building had a further consequence in that their portrayal was largely masculine, in striking contrast to the revolutionaries' iden-tification of the nation through a predominantly feminine symbolism. The new imagery had male military bodies at its core, bodies which defined the character of the Empire by contrasting them with those of their enemies.[34]

While Napoleon encouraged these portrayals and expressed approval for the work of those painters who specialised in military scenes – Prud'hon and Lefèvre, for instance – there is little to suggest that he had any real appreciation of art for its own sake. What he did appreciate was the influence art could exercise, and from early in his career he saw patronage as a valuable tool to manipulate opinion and build his reputation as a leader in the cultural domain. Of course, the painters concerned made a good living from state patronage; there was an annual budget of sixty thousand francs expressly reserved for purchases of 'new, high-quality pictures and for encouraging the art of painting'.[35] But they could also expect to capitalise on their fame in the market place, as the private art market revived under the Empire. The revolutionary age of austerity was at last over, and artists and craftsmen, from portrait painters to landscape gardeners and the makers of fine porcelain, saw their business revive. The return of some of the great noble families from emigration, when added to Napoleon's own taste for luxury, meant that those artists who had suffered most grievously during the Revolution now had fresh opportunities for sales, and hence for profit. The strong bond between Napoleon and his artists was mutually beneficial.

The benefit that Napoleon could derive from art is exemplified by the flurry of paintings recording and commemorating the Egyptian Campaign. The military effort, as we have seen, was an undisputed failure, with the remnants of his army returning in tatters to France and an important part of the artistic plunder, including the Rosetta Stone, falling ignominiously into British hands before it could be brought back to Europe. Yet, even at the time, Napoleon had insisted that these engagements would provide the subject matter for dramatic history paintings; and throughout the Empire such paintings became regular highlights of Napoleonic salons. It did not concern him that the battles had been lost, or that some of the scenes depicted were more invention than historical truth. Most important was the opportunity to paint scenes that would etch themselves on France's imagination, and appeal to the colonial ideal that had begun to dissolve with the loss of Quebec in the Seven Years War and the Peace of Paris that followed. In the paintings of Gros, Girodet and Lejeune, a new colonial idyll was developed that could appeal to the France of the early nineteenth century and to the post-revolutionary world. The paintings nodded in the direction of the current fashion for the exotic and the oriental, lingering lovingly on the vivid cloaks and glinting weapons of France's opponents. But they were not intended only to dazzle or entertain: they invoked memories that placed the French in the direct line of other great empires, whether of Egypt or of Rome. And by contrasting the French with the Syrians or Egyptians, the paintings also played to ideas of national stereotypes, that pitted, in Todd Porterfield's words, 'French science, morality, masculinity and intellectual rigor against supposedly representative traits of Easterners: fanaticism, cruelty, idleness, vice, irrationality, deviance and degeneracy'.[36] The French encompassed the highest values of civilisation; they could admire these paintings and feel good about themselves.

Napoleon had neither the time nor the expertise to exercise artistic judgment on his own account, and understood that he needed an artistic director, someone who could develop a national policy of collections and take charge of the masterpieces. Many of these had been pillaged from Germany, Italy and elsewhere, and would be placed in the new museum Napoleon intended to found in the Louvre. The man he chose for the task was Dominique-Vivant Denon, an engraver and former royal curator in the Old Regime, who had gone with Napoleon to Egypt where, accompanying Desaix's army, he had travelled widely in the countryside and both written about and sketched the hundreds of antiquities he came across.

Denon was an indefatigable traveller who, on his return to France in 1802, published his findings, and his sketches, in his *Voyage dans la Basse et la Haute Egypte pendant les campagnes du Général Bonaparte*, a book that brought him instant fame, as much for his descriptions of the countryside and of everyday life in Egypt as for the technical detail on the ruins.[37] He commented on the Egyptians' costumes and their diet, and noted the extremes of wealth and poverty that characterised urban society in Cairo. He lived through the Cairo uprising with all its extremes of violence and cruelty, yet noted that the ringleaders were atypical of the citizenry as a whole.

'While murder was devoutly preached from the galleries of the minarets, and while the streets were filled with death and carnage, all those in whose houses any Frenchmen were lodged were eager to save them by concealment and to supply and anticipate all their wants'.[38] Denon's descriptions were rich and detailed and, like all eighteenth-century travellers, steeped in the travel literature of the age, foremost among them the writings of Volney. Passing through Alexandria, for instance, he noted that everything he saw confirmed Volney's graphic account of the city, to the point where, on rereading him several months later, all the shapes, colours and smells came flooding back to him.[39] If Napoleon warmed to Denon's writing, he also trusted his politics, for Denon was a committed disciple. Describing the Battle of the Pyramids, he had concluded, with a degree of literary licence, that 'a handful of French, led by a hero, had just subdued a quarter of the globe'.[40] It was not true, but it was the sort of distortion that appealed to the Emperor.

Vivant Denon was appointed in 1802 as the first director of Napoleon's grand project for an imperial art gallery to be formed out of the Louvre, and he would retain the post until after the fall of the Empire in 1815. It gave him great influence over the artistic taste of his generation in his effective management of Napoleon's cultural policy. He built up the collections in the Louvre and at Versailles, as well as arranging salons and giving help to struggling artists. The Louvre he inherited from the Revolution was a museum which had been established with a clear republican mission: as the Girondin minister Jean-Marie Roland explained to David in 1792, 'The museum must demonstrate the nation's great riches. France must extend its glory through the ages and to all peoples: the national museum will embrace knowledge in all its manifold beauty and will be the admiration of the universe.'[41] Under the Empire the purpose of the museum became less educational and more celebratory, a storehouse for the culture of Europe and the conquests of Napoleon's military triumphs. Art works were sedulously pillaged from public galleries and private collections in Italy, Germany, and across Europe, and brought back to Paris where they were displayed in chrono-logical sequence to reflect the evolution of culture, building, of course, to the great painters of Napoleon's own day.[42]

In the streets of Paris, too, large numbers of public buildings and monuments proclaimed the glory of the regime and acted as everyday reminders of imperial military triumphs. If Napoleon disliked statues of himself, which would have recalled too directly the reigns of long-deposed monarchs, he aimed to make Paris a city of rare beauty, a fitting capital for his Empire. The obelisk on the Place de la Concorde recalled the splendours of an empire he had overcome; the Pantheon commemorated contemporary heroes; the Trajan column in the Place Vendôme conjured up memories of classical Rome. The triumphs of his armies are proclaimed on the Arc de Triomphe, designed for the Emperor though not completed until the 1830s. In architecture, classical facades dominated in the perfectly balanced, if emotionally cold, frontages of buildings such as the Madeleine or the French parliament building, the Palais Bourbon. Napoleon was not the last French leader to dream of leaving a permanent mark on Paris – the presidents of the Fifth Republic have in turn bestowed their architectural trademark on the capital – but few have left such a range of palaces and monuments.[43]

Napoleon jealously guarded his reputation as a patron of the arts, since generosity and patronage were part of his image as a monarch. He was determined to show that he was more than a great warrior, and that he brought peace, culture, and civilisation to the territories he ruled. His artistic interest extended beyond painting and the plastic arts. He saw himself as a patron of music, too, and through the Comte de Remusat he intervened directly in the selection of prizewinners in the annual competition at the Imperial Music Academy. Like the Bourbons before him, he showed an interest in the plays that were staged in the Paris theatre, and most particularly in the performances staged at the Paris Opera, which he attended regularly when he was in the city. He even insisted on playing a role in programme selection, which allows one recent historian to talk of Napoleon having a *politique de la scène*.[44] This was especially so during the years of his great victories, when operas and plays often made specific reference to his achievements but, shrewdly perhaps, he maintained tight control over the Paris stage throughout the Empire. For there can be no mistake about his intentions, or the root of his artistic interest. Like everything he did, his motive was political before it was cultural. Patronage of the arts was yet another aspect of imperial power.

From the Peninsula to Leipzig

In 1807, as we have seen, Napoleon was at the very zenith of his power. In a face-to-face negotiation with Tsar Alexander I on the Niemen, he had effectively divided Europe into French and Russian zones of influence to the exclusion of defeated powers such as Austria and Prussia – as well, of course, as Great Britain. The glorious surroundings, the trappings of imperial authority, the intimacy of the moment – allies and even advisers were excluded from the meeting of the two emperors – all served to emphasise that this was a very personal triumph, one that might yet allow him to be perceived by the French people as a man of peace. Yet the accords drawn up at Tilsit held the seeds of future conflicts. Those rulers who had not been involved in the negotiations were unlikely to accept with good grace a treaty imposed on them by France and Russia; their feelings of resentment would smoulder until they had an opportunity for revenge. The King of Prussia, in particular, had reason to feel aggrieved, since his lands were cavalierly carved up in the interests of the two empires to his east and west. Prussia lost a third of its territory and nearly half its population, with its share of Poland remodelled into the Grand Duchy of Warsaw and placed under the hereditary rule of the King of Saxony.[1] Prussia would bide her time, restructure her armed forces, and seek new alliances; in this part of Central Europe Tilsit was an invitation to further warfare, and it is surely unsurprising that the Grand Duchy did not survive Napoleon's fall. Many of the German princes whose loyalty Napoleon had bought with favours and honours became increasingly restive as the Emperor rode roughshod over their interests, while their subjects were attracted to the new forces of German nationalism.

Tilsit would prove a short-lived triumph for Napoleon, exposing him to the resentments and jealousies of others. It left him with responsibility for a Europe-wide empire, to be sure, but also vulnerable to the perils that wide-flung territories and distant frontier zones imposed. Stable government depended increasingly on gaining the cooperation of local rulers and local elites. In particular, Napoleon was overly dependent on the support of Alexander I to maintain his territories to the east, to the extent that Russia became, in Luigi Mascilli Migliorini's phrase, 'the keystone to the stability of the Empire's eastern frontier'.[2] The foreign policy successes of the early years came with dangers of their own.

It was not only a question of defending these far-flung borders, difficult as that might at times appear. The sheer geographical extent of the Empire took the Napoleonic system into new political zones, which had hidden perils of their own. French territories were not all contiguous with France itself; at its height, the Empire also controlled provinces along the Adriatic, in Istria, Croatia and Dalmatia, which bordered on Russia and the Ottoman Empire. In the Balkans and the Near East, Napoleon had dreamt as late as 1806 of creating alliances with both Turkey and Persia, a triple alliance that would help France to ward off Russia and attack British India. But by the following year his priorities had changed because the speed of his victory against the Tsar obviated any further need for aid from Persia or Turkey; while relations between the two Near Eastern powers, never good, had disintegrated into open warfare. Napoleon had to choose between them: he decided that the stability of the Ottoman Empire was threatened by internal decadence, and so he opted to abandon the Ottomans for the sake of a Persian alliance.[3]

This, too, would have serious diplomatic consequences, alarming both the British and the Russians and alerting foreign governments to his further ambitions beyond Europe. It was also a reminder that, however great France's military power, the Emperor could not force others to share his interests or bully them into unnatural friendships. Besides, inside the envelope of the Napoleonic Wars there would be areas of conflict that had little to do with France, but which reflected local goals and regional animosities. The Europe-wide wars provided a context in which ambitions could be realised and old scores settled. A military coup in Sweden in 1809, for instance, overthrew Gustav IV and provided Russia with an excuse to intervene; Finland then battled to secure liberation from two centuries of Swedish rule, and a popular insurrection broke out in the Tyrol against Austria. None of this had much to do with Napoleon's Empire, at least not directly. Nor, ostensibly, did the first murmurings of a Spanish-American revolution in Venezuela in 1810, though the insurrectionary mood was fired by news of Napoleon's invasion of Spain. The revolutionary leaders in Latin America, like Francisco de Miranda, were profoundly influenced by France's revolution and looked for inspiration to its iconography.[4] Conflict in one area created aspirations elsewhere in the world, thus transferring the Napoleonic Wars on to a world stage.

Elsewhere in Europe, the demands of Napoleonic administration served to whip up opposition and stimulate a desire for national autonomy. Throughout Germany it sowed the seeds of a new German nationalism that would be a powerful force in the Wars of Liberation in 1813, while Russia and Austria continued to cast covetous eyes on Napoleon's Grand Duchy of Warsaw. Napoleon himself showed no desire to end the war, or to accept that the balance of power established at Tilsit was in any sense definitive. Rather, he argued that further wars of expansion were needed, that further punishment must be meted out to those, like Britain, that had not been conquered, if the stability of the Empire was to be guaranteed and the formation of new coalitions averted. He may, of course, have been right here, in the sense that the dynastic rulers of Europe were unlikely to accept as legitimate the patchwork of client states with which the Emperor had surrounded himself, most often with one of his relatives at its head. It was not only the King of Prussia who was harbouring resentments or biding his time. Austria, too, humiliated by Napoleon in battle and humiliated again diplomatically by the dissolution of the Holy Roman Empire, had good reason to seek revenge. And internally, across much of Europe, there was the danger of restiveness as people suffered the full weight of taxes and requisitions, the burden of conscription, and the intrusion of imperial administration and policing. For a while, until around 1808, it must have appeared that the Napoleonic system was working well, introducing efficient government and attracting local notables to its service; and from Belgium to Venice and across much of German Central Europe, landowners, merchants, lawyers and even the great noble families seemed ready to attach themselves to the imperial standard. But already there were serious fissures below the surface, and in the years that followed Napoleonic Europe would be engulfed once more in war and crisis.

At the root of the crisis was Napoleon's determination to attack Britain's trading and economic power, which he believed, with some reason, to hold the secret of her military success. The destruction of her commercial wealth and the impact this would have on the City of London would, he argued, force the British government to sue for peace and thereby remove his most implacable opponent. He would claim that this policy was forced upon him by Britain's dominance at sea after Trafalgar, and the aggressive use that she was making of her naval superiority. In London, the Portland administration showed no desire to treat with the Empire and, even more than its predecessors, seemed set on a fight to the death. The French response was to implement the Continental Blockade, with the aim of cutting off the coasts of Europe from British shipping.[5] Britain's response was immediate, and it was openly aggressive – an attack on Denmark in 1807 in which the British fleet bombarded Copenhagen, causing thousands of civilian deaths, and seized the Danish navy before it could fall into Napoleon's hands. For Britain had good reason to fear the effect of Napoleon's blockade, at least until such time as she had found new markets for her goods, and she put intense pressure on her allies to break it. Knocking out the Danish navy was necessary, the British felt, if they were to maintain command of the seas and control the coastline of Europe.[6]

Napoleon did not doubt that he would bring Britain to her knees. As a strategy, the Continental System he had initiated was by no means an unpromising idea, nor was it certain in 1806 that the British could undermine it. However, as mentioned earlier, it was harder to enforce than Napoleon had envisaged and was proving deeply unpopular, even in parts of France. Across the Empire the Continental System was resented, and blamed for creating shortages and forcing up prices; it was also seen, quite justly, as a French policy to promote French interests, often at others' expense. [7] In the short term, the great European ports were savagely affected, losing their domestic commerce and becoming increasingly dependent on neutral shipping. In the longer term, merchants devised their own strategies to subvert the policy, and many managed to carry on in trade.[8] But the policy, as a device designed to undermine Britain, clearly failed. Meanwhile, in ports like Hamburg, the misery it caused and the sense that they were being exploited for the benefit of France left a burning sense of resentment which helped to militarise opinion and persuade a commercial civil society to take up arms against the Empire.[9]

It was Napoleon's determination to enforce the Continental System that led most immediately to the extension of the war, to force other rulers to implement the Berlin and the later Milan Decrees and to close their ports to the British. This brought heightened tensions in much of Italy and led to the occupation of the Papal States. More importantly it explains Napoleon's fateful decision to invade Spain. Spain was not a hostile power; indeed, the Spanish monarchy had been counted among the Empire's military allies, albeit a rather lukewarm and inefficient ally at times. But the Spanish court was a hotbed of cabals and factions, some strongly anti-French, and the King's chief minister, Manuel Godoy, was plotting to tear up the French alliance and cross the Pyrenees. This treachery alone was enough to persuade Napoleon that the time had come to take firm action, but just as important was the threat that Iberia presented to the Continental System, Lisbon in particular offering a major entry point for British goods on the continent. In October 1807 French forces had crossed the Spanish border and invaded Portugal, the first of three invasions within four years, and in May 1808, at Bayonne, Napoleon bullied the King of Spain, Charles IV, into signing over his rights to the throne and forced his son Ferdinand to abdicate. He then brusquely transferred his own brother, Joseph, from Naples to replace Charles as King of Spain.

At Bayonne, Spain was transformed into yet another imperial satellite, or so it appeared; in the event, the arrival of the French, with their customary demands for heavy taxes and military levies, triggered widespread popular resistance in support of the Bourbons, including a bitter insurrection in Madrid that would be immortalised by the Spanish artist Goya. Provincial risings followed in many parts of the country, pinning back French forces, and by the end of 1808 the British army had liberated Portugal. It was now clear that the French were engaged in a different kind of war from those they had encountered on the plains of Central Europe. Many Spaniards remained deeply loyal to their royal family, now exiled in Brazil, and saw Joseph as a usurper and the puppet of a foreign power. Their acquiescence could not be taken for granted as it could in many of the German electorates, where Napoleon sealed deals with their rulers and ensured that their subjects' loyalty remained undivided. This would be a war against civilians and partisans as well as regular soldiers, a guerrilla war, in which it was difficult to distinguish soldiers from villagers, fought against an enemy that melted away into forests and mountain passes. It was something new in the imperial era: a people's war that Napoleon found he could not win, a war that dragged on miserably and drained French manpower and resources.[10]

Of course, France did not go into Spain unprepared, and the army that Napoleon sent across the Pyrenees was a powerful military unit of around one hundred and twenty thousand men, certainly the best trained and equipped in Spain at the time, even if it was composed mainly of raw conscripts and second-line troops transferred from war in Italy. In the early stages of the war the army advanced across the north of the country meeting only limited resistance, but Spanish opinion rallied against the French, with the opposition centred in provincial governments and local juntas. Militarily, the Spanish army itself was in poor shape, badly neglected during the years of Godoy's government, and the major military operations against the French were led by the British under Wellesley, for whom the Peninsula was the principal theatre of operations. Soon, around twenty-three thousand British troops were assembled in Portugal, the base from which the British defended the Portuguese and launched attacks on French positions, with both Spanish and Portuguese troops playing a secondary role alongside them.

Until 1809 it looked as though the French invasion would succeed. They had put down the majority of the insurrections they had encountered in the northern areas of the country and, with the exception of a surprise defeat at Bailén in 1808, they had systematically defeated the Spanish army in open battle. But then the political climate in Europe changed dramatically. In response to the Tyrolean rebellion Austria re-entered the war and looked to form a new coalition against France. Napoleon hurriedly returned to Paris, leaving the day-to-day conduct of the Peninsular War to his marshals while he concentrated on hostilities in the east. And, increasingly, it was not the Spanish army that the French found themselves pitted against, but the guerrillas on the one hand, and the British army on the other. The British, from their base in Portugal, proved more than a match for them on the battlefield, where Wellesley – soon to be created Viscount Wellington – would prove a skilled tactician. But for the average French soldier thrown into the cauldron of the Spanish war it was the unfamiliarity, and often the sheer savagery, of guerrilla warfare that left the deepest mark. Officers' memoirs and soldiers' letters agree in expressing a hatred of the Spanish front that was unequalled in their previous experience of warfare. As one French officer recalled, no one could be trusted: 'Treason was a constant risk, day and night, whether at the other side of the road or at the head of one's bed. Everyone was to be feared, even those seemingly hospitable people who took you in to their homes.'[11]

Increasingly, France found herself at war with what must have seemed like the entire population. Joseph failed to win popular support for his government, and the French army became embroiled in an increasingly brutal, ruthless and repressive campaign against Spanish irregulars, the guerrillas who have gone down in nineteenth-century Spanish history as nationalists and freedom fighters. Their motives were almost certainly more mixed, many of them choosing service in the *guerrilla* less from political idealism than as a means to combat poverty or escape conscription into the official army; and some of those who led the guerrilla bands were little better than robbers and bandits.[12]

Their reputation among the French troops was characterised by tales of torture and cruelty: they ambushed French columns in impenetrable mountain areas, cutting off stragglers and subjecting them to sadistic torture before mutilating and killing them. In parts of southern Spain, notably Andalusia, civilians joined in these acts of cruelty, and there were horrific tales of soldiers being buried alive in sand and left to die in the sun, reports of mutilation and, worse, decapitation, and of men having their genitals cut off and stuffed into their mouths – watched by the entire village – in a final, repugnant act of sexual humiliation.[13] It is impossible to guess how much these tales were exaggerated or a single incident multiplied many times in the retelling. But like any act of terrorism, it had the effect of destroying French discipline and inviting retaliation; and the French were not slow to oblige, hanging partisans from olive trees and inflicting collective punishment on entire villages suspected of aiding the guerrilla fighters. Like the civil war in the west of France in the 1790s, which was also fought against peasants, the war in Spain sparked hatreds that would be difficult to quench. For a trained professional army, accustomed to fight in battle formation, it was a miserable and often frightening experience and led many of the French soldiers to regard their Spanish opponents as barbaric and uncivilised. This was an opinion that some of Wellington's troops, their supposed allies against the French, confessed to sharing. Exacerbating the poor relations between the invading army and the local population, the French often equated Spanish backwardness with the excessive piety of a people who had emerged from the eighteenth century untouched by the Enlightenment. They further fuelled the animosity of local people by pillaging and desecrating churches in the regions the army passed through, where, as one historian has remarked, 'French troops behaved as if they were charged with the de-Christianisation of the province'.[14]

If the French were harassed by the guerrillas, they were not, however, defeated by them; the Peninsular War would be won by the British army, aided by the Portuguese and some Spanish divisions, in regular fighting. Three times the French invaded Portugal to try and dislodge the British army, and three times, in 1808, 1809 and 1811, they were driven back. The British army was helped in no small measure by the Portuguese policy of destroying their crops and farmsteads and retreating behind the walls of Lisbon to thwart the French attack. But in Spain itself Wellington's only significant incursion – an attempt to take Madrid in 1809 – had ended in failure, and the British had retreated to Lisbon, leaving the defence of Spain to the severely mauled Spanish forces. In the years that followed, the French marshals entrusted with the Spanish campaign scored significant military successes, conquering Andalusia and Extremadura in the face of fierce resistance. But the British understood how seriously other war fronts were distracting Napoleon from Spain and how rapidly they were consuming French military resources. It was now decided to increase troop deployment in the Peninsula and to push on into Spain, beginning in the south and with the liberation of Madrid. The tactic worked brilliantly. With the French now fighting major campaigns in Germany and Russia, Wellington had, by 1813, driven their armies out of every Spanish province except Catalonia. By the following year the Peninsula was lost, and Ferdinand VII, who had been held captive in France for most of the war, was able to reclaim his throne.

Napoleon's strategic approach had come badly unstuck in Spain. He had not secured the acquiescence of the population to Joseph's kingship, and this left the country a prey to insurrection. And his troops had been unusually vulnerable to attack from the guerrillas. The tactic of seizing territory by means of a rapid manoeuvre, with the aim of engaging and destroying the enemy's army – a tactic that he had used so deftly elsewhere – failed him here. His forces were held off by guerrilla attacks in the inhospitable mountain country of the interior, or delayed by the need to send out foraging parties if men and horses were to be fed. And with little cooperation from the local people, rations and fodder were often scarce, or had to be wrenched from the peasants' grasp by threats and violence. In hostile terrain of the sort the French encountered beyond the Pyrenees, the wisdom of a logistical policy that had remained intact since the Revolution, that of exporting the supply problem and living off the land, was less assured, and the army's march was continually slowed by the need to stock up from local granaries.[15] There were other problems, too. With Napoleon's attention diverted by other theatres of war, he spent little time in Spain, leaving campaign decisions to his marshals, who certainly showed little of the political under-standing that was necessary to win over public opinion. They, too, were shunted around to serve the interests of the wider war, and the abler marshals, like Soult and Marmont, were removed from Spain to serve in what Napoleon regarded as the more sensitive war zones of Central Europe. Those who remained were of only moderate ability, and it is hard not to conclude that Napoleon systematically underestimated the threat he faced in Spain, giving insufficient credit to Wellington as a commander and showing contempt for the guer-rillas. He would pay dearly for it, as the Spanish Ulcer pinned down nearly two hundred thousand French and Allied troops, thus restricting his ability to move against Russia and Central Europe.[16]

Perhaps Napoleon also failed to understand the resentment that his rapid victories over the great European powers had created, or the extent of their anxiety about his future ambitions. After 1806 both Prussia and Austria, which had both been humiliated in war by the French Emperor, planned major reforms of their military structures, attempting to learn from Napoleon's tactics and prepare themselves for a future war of revenge. Austria in particular saw a new war as inevitable and encouraged expressions of German nationalism; in 1808 the Archduke Charles established the Landwehr throughout Austria and Bohemia, with compulsory military service for all men between eighteen and forty-five. In Russia, too, Alexander I was biding his time, temporarily focusing on military objectives closer to home, in Finland and Turkey, yet fully aware that Russia would need to fight another war against the Empire.

Britain was equally convinced of the need to defeat Napoleon, but Canning saw little advantage to be gained from spreading Britain's military resources, preferring to concentrate on the struggle in the Peninsula where he believed that the French were most vulnerable. Besides the Peninsular campaign, Britain deployed her traditional weapon against French hegemony – the Royal Navy – responding to the Continental System by imposing a blockade of the French coastline. This strategy was reasonably effective as it seriously cut the volume of French commercial shipping, though, after 1808, developments elsewhere weakened its impact, from the growth and diversification of British trade to an explosion of smuggling along the Channel coast.[17] Britain had, however, no need for concern, as her stronger and more diversified economy and the support of international finance provided her with a decisive advantage. Britain could simply run up debt, thanks to the money markets and the people feeling secure in the belief that their credit was safe. International merchants, industrialists, landowners, planters, banks and speculators all rushed to buy into London. Napoleon enjoyed no such confidence.[18]

In Central Europe and in Italy conflict continued, fired by revolts and popular insurrections against the Empire, while Napoleon's contemptuous treatment of the Pope – who was seized and imprisoned by French forces in 1809 – outraged Catholic opinion across Europe. There was talk of a new military alliance against France, but in April 1809 Austria broke ranks and, buoyed by public opinion and a new surge of nationalism, resumed the war against Napoleon on her own; of the other powers only Britain signed up to the so-called Fifth Coalition. The Austrian Emperor, Francis II, and the majority of the archdukes believed that, with the French bogged down in Spain, they should seize the moment to re-establish Austrian dominion in southern Germany and Italy. Austria's army was in better shape than it had been four years earlier, while Napoleon seemed ill-prepared because of his heavy involvement in Spain. He had at his disposal some ninety thousand men of the Army of the Rhine, to which he added around a hundred thousand allied troops, mainly Germans, Dutch and Poles. To plug the gaps, he then called up a further one hundred and forty thousand conscripts, so that by March 1809 he had effectively assembled a new army in Germany, some three hundred thousand strong.[19] He did so in record time, forsaking his customary meticulous preparation; the consequence was a messy campaign that saw Napoleon defeated by the Austrians in a bloody encounter at Aspern-Essling, in which Lannes and a number of generals were killed. Napoleon rallied, defeating the Austrians at Wagram and forcing them to sue for peace at Schönbrunn. But the victory bore none of the mystique of his earlier campaigns. There were enormous casualties on both sides, and the French were too exhausted to destroy the enemy. The Emperor's military reputation was left tarnished by a campaign chiefly remembered in Germany for the failed insurrection of the Tyrolean patriot Andreas Hofer.

Napoleon's ambition, however, was not satisfied, and his attention soon turned to Russia. He was disappointed in the fruits of his Russian alliance and was angered by Alexander's reluctance to implement the Continental System and exclude British trade. When the two emperors had met at Erfurt in 1808, Alexander had looked to the French for concessions over Constantinople, but got none.[20] Napoleon was also irritated by the cool reception to the proposal that he might marry a Russian princess after he divorced Josephine. He had, however, other, more political, reasons to distrust his Russian ally: Alexander had not stood by when he saw the French stretched on other fronts, but took advantage of Napoleon's distraction in Spain to pursue his own traditional foreign policy objectives in Eastern Europe.

Within what Russia saw as her sphere of influence she was defiantly expansionist, going to war with Sweden in the north and with Turkey in the south. From the Swedes, Russia took Finland and Aaland, in the process unleashing a constitutional crisis in Sweden that would overthrow the reigning monarch and make the former Napoleonic marshal, Bernadotte, the Swedish Crown Prince. This Alexander saw as an opportunity rather than a threat. He sought Bernadotte's friendship and tried to force a schism between him and his former Emperor; and Bernadotte, flattered by the Tsar's attentions, outraged by Napoleon's seizure of Swedish Pomerania, and attracted by Alexander's offer of a free hand against Denmark, agreed to commit Sweden to the Russian cause.[21] But this was not the only reason for Napoleon's rupture with Alexander. Even more provocative was Alexander's decision in 1810 to break formally with the Continental System, and he was soon demanding that Napoleon recognise Russia's right to trade with neutrals, which undermined the economic strategy of the Empire.[22] There were also persistent rumours of an imminent Russian attack on the Grand Duchy of Warsaw, a loyal French ally in the region. Russia was posing a threat to the very sinews of the Empire.

For all these reasons, relations between the two emperors cooled rapidly, and both understood that they would have to fight another war. By 1811 Napoleon was drawing up plans to assemble a *Grande Armée de la Russie*, calling upon his allies across Europe to make contributions of men and materials. His intentions were clear. Alexander and his chief minister, Speranski, were also building up their military strength, initiating army reforms and, crucially, making peace with Turkey in 1812, which released more forces for national defence. Timing was everything. In 1811 the Russians had feared being overrun by Napoleon. A year later, with his army enlarged and reformed by Barclay de Tolly and his strategy in place, Alexander was more confident that he was now in a position to take full advantage of Russia's vast territorial expanse to repel any French invasion. What he may have underestimated was Napoleon's capacity to shrug off his losses in the Peninsula and create a massive new army six hundred thousand strong, including a huge cavalry force of eighty thousand.

It was in one sense a remarkable achievement: an army drawn from across occupied Europe, its men forcibly conscripted, the horses compulsorily purchased for army service. In France itself, if the levies were met, it was in the face of glum fatalism and occasional sparks of resistance. But barely half of the soldiers were Frenchmen. The fourth corps was one-third Italian, while the fifth (under Poniatowski) consisted entirely of Poles. Others were drawn from Bavaria, Saxony, Westphalia, Austria and Prussia, and those corps that were predominantly French were augmented by foreign auxiliaries from Switzerland, Spain, Portugal, Croatia, Poland or the Confederation of the Rhine. Even the Imperial Guard had brigades of Portuguese and Hessian cavalry.[23] Yet by the summer of 1812, with Austria and Prussia offering support, this huge army was already marching eastwards and the first units had crossed the Niemen.[24] The Russian campaign, which must surely be seen as Napoleon's most audacious military gamble, was under way.

If it was audacious, it was also foolhardy. Napoleon's timing in launching a mighty campaign against the huge expanse of the Russian empire could scarcely have been worse. A large contingent of his forces was still cut off in Spain; and in Central Europe there were increasing signs that his German empire was becoming restive. This was a war that would be fought on enemy terrain – the open steppes of Russia – where the French had little feel for the topography and low tolerance for the extreme cold of the Russian winter. These conditions handed a huge advantage to those with local knowledge. Napoleon seems to have recognised all this and yet still felt driven to fight the Russians rather than make the political concessions that peace-keeping would require. One of the Emperor's closest aides, Armand de Caulaincourt, would recall in his memoirs the warnings he had given to Napoleon at the time. 'I described the country to him, the climate, the advantage the enemy would have in allowing him to advance and wear himself out by marching without the chance to fight. I also recalled to him the privations and discontent of the troops during his last campaign in Poland.' But, Caulaincourt reports sadly, 'to all my argument his reply was that *I had turned Russian, and that I understood nothing of great affairs.*' Napoleon did not reconsider; he insisted that he had no choice, and that it was

Alexander who wanted war.[25] Though this was a self-servingly partisan view, he was not, of course, entirely wrong. Russia was not dedicated to maintaining peace; Alexander, too, had predatory instincts, and his army had been preparing for war since 1810.[26]

The story of the Moscow Campaign is among the best-known battle histories of all time, thanks in large part to the fictional account presented in Tolstoy's epic novel of the period, *War and Peace*. Here Napoleon is shown to hesitate fatally and the French army to blunder and delay till it was thwarted by a combination of the Russian winter and the stout heroism of the Russian people. What Tolstoy downplays is the skill of the Russian commanders and the tactics they adopted to frustrate the invader – tactics well suited to their strengths, to the landscape, and to the logistical shortcomings of the enemy. Napoleon, as always, chose to live off the land, foraging for food in the countries he passed through, with the result that much of Central Europe had been denuded of grain and fodder crops during the passage of the French army, while horses and cattle had been seized to mount the troops and provide food on the hoof. Rather than engage the troops in battle, Russian commanders withdrew before them, retreating hundreds of miles into the interior, thus drawing the French into the empty, barren steppes while destroying food supplies as they went. Napoleon sought a decisive victory in Russia, but his tactical goals were vague and his strategy amounted to little more than hunting down the Russians to defeat them. And the Russians eluded him. Their armies under Kutuzov and Barclay de Tolly continually frustrated Napoleon, avoiding engagement on any other than their own terms, while pulling him further and further into the interior. The Russian generals had made their calculations carefully; they accepted that if they were drawn into open battles to defend their territory they had little chance of success against Napoleon's seasoned troops. Barclay de Tolly had been forbidden by the Tsar to adopt an offensive strategy; his task was to defend Russian territory, and this he did, drawing back, harassing Napoleon's positions, and goading the Emperor relentlessly, almost taunting the French to pursue him towards Moscow.[27]

In the first weeks the fighting consisted of little more than irregular skirmishes in a silent countryside of smoking barns and burned-out villages, as the pace of the French advance slackened and the army grew weaker from the effects of heat and fatigue. Then, behind carefully prepared defences, the Russians at last gave battle, first at Smolensk in August, then at Borodino in September. Neither battle was conclusive; certainly neither was a great tactical Napoleonic triumph. The carnage was frightful, the losses shocking on both sides. Each time the Russians withdrew after the battle, and each time Napoleon was lured further into the Russian heartland. Seven days after Borodino, he entered Moscow – but this was a Moscow that had been torched by the Muscovites and now lay in ruins, sacrificed by the Russians in a bid to halt the French advance. As can be seen in a letter to Marie-Louise, Napoleon shared the horror of his men on seeing Moscow burn before his eyes: 'I had no conception of this city. It had five hundred palaces as beautiful as the Elysée, furnished in French style with incredible luxury, several imperial palaces, barracks, and magnificent hospitals. Everything has disappeared, consumed by fire over the last four days.'[28] An integral part of European civilisation had been lost.

But for the French army the worst was far from over. Faced with an empty city, and unable to access fresh supplies, Napoleon now faced the prospect of a long retreat, harried by the Russian army, and with winter closing in. Napoleon fatefully delayed his departure from Moscow until mid-October, and almost at once hit difficulties. He had intended to return by a more clement southerly route, but at Maloyaroslavets, south of Moscow, he was cut off by Kutuzov and forced back north, retracing the same route that he had followed on his advance eastwards – the same burned villages, the same scarred landscape, where any food there may once have been had been already pillaged and consumed, the same harrying from Cossack soldiers. In late October came the first frosts of winter, and by the time the army reached Smolensk in November the thermometer had dipped to minus twenty or thirty degrees centigrade.

France's troops were weak, sick and hungry. Men died by the roadside, some pleading with their colleagues to end their misery lest they fall into Russian hands; those taken prisoner risked being stripped of their clothes and possessions by the Cossacks and sold to Russian villagers, a fate which they equated with slavery and a slow, cruel death. Many more froze to death in their sleep. They ate what little they could find to keep themselves alive; life became a lottery, survival dependent on desperate makeshift measures. Increasingly, they were reduced to eating their own horses when the animals died of starvation, or simply slaughtered them for food. A French officer wrote from Smolensk: 'The army has been without bread on its march, but it did have large numbers of horses which had died from exhaustion, and I can assure you that a slab of horsemeat, sliced and cooked in a pan with a little fat or butter makes a very reasonable meal.'[29] In these desperate weeks it was probably the only 'reasonable meal' they could hope for. The retreat had turned into a human disaster, as disorganised as it was poorly planned. Some sixty thousand men died on the march, and the supplies which Napoleon had ordered for Smolensk proved woefully inadequate. Food intended to feed the army for two weeks was consumed by desperate soldiers in just three days. Any thought the Emperor may have had of wintering in the city had to be quickly abandoned.[30]

It was little comfort that the Russians, too, had suffered mass desertions and seen men and horses die in their thousands. Kutuzov and Wittgenstein, the general charged with the defence of Saint Petersburg, made no effort to engage the French, contenting them- selves with harrying tactics as the ragged, dishevelled army plodded westwards in search of safety. The final hurdle was the Berezina river, which they had to cross to find that safety, and here Napoleon showed some of his old decisive flair, ordering his sappers to build pontoons – temporary bridges that would allow the men to make their way across the bloated river. Despite constant harrying and sniping, most of the remaining troops survived the ordeal, though they still faced the misery of frostbite and near-starvation on their long march home.

Napoleon himself left his troops under Murat's command and hastily returned to Paris. But there was no way he could disguise the scale of the catastrophe. In the course of the Moscow Campaign he had lost the largest army of the entire war, possibly the largest in European history. The losses were stupefying. Though there are no definitive figures, no records of many of those who perished, it has been estimated that some five hundred and seventy thousand men and two hundred thousand horses did not return. The famed Imperial Guard, once fifty thousand strong, had been reduced to a meagre rump of fifteen hundred men.[31] And Napoleon's prestige as a military strategist and battlefield tactician, which more than anything guaranteed the loyalty of his troops, was now seriously damaged, although their continuing affection for him would suggest that there was more to his personal chemistry than military success. What the Moscow Campaign demonstrated was that the remarkable military abilities he had shown as a younger man were fading; he was less supple, more corpulent, and more fatigued by long days in the saddle. His health, too, was beginning to desert him; he complained of problems with his digestion, and it has been suggested that he was suffering from the early stages of duodenal cancer. He could no longer maintain his gruelling work ethic and increasingly depended on his marshals to make key military decisions, despite the fact that they were of variable ability and did not always enjoy his full confidence. The marshals of 1813 did not always display the same qualities as those of the early years. Napoleon had never learned to delegate, and had tended to promote those most loyal to him. His failure to develop the talents of his officers or to reshape the higher command system of the army was a source of weakness that would be increasingly evident in his final campaigns.[32]

Russia had serious international consequences too. The scale of Napoleon's defeat put his earlier conquests in jeopardy when the other European powers realised the full extent of French military weakness. In Spain, the withdrawal of French troops to serve in the east provided the British with an opportunity to mount a major offensive that left the whole of southern Spain, along with border fortresses at Badajoz and Ciudad Rodrigo, in Allied hands. Wellington also won a major battle against the French at Salamanca, which again served to puncture the reputation for invincibility of the imperial armies and gave new hope to both the British and the guerrillas. In 1813 he attacked the northern fortresses of Pamplona and

San Sebastian before repelling the French, now under Soult's command, at the Battle of the Pyrenees. By November Wellington had advanced to the frontier, pushing Soult back on to French soil, and the remaining months of the campaign saw the British lay siege to Bayonne before attacking Bordeaux and Toulouse. The very last action of the war, in April 1814, was a bloody engagement between the British and the garrison at Bayonne.[33] It was a final humiliation for the French. In the far south-west of France the once mighty imperial army had shown that it was now incapable of defending France's own territory.

If the Russian campaign paved the way for a British victory in Spain, in Central Europe it produced a diplomatic revolution that shattered Napoleon's alliance system and heralded the end of the Empire itself. The Emperor had piled too much misery and humiliation on the other crowned heads of Europe to escape their vengeance when they believed their moment had arrived. Towards the end of his life, from exile on Saint Helena, Napoleon would look back with regret on the debacle in Russia, but ascribing it to the Russian winter and to misfortune rather than to his own overweening ambition or tactical misjudgements. It was the moment, he decided, when 'fortune ceased to smile on me'. But there was more than self-justification here; he was expressing genuine regret. He recognised the damage that had been done to his army and military capacity, but also to his reputation. 'I should have died at Moscow,' he lamented, with more than a touch of self-pity. 'Then I would probably have had the reputation of the greatest conqueror of all time.'[34] It was the reputation he craved, but which would elude him.

Even during the Russian Campaign, the first tentative steps towards a Sixth Coalition against France were being taken, beginning with an alliance between Britain and Russia in response to Napoleon's march eastwards. In 1813, this rapidly extended to encompass Prussia, Austria, and other German powers now awakened to the scale of Napoleon's defeat by the sight of his famished and bedraggled troops retreating across Poland and northern Germany. They were also increasingly pressured by popular feeling at home, which no longer saw France as a fount of justice and citizenship, but as a colonial power intent – seemingly without end – on taxing them, conscripting their sons and requisitioning their goods and livestock. Before the end of the Russian campaign Napoleon's Prussian allies were abandoning him. Prussian units were deserting in large numbers and fleeing the imperial cause, while some leading Prussian officers, among them the great military strategist Clausewitz, were so appalled by the threat Napoleon posed to their country's independence that they travelled to Russia to advise the Tsar and steel his resolve to carry on the struggle.[35] Some soldiers, cut off in Russia during Napoleon's retreat, offered their services to the Tsar. In doing so there is no doubt that they were exceeding their orders since, for the Prussians, their alliance with Napoleon served a serious purpose: that of guaranteeing their security. Now, however, with the Grande Armée in tatters and Napoleon's invincibility punctured, many in Central Europe thought the moment ripe to renege on that alliance and unite against him. As well as Russia and Prussia, who had signed their military alliance as early as February 1813, Britain promised financial contributions to the war effort, and Sweden pledged her support for the Allies. In August, Austria declared war after Metternich convinced himself that Napoleon had no further interest in peace. Frederick William in Prussia did not hesitate to summon up the language of German nationalism to rally opinion against the

French, while the Tsar seemed intent on freeing all Europe from Napoleon's control. A new phase of the Wars, known in German history as the Wars of Liberation, had begun.

Napoleon had had warnings of the strength of European opinion and the dangers of a new German war. His brother Jerome had already advised him in 1811 that a new war in Europe would unleash popular insurrections 'in all the provinces between the Rhine and the Oder'; while Caulaincourt, a consistent critic of the Russian campaign, continued to discourage further military aggression.[36] But Napoleon paid no attention to their pleas, showing within days of his return to Paris that he was intent on raising a new army to replace the men lost in Russia, whatever the cost for a country that was becoming increasingly drained of manpower. He was eager to resume the conflict, eager to gain revenge on those he believed had betrayed him. That was not quite the story he reserved for posterity, however. Had peace been concluded at Moscow, he told Las Cases in 1816, it would have been the last of his military campaigns, a peace that finally would have guaranteed national security. 'A new horizon, new projects would be undertaken, all devoted to the wellbeing and prosperity of everyone.'[37] This can only be dismissed as fantasy. A series of imperial edicts incorporated national guardsmen into the regular army and called up recruits from the 1814 conscription roll, while the French provinces were required to provide twenty thousand men, trained and equipped, for the new campaign. Astonishingly, France responded, despite the enormous cost in men and taxes.

Within months Napoleon again headed an army of more than two hundred thousand men, though it did not bear comparison with the superbly trained forces he had led in previous campaigns.

The infantry was raw and lacked battle experience, and even more damagingly the cavalry was critically short of horses of the necessary quality. Most of the one hundred and seventy-five thousand horses that had left for Russia never returned, and the army had no choice but to requisition such horses as it could find, or call on French civilians to volunteer their riding horses for military use. The French countryside could not supply more; besides, many of France's strongest cavalry horses had traditionally come from northern Germany, whose resources Napoleon could no longer exploit, though even here there was a serious shortage of horses for supply and artillery transport.[38] The new campaign was a rushed affair, launched without the careful logistical build-up it required, which was a reflection of Napoleon's impatience. His adversaries were stronger, too, buttressed by military reforms, supported by at least a modicum of popular opinion, and subsidised by the British treasury to the tune of over ten million pounds. But this was more a victory for the old European aristocracies than for the new forces of nationalism. Napoleon had started out by launching his army into Saxony, scoring early successes over the Russians and Prussians at Lützen and Bautzen in May 1813, and forcing the allies to seek a brief armistice. But his refusal to accept the mediation of the Austrians at Dresden in late June brought Austria into the war, and thereafter the French were heavily outnumbered and increasingly outfought. Despite beating an allied army at Dresden, the French suffered a series of minor defeats in August and September that forced Napoleon to concentrate his forces around Leipzig.

Here, in October, was fought the decisive battle of the war in Central Europe, the Battle of the Nations, where the French took on the combined armies of Austria, Prussia, and Russia, their numbers supplemented by several of Napoleon's former German allies who, sensing which way the wind was blowing and threatened by popular insurrections at home, now threw in their lot with his enemies. Leipzig was a bloodbath, with huge losses on both sides; French deaths were estimated at fifteen thousand, while a further thirty thousand were wounded. It was a decisive defeat for Napoleon, which forced him to retreat to Mainz, then on to French territory. Even the inner empire was now collapsing as he was forced to throw reservists and boys of seventeen – the conscripts of 1815 – into the fray. The northern Italian states had already fallen to the Austrians; now it was the turn of the lands on the west bank of the Rhine, Holland, and then Belgium. By the beginning of 1814 Blücher's army had crossed the Rhine, leaving the final stages of the war to be fought on home turf, in eastern and northern France.[39]

The *Campagne de France* would drag on for three increasingly desperate months before Marmont decided, on 31 March, that further resistance was futile and, seemingly on his own initiative, sued for the armistice that ended the war. The Allies now enjoyed clear military superiority over France, and the French army suffered from both a breakdown in its command structure and a sapping loss of morale. Desertion levels soared. Within a month the marshals were forced to abandon the Rhine and retreat to the Marne, evacuating territory in the hope that they could play for time and regroup.[40]

Predictably, Napoleon did not give up without a fight, winning a number of minor engagements against both the Austrians and the Prussians before cutting off the advance guard of a joint Prussian and Swedish army on the plateau of Craonne in early March. Significant reverses followed, however: first at Laon at the hands of the Prussians and Swedes, then at Arcis-sur-Aube, where he was forced to withdraw by the Austrians and Russians; thereafter, the Allies decided to march directly on Paris and put an end to French resistance. Surprisingly, perhaps, given the disruption he had brought to the European political order, they were still willing to negotiate with Napoleon, offering to maintain him on his throne and leave France with her 1792 borders. This fact alone allowed the Emperor to emerge from his defeat with some dignity. So did the manner of these last weeks of fighting. In Spain and Italy, Croatia and Russia, wherever the French had encountered guerrilla activity, they had denounced it as brigandage and the work of criminals. Yet when France was invaded civilians rose in arms to help their troops, and brigandage was magically transformed into the patriotic courage of partisans, fighting to defend their communities against the invader. Theirs was a hopeless cause, but many men, simple peasants in the main, chose to die for it. That the French did not lie down before the invading armies became something of a badge of honour in the last days of the war. It restored a little lustre to the cause, and helped to stoke the Napoleonic legend of a brave and glorious defeat.[41]

1 2

The Hundred Days

Defeated, sick, and reportedly contemplating suicide, the Napoleon who returned to France in the spring of 1814 was a sadly diminished shadow of the Emperor he had been only a few months earlier. He had wanted to fight on, but superior Allied numbers, high desertion figures, and hunger in the ranks of his army all conspired to deny him the option of a favourable military outcome. In Paris there was a political vacuum as some of those on whom he had depended for support abandoned him – or hesitated to commit themselves to him while they weighed up his prospects of survival. The Emperor was no longer the master of the situation; he wanted to believe that he could conclude a peace on the basis of the terms held out to him at Frankfurt and sought to play on the different ambitions of the Allied powers as he looked to a political solution that would leave France intact and his imperial authority assured. But that was not going to happen. By refusing to make peace when it was on offer, and by allowing France to be invaded, Napoleon had weakened his own negotiating position and abandoned the initiative to the victors.

From Chaumont he made peace overtures to the Allies, sending Caulaincourt to the enemy camp to negotiate on his behalf, but without success. The Emperor's envoy was not even granted an audience. The other leaders had no reason to trust Napoleon or to believe his promises; they were no longer interested in making concessions but wanted to press on to Paris and drive home their victory. And Napoleon found himself unable – in either his own or his country's interests – to exploit important tactical differences between his opponents. By the end of March the French army was effectively beaten and the Allies were at the gates of Paris. There was little defence. Napoleon had baulked at building fortifications around his capital and, beyond the incomplete *octroi* wall and a few trenches and redoubts, the city was undefended when the Allies attacked.[1] Paris was occupied, and although Napoleon, camped at Fontainebleau, considered one last assault on his capital to dislodge them, his plans came to nought. They were undone as much by his supporters and by public apathy as they were by the Allies.

For it was Napoleon's own marshals, the men he had entrusted with the defence of Paris and the command of his armies, who took the decision to hoist the flag of surrender. They were encouraged in this by Napoleon's brother Joseph who, as lieutenant-general in Paris and head of the Regency Council, had lost all taste for further bloodshed and saw his main responsibility as preventing the Emperor's young son from falling into enemy hands. On 29 March he ordered a reluctant Empress to escort the young king away from Paris, taking him first to Rambouillet, then to the comparative safety of Blois. Within days, however, they were on the move again, this time to join Marie-Louise's family in Vienna, back at the Austrian court. This deprived Napoleon of his last diplomatic card and removed any lingering chance that the Allies would allow the boy to accede to the throne as his father's successor.[2] Increasingly, by early April he accepted the possibility that he would lose his throne, and planned to abdicate in favour of his son, establishing the imperial line and providing an honourable exit strategy. But here, too, he was doomed to fail. Ever open to conspiracy theories, Napoleon was quick to smell treason among his marshals and ministers. Marmont, who authorised the surrender of Paris, quickly rallied to the Bourbons, and those marshals who surrounded Napoleon at Fontainebleau – among them close advisers like Lefebvrc and Macdonald, Oudinot and Ney – refused to march on the capital, anxious to avoid firing on Parisians. Behind the scenes, politicians lobbied and plotted, most notably the cunning, unscrupulous figure of Talleyrand, who in these vital few days became a powerful advocate of the Bourbon cause. Talleyrand was highly persuasive, urging Tsar Alexander I, Frederick William of Prussia, and the Austrian Emperor Francis I to reject a negotiated peace and demand unconditional surrender.[3] Deals were struck about the future without even consulting the Emperor. Napoleon was outraged; he had been out manoeuvred, and, as he continued to protest, betrayed.[4]

The Empire was over, and it was over on Allied terms. Napoleon would neither be granted the peace with honour that he had held out for, nor would he be allowed to hold on to his throne. At this point the most determined of his adversaries was Russia's Alexander I. The Tsar refused all forms of political compromise and quite unambiguously demanded that Napoleon abdicate and renounce all claim to the French throne. The Emperor was left with no choice but to agree, and on 6 April 1814, by the Treaty of Fontainebleau, he signed a letter of abdication, receiving in return the right to retain his imperial title, sovereignty over the tiny island of Elba (which even he dismissed as a '*royaume d'opérette*'),⁵ and an income of two million francs a year, to be paid to him by the French government. There were other small concessions, too: clauses in the treaty gave the Empress the title of Duchess of Parma, and made financial provision for various members of the Bonaparte clan. But all that was mere window-dressing. What mattered was that Napoleon Bonaparte, the self-created Emperor of France, was stripped of his power, and that his claim to dynastic legitimacy was firmly rejected. Europe could breathe more easily, safe in the knowledge that, once banished to Elba, the man they regarded as a usurper and a serial aggressor could do them no further harm. Any settlement concluded in 1814 had to be acceptable to the European powers, and they were not in a forgiving mood. The restoration of Louis XVIII may have been accepted by the French and championed by some of their number – with Talleyrand, as ever, to the fore – but the final decision was not theirs to make. This was a settlement by the Allies for the Allies – something that France was not allowed to forget.

A fortnight later, on 20 April, Napoleon left Fontainebleau for his new kingdom. As ever, his exit lines were carefully prepared, his sense of betrayal intact. He spoke with dignity, even with warmth, of his British opponents, who, he said, had always behaved properly in war and whom he therefore respected. But he remained bitter in his condemnation of the French Provisional Government, which, he believed, was loading him with petty restrictions that were insulting and demeaning. The new Minister of War, for instance, had ordered the withdrawal of guns and stores from Elba, displaying the government's distrust of their prisoner and leaving him without the means to defend himself – not, he insisted, against his fellow Frenchmen, but against the raiders and Barbary pirates who were still the scourge of the Mediterranean. Napoleon was scathing in his dismissal of the new government, accusing them of cowardly collaboration with the enemy and questioning their legitimacy. He seemed keen to draw a clear distinction between his British captors and representatives of the Bourbons, with whom he refused to have any dealings. His treaty, he said, was not with the French monarchy but with the Allied governments, and he looked to those governments to fulfil their obligations to him.[6] In the same spirit, once he had reached Fréjus, where both a British frigate and a French corvette waited to escort him to Elba, he avoided all communication with the French. On being told that the French captain had instructions from his government to embark him and take him to Elba, Napoleon took pains to insist that he travel on the British vessel.[7]

Despite his repeated claims to represent the patriotic instincts of his people, there is little to suggest that they shared his outrage. In Paris as in London, cartoonists mocked Napoleon's little kingdom, with its toy defences and its travesty of an imperial court. An English caricature showing the deposed leader being welcomed by the savage inhabitants of the island was entitled 'Napoleon dreading his doleful doom, or his grand entry on the isle of Elba.[8] Another popular image, first printed in London, then widely circulated in France, mocked 'the jay stripped of his borrowed feathers', and depicted Napoleon being plucked of his peacock feathers by two crowned eagles.[9] French caricaturists were equally dismissive, depicting Napoleon as a murderous tyrant, half covered in a tiger skin, with a handsaw replacing the hand of justice and papers scattered on the ground to remind the onlooker of his savagery: one read 'conscription', the others 'Spain', 'Moscow', and 'Jaffa' – reminders all of the cost in blood of his regime.[10] Across Europe relief and glee mingled easily. Even in France itself there were few outside the army who did not share that relief, happy at least that the Emperor's fall from grace meant a respite from war and from the dreadful tax in blood they had paid for it. Some did not hesitate to blame Napoleon personally or to accuse him of being unmoved by the loss of so many young lives. A proclamation by the department of the Seine on 2 April was unambiguous in its condemnation of the Emperor, reminding the inhabitants of Paris that he alone was responsible for the miseries they had endured. 'You owe all the woes which have befallen you to one man and one man alone,' it intoned, a man who 'year after year has decimated your families by his continuous conscription.'[11] There were many in France who, in the immediate aftermath of the defeat and invasion, thought of Napoleon as the cause of their troubles and were prepared to welcome any ruler who promised them a respite from war.

On 3 May Louis XVIII made his official entry into Paris, his coach drawn by eight white horses and his arrival greeted with church bells and a salvo of artillery fire. To judge by contemporary accounts, the city reacted with caution rather than exuberance; people lined the streets or looked down from their balconies, but did so quietly, driven more by fear and curiosity than by joy. There were royalists among them, of course, cheering for the Bourbons and the white flag and shouting their hatred for the tyrant they had toppled. But they were a minority. Most people were less concerned by the change of regime than by the prospect of peace, and the dominant emotion was relief that the war was over, that civilian life could resume, and that future generations of young men would be free of the obligations of conscription.[12]

There was no clamour for a return to Bourbon rule. But the draining effects of over twenty years of war were taking their toll, with high prices, shortages, and the loss of sons, servants and horses, all in the name of patriotism and the Empire. Bemused, often unenthusiastic, Parisians looked on as momentous changes took place in their midst and peace was restored. The treaty was signed at the end of May and the Allied armies then began their withdrawal. On 4 June, in the presence of the new king, the charter was read before the two Chambers, and though it provided the constitutional framework by which Louis was to rule the country, the symbolism of monarchy would prove powerful, especially for a nation and a generation that had known only revolution and empire. 'The period of revolution and wars was over', wrote Henry Houssaye during the most republican years of the Third Republic, and it seemed as if nothing had changed; Louis XVI might still be on the throne. 'Hereditary monarchy and the authority of divine right were re-established; the legitimate king was in the Tuileries, on the throne of his ancestors, in "the nineteenth year of his reign."' But that did not mean that these changes were consented to, or approved by the population; many in France were bewildered and confused, while others, especially in the army, refused to accept the consequences of defeat. If Louis promised an amnesty to his opponents, he did not extend that to regicides. Those who had voted Louis XVI's death were to be banished from his realm. And the restored monarch soon started to snub former revolutionaries, however willing they might be to serve him.[13] The country was not reunited; as Houssaye perceptively added, the Bourbons may have been restored to the throne, but 'all that remained was to govern.'[14]

The difficulties of the new regime were greatly increased by Napoleon's refusal to accept his own defeat, by the dreams and the resentments he took with him to Elba. His proud words of farewell to the officers and men of the Old Guard in the court-yard at Fontainebleau, as he left on his journey to Elba, contained more than a suggestion of the perils to come. '*Adieu, mes enfants,*' he addressed them with an almost paternal affection, 'would that I could press you all to my heart.' Instead, as his men lined up before him, he solemnly kissed their standard. Between the soldiers and their commander there was a genuine bond, built on the many painful campaigns they had shared and the moments of glory they had revelled in together. At Fontainebleau, Napoleon's gesture was not innocent. Rather, he was sealing that bond for the future, revealing very publicly the love and esteem in which he held those who served him. The report of the ceremony offered no commentary but let the poignancy of the moment shine through. 'The silence was broken,' it noted, 'only by the sobs of the soldiers.'[15] Many who were there, like many others who had seen service under him, continued to revere him and to look back on their years in the Grande Armée with affection and nostalgia as a period of adventure and comradeship, when they had been plucked from their cottages and workshops and helped to make history. With peace restored and the Bourbons deeply suspicious of their political motives, they felt poorly rewarded for their years in uniform, pensioned off or placed on half-pay, the years of dreaming brought to a sudden and savage end. Among them were romantics who dreamed that Napoleon would return to lead them again, and they held on to their sacred relics of war – the medals, the tricolour cockades, the eagles – in the hope that they might see further service.[16] For them, Napoleon would always be their leader, the commander who had shared their sufferings and had inspired them to greatness; a soldier's soldier who had risen through the ranks of the army and had brought them glory, honour and national pride.

The conditions of his exile were in no sense Spartan, though after his long years at the heart of a Europe-wide empire, Elba must have felt curiously remote, even for a man brought up in Corsica. He was accompanied from France by three collaborators who had volunteered to share his exile, Cambronne, Drouot and Bertrand, and once on Elba his entourage included two secretaries, a butler, a doctor and a considerable domestic staff. There were also the officers of the small military force he maintained for ceremonial occasions and for the island's defence. He lived comfortably, if simply, in the Palazzina dei Mulini in Portoferraio, where he spent long hours outside in the garden overlooking the Tyrrhenian Sea. There was no prohibition on receiving visitors; indeed, he maintained regular communication with the outside world, mostly through the sea-link to Naples where Murat was still (temporarily) in power. For political reasons, the government refused to allow the Empress Marie-Louise, or their son, the King of Rome, to visit him on Elba, but the Bonaparte family rallied round. He entertained his favourite sister Pauline, while his mother, Letizia, showed solidarity with her son by electing to live with him in his new kingdom. Of the other women in his life, Maria Walewska also came to visit, with their four-year-old son, Alexander, the pair being smuggled secretly on to Elba, where

Napoleon preferred to receive them in private, in a simple cottage in the mountains at the far end of the island, far removed from public gaze. Josephine, to Napoleon's profound sorrow, never made the journey. She died at Malmaison on 29 May, within weeks of his arrival on Elba.[17]

During the ten months he spent in Portoferraio Napoleon retained much of his astonishing energy, which he now transferred to the land and to improving the quality of life of the islanders. He had, as ever, no shortage of plans or projects, from new crops to irrigation schemes and plans to improve the profitability of iron-mining, all of which brought him the lasting respect and affection of the islanders.[18] And he dreamed up building projects of his own. The unofficial British representative on Elba, Neil Campbell, remarked in one of his regular despatches to London that Napoleon was 'engaged in perpetual exercise, and busy with projects of building, which, however, are not put into execution'.[19] But with the passage of time Campbell began to notice a significant change in the Emperor's concentration. On 20 September he wrote that 'Napoleon seems to have lost all habits of study and sedentary application. He has four places of residence in different parts of the island, and the improvements and changes of these form his sole occupation. But as they lose their interest to his unsettled mind, and the novelty wears off, he occasionally falls into a state of inactivity never known before, and has of late retired to his bedroom for repose during several hours of the day.' Campbell rushed to add that the Emperor's health was still excellent, and that he was often in good spirits. He did not raise questions of boredom or depression. 'I begin to think', he concludes, 'he is quite resigned to his retreat, and that he is tolerably happy, excepting

when the recollections of his former power are freshened by sentiments of vanity or revenge, or his passions become influenced by
want of money, and his wife and child being kept from him.'[20] It
was an intelligent guess based on his observations, but, as events
soon proved, a very mistaken one.

Napoleon, it turned out, was both bored and frustrated with
what life could offer on a small Mediterranean island. He was not
content, as he had told Campbell he was in the course of a private
conversation, to 'lead the life of an ordinary justice of the peace';
and he certainly wanted more from the world than 'my family, my
little house, my cows and mules'.[21] But then he never had restricted
himself to such a domestic arena. As a ruler, albeit of a tiny state,
he had set about providing for its defence, against both an Allied
attack – never a likely occurrence – and the more probable incur-
sions of pirates from the Barbary coast. To this end he raised an
army of just under two thousand men, which included more than
six hundred former members of his Imperial Guard who elected
to follow him out from France; among these were a small number
of Poles and Mamelukes who remained loyal to his person. And
given that Elba was an island, and that any attack must come from
the sea, he also built a small navy with at its heart the French frigate
Inconstant which had accompanied him from Fréjus. Elba's navy
had around a hundred sailors and was used mainly to sail to the
mainland on missions for Napoleon and his family. But we should
not underestimate the importance of this tiny force to Napoleon's
ambition. The Emperor himself still cut a military figure. He took
a deep personal interest in his troops, reviewing them on the main
square of Portoferraio, reminding them of their loyalty to France
and of their duty to the people of Elba. In all, the army and navy

consumed three-quarters of his annual budget.[22] They would also form the kernel of his support when the moment came to invade the French mainland.

That moment came in early March 1815. Napoleon had kept in touch with events in France throughout the winter and had learnt from his correspondents a great deal to give him hope. The initial goodwill of the French people towards Louis XVIII seemed to have faded. The King had never succeeded in harnessing popular enthusiasm, and the first months of his reign had done little to increase his support. Many resented the dynastic symbolism of the restored monarchy, the insistence on the white Bourbon flag, and the return of the Catholic clergy to the inner councils of state. Taxes had risen in a period of economic austerity, grain prices had increased sharply, and the presence of an army of occupation and the imposition of a large indemnity dispelled any vestige of glory and national pride. Napoleon's sources told him that the regime had become unpopular with the people – those who still shared the values of the Republic and gloried in the name of the nation. Many of Napoleon's fellow countrymen had started to look back on his reign with a tinge of nostalgia, remembering a time of good harvests and affordable bread. It was, he convinced himself, the moment to offer the French people an alternative, the moment to take action. What followed was a bizarre adventure story. Napoleon chose a moment when Campbell was absent from the island and there were no British naval vessels in the vicinity, and left Elba for ever. He took with him a handful of ships, some forty horses, and a small number of troops – just six hundred and fifty men of the Guard, plus a hundred Polish lancers and a handful of Corsican and Elban volunteers.[23] With this puny force he crossed the Mediterranean to the south coast of France, landing safely on the coast near Antibes, from where he began his march northwards towards Paris and the resumption of power.

The idea seemed ridiculous, the pitfalls innumerable. But Napoleon, above all, was a gambler who believed in his abilities and in his power to charm and persuade. He was helped, of course, by the slowness of communication in the French provinces, so that no one in Paris knew anything about his return till 5 March, four full days after his landing. The journey was long and arduous, through the foothills of the Alps along what is today dubbed the *Route Napoléon* by the tourist authorities, to Grenoble, then Lyon, and on through Burgundy to the capital. Along the southern part of the route his little army passed through divided and embittered communities, the sorts of places where royalists lurked and villagers were embroiled in White Terror and revenge killings. Yet the journey proved almost unreasonably easy. During the first days the party encountered no opposition, no soldiers, no challenge to their progress. As he moved north, and as word spread of his approach, local people began to join him: villagers, peasants, men dazzled and overawed by his reputation or attracted by the promise of liberty he appeared to hold out. Popular crowds greeted him rapturously in the bigger cities where he passed, first Grenoble, then Lyon. When soldiers did appear, sent by the new government to stop him, his charismatic charm did not fail him. At Vizille, Lyon and Auxerre the units that had been sent against him were won over to his side.

Near Grenoble, in one of the most famous incidents of the whole adventure, he was approached by several French regiments with orders to arrest him. Opening his greatcoat to expose his chest, he called on them to recognise him and challenged them to carry out their orders: 'If there is one among you who would kill his general, his Emperor, he may; here I stand'.[24] No one moved. The same emotional appeal worked for generals and men of the line; at Grenoble civilians mingled with his troops and he was assailed with enthusiastic cries of *Vive l'Empereur!*[25] When Marshal Ney, having taken an oath of loyalty to Louis XVIII, was sent to arrest him, his resolve failed as soon as he met Napoleon face to face. With every day the little army that had left Antibes posed a greater threat to the Bourbon regime. With every day, the *vol de l'aigle* gained a further hold on the popular imagination. Every step Napoleon took seemed to add further lustre to his romantic legend.

On 20 March, little more than a fortnight after disembarking on the south coast, Napoleon was back in Paris, where he at once occupied the Tuileries, his former palace, hurriedly abandoned by a fugitive Louis XVIII. But he no longer presented himself in all the finery of the Empire, or played on the pomp of his imperial office. Rather, in a quite remarkable act of political theatre, he spoke directly to the populace, presenting himself as a man of the people, wronged by foreign tyrants and British treason, and appealing directly to the tradition of the French Revolution. He showed that, unlike Louis, who had learned nothing and forgotten nothing during his years of exile, he had learned a great deal and was willing to make important concessions in order to woo opinion. Over the years of the Empire, the rights and liberties of Frenchmen had been whittled away as the power of the state was reinforced, conscription extended, and policing reinforced. Yet, during the Hundred Days Napoleon did not tire of expending effort on gaining support from former republicans who feared discrimination at the hands of the monarchy. He drew attention to the new government's attempts to appease the Church and welcome back priests from emigration. He pointed to the danger of their seizing back church lands that had been sold off during the Revolution. He offered liberal reforms and wider voting rights, and sought to win the support of the bourgeoisie by confirming the abolition of feudalism, banishing those émigrés who had returned to France during the Restoration, and expropriating their landed estates.[26] He restored the Legion of Honour, the award which more than any other imposed military values at the very heart of civil society; this appealed to the spirit of the army, placing solidarity and the defence of the public good above selfish materialism.[27] And he unashamedly tapped into what he believed to be a potent seam of popular opinion: fear of a return to the Old Regime, using a language of anti-privilege that the Jacobins could hardly have bettered. 'I have come,' he insisted, 'to save Frenchmen from the slavery in which priests and nobles wished to plunge them,' adding ominously that 'I will string them up from the lampposts.'[28]

If that was little more than empty rhetoric and an attempt to capture something of the flavour of republican sentiment, his constitutional reforms did represent something of a break with the authoritarian tone of the later Empire and a return to the more consensual politics of the Consulate. Not that the *acte constitutionnel* of 1815, which contained his principal reforms, can be seen as a model of democratic practice. In essence, it amended the constitutions of the Consulate and Empire to take account of the Bourbon Charter of 1814 and to reaffirm the principles of individual liberty and of equality before the law: freedom of religion and the free expression of opinion were guaranteed, property was declared inviolable, and, in a significant shift of policy since 1812, the Emperor promised that no part of French territory would in future be placed under siege unless France was invaded.[29] Legislative power was to be shared by the Emperor and two chambers, one composed of hereditary peers nominated by Napoleon, the other of deputies elected indirectly, through a two-tier electoral process. The act was to be ratified by the people in a plebiscite, though opinion differs on just how significant this consultation was. For some, the low turn-out and the apathy among young voters suggest that the constitution failed to ignite the public, and they point out that Bonaparte's supporters were only half as numerous in the Hundred Days as they had been during the Consulate.[30] Others minimise the significance of the fact that only 1.3 million Frenchmen bothered to record their vote. There was little local encouragement to do so, no intervention by prefects or sub-prefects, with the consequence that around a third of the registers sent out to mayors to record the votes of their constituents were returned entirely blank.[31] Any popular enthusiasm for the regime was more about the person of the Emperor than about constitutional rights.

There is no reason to believe that Napoleon was enthusiastic about this new, more liberal empire, which had been largely forced upon him by his collaborators, those men to whom he turned in 1815 to establish civil government, many of whom were committed to peace and lukewarm about his prospects of uniting the country. Some were longstanding imperial allies, like Fouché, who returned to the Ministry of Police, or Cambacérès, who was charged with the Ministry of Justice. Caulaincourt was made Foreign Minister, Maret Secretary of State and Davout Minister of War, with Decrès Minister for the Navy. Two of the Emperor's staunch supporters, Boulay de la Meurthe and Regnaud de St-Jean d'Angély, became heads of section in the Council of State. Other pillars of the new regime were more surprising choices. They included men who had previously quarrelled with Napoleon over his authoritarian appetites, or his contempt for the institutions of the Republic. Lazare Carnot, for instance, was a staunch republican who had refused to serve the Empire after 1804 but had rallied to Napoleon in 1814 when France was invaded; he agreed to stay on as Napoleon's Minister of the Interior, convinced that he was now committed to a more liberal empire, and that this represented the only remaining hope of rescuing something from the revolutionary legacy.[32] Perhaps most surprising of all was the man to whom the Emperor gave responsibility for drafting the new constitution, the noted liberal thinker Benjamin Constant. Constant, having proclaimed his opposition to the Emperor's taste for dictatorship, now made it his priority to restrain his excesses through parliamentary controls. What emerged through the *acte additionnel* was something akin to constitutional monarchy.[33]

If Napoleon managed to persuade a percentage of French domestic opinion that he had changed his spots and wished to represent the interests of his people, he enjoyed no such success beyond his national boundaries. Across Europe the leaders of the Great Powers were in no mood to compromise, continuing to view him as a usurper and a threat to the peace of the entire continent. And though in the various lands Napoleon had annexed or conquered there were groups of powerful and eloquent defenders of his regime, they were drawn from the educated elite – the lawyers and judges and professional administrators – seldom from the population at large. The masses, and especially the rural masses, continued to view the Napoleonic state as an artificial imposition, what Michael Broers has called 'the practical expression of an alien elite culture'.[34] The Allies saw no reason to hesitate or play for time; to their eyes Napoleon was an outlaw, and the constitutional arrangements he offered France a total irrelevance. Indeed, as soon as news reached them of Napoleon's escape from Elba, the European monarchs understood that there was no alternative to war, a war which they would declare in order to force a second abdication. As early as 7 March 1815, Metternich summed up the Allies' mood, writing that Napoleon 'appears anxious to run great risks. That is his business. Our business is to give to the world that repose which he has troubled all these years'.

Francis I committed himself to using military force if necessary to dislodge Napoleon once more from his throne. 'Go at once and find the Emperor of Russia and the King of Prussia,' he instructed. 'Tell them that I am prepared to order my armies once again to take to the road to France. I have no doubt that the two Sovereigns will join me in my march.' The Austrian Emperor was, of course, right. The Allied powers worked together to produce a concerted policy, and on 13 March issued a joint declaration in the name of Austria, France, Britain, Prussia, Russia, Spain, Portugal and Sweden. Once again drawing a clear distinction between Napoleon and the French people, they undertook to provide 'the King of France and the French nation' with all the help they required to restore what they termed 'public tranquillity'. At the same time they noted that 'Napoleon Bonaparte had placed himself outside the pale of civil and social relations,' and that he stood condemned as 'the disturber of world repose'.[35]

The course was again set for war. On 25 March the four major Allied powers, Austria, Britain, Prussia and Russia, undertook, by the Treaty of Vienna, to rally their armies against Napoleon so as to disable him and prevent him from causing further trouble.

Castlereagh hammered the point home in a dispatch to Wellington, insisting that troops be deployed on 'the largest scale', with Allied forces 'inundating France from all sides'.[36] Even some of Napoleon's closest allies viewed this prospect with ill-concealed unease, the more so as it necessitated yet another round of conscription, draining the country of still younger men and boys and arousing public discontent across the length and breadth of France. After watching the decimation of two armies during the retreat from Moscow and at Leipzig, and with the greater part of those who returned in 1814 now retired or decommissioned, the renewal of hostilities meant the creation of yet another new army with which to confront the Allies. France was exhausted, her local communities crying out for peace; yet by mid-June Napoleon had assembled a force of one hundred and twenty thousand men, with which he crossed the frontier into the Netherlands, driving a wedge between British and Dutch forces under Wellington and the Prussians of Blücher.[37] His final campaign against his enemies, now ranged against him in a seventh coalition, had begun.

Napoleon was deaf to those of his ministers who counselled caution, who shrank from squandering yet more blood on the battlefield in a cause which they deemed already lost. And he had spilt plenty – one of the charges that would always be mounted against him by those seeking to diminish his stature as a military commander. His ability to draw on a mass conscript army meant that he had large numbers of soldiers, often raw and ill-trained, at his disposal, and he often gave the impression that he cared little about losses, that men could always be replaced and that their lives came cheap. Indeed, he famously boasted that he had grown up on battlefields and 'cared little about the lives of a million men'.[38] Some have estimated these losses much higher; the nineteenth-century historian Hippolyte Taine suggested that Napoleon's wars killed one million seven hundred thousand men born within the limits of pre-revolutionary France, besides a further two million Europeans, both allies and foes.[39] Though these figures are probably exaggerated, the scale of losses, whether from wounds sustained in battle or from fevers and disease, was unprecedented. To a degree this reflected the manner of fighting: the growing use of artillery, the resort to ever more mobile guns, and the increased firepower of these guns in battle. Jean-Paul Bertaud has told the story movingly, in raw statistics. If the French artillerymen fired twenty thousand cannon balls during the battle of Valmy, at Leipzig they fired a hundred thousand. Artillery aimed to kill, to mow down their opponents in a largely anonymous slaughter. And with every campaign the carnage grew worse. If losses were around six per cent at Fleurus in 1792, they had risen to fifteen per cent at Austerlitz in 1806 and thirty-one per cent at Eylau the following year. At the upcoming Battle of Waterloo, casualties would hit a staggering forty-five per cent.[40] Not without reason was Napoleon accused by his enemies of being a cruel and heartless butcher, prepared to condemn thousands to die in pursuit of glory.

Once again Napoleon faced the problem of manpower. With the Allies able to muster a million men, he was yet again forced to raise an army virtually from scratch. It proved a Herculean task, though by the end of the spring extraordinary progress had already been made. In March, all non-commissioned officers were recalled to the colours, and by the end of April he could put four armies and three observation corps in the field. Money was quickly raised, and tens of thousands of horses prepared for battle.[41] But time was short, too short to allow him to assemble the army of eight hundred thousand of which he talked. Already a Prussian army under Blücher and an Anglo-Dutch army under Wellington were taking up position in the Netherlands, leaving Napoleon little choice but to launch a quick pre-emptive strike against them. This he achieved with remarkable precision. He imposed a total news blackout, and spread false intelligence to unnerve his opponents. On 2 June he ordered the one hundred and twenty-four thousand men who made up the Armée du Nord to a position just south of the Belgian border, seemingly without provoking any response from the Allies. His tactic was working like a dream. Ten days later he left Paris to take personal command of the army, without his opponents realising what was happening around them. As late as 13 June Wellington was still reassuring London that it was unlikely Napoleon would leave Paris – just two days before he launched an incisive attack to separate the Allied armies and prevent them from forming a united front.[42]

Hostilities were joined quite dramatically on 16 June, when the French army attacked both the Prussians and the Anglo-Dutch army to the south of Brussels. At Ligny, Napoleon engaged the Prussians and scored what turned out to be his last victory in the field, though it was less decisive than he would have liked since it left the Prussian army able to re-form and fight on. It was a bloody encounter, pitting around eighty-three thousand Prussians against sixty-three thousand Frenchmen, and few prisoners were taken on either side. Napoleon read the battle well, but credit for the victory did not lie with him alone: of his generals, Gérard was far-sighted and tactically shrewd, but the victory can also be ascribed to the quality of those under his command, especially his junior officers and non-commissioned officers.[43] The significance of Ligny was diminished, however, by events elsewhere in the field. An army of twenty thousand men under Drouet d'Erlon, instructed to keep the English in their sights, was harassed and delayed. At the same time, Ney failed to take the key crossroads of Quatre-Bras from the Anglo-Dutch army, which allowed Wellington to pull back towards Brussels.[44] The French had sought to destroy the two armies individually so as to avoid having to face their combined onslaught, but neither battle was decisive and the Allies were able to regroup. The blood shed at Ligny and Quatre-Bras by the Prussian and British armies had served its purpose: it had bought the Allies time. Wellington and Blücher were far from defeated, and two days later they would engage Napoleon again, much more decisively, at Waterloo.

The Battle of Waterloo was an evenly matched affair, and one in which Napoleon again demonstrated his qualities as a commander and a strategist. He understood only too well that this was a life-or-death struggle, an engagement he had to win if he was to survive, and his principal aim after Quatre-Bras was to force the British to engage him before they had the chance to join forces with Blücher's Prussians. The French opened the attack with a frontal assault, led by Napoleon's brother Jérôme, against the right flank of the British army near the fortified farm of Hougoumont. At the same time Napoleon ordered an infantry attack on the main body of British troops at La Haie Sainte. Both manoeuvres were carried off with a certain *élan*, but both failed to dislodge the enemy, necessitating a third assault. This was a cavalry charge led by the brave if headstrong Ney, which was also repulsed by the British squares. The British lines had held firm. Worse, from the Emperor's point of view, was the fact that Grouchy, whom he had sent with thirty thousand men to find and pin down Blücher, had not succeeded in locating the Prussian army; and though he was within earshot of the battle, he had stuck limpet-like to his instructions instead of turning back to add fresh troops to the French attack. Should Grouchy be held to blame – as Napoleon did not hesitate to do from his exile on Saint Helena – or was the Emperor's own strategy at fault? Whatever the cause, it proved a fatal blunder, and when Blücher himself turned up on the battlefield, his Prussian forces emerging through the smoke and mist to add weight to Wellington's Anglo-Dutch army, the game was surely up. It was not in any sense a rout; indeed, Wellington would famously describe it as 'the nearest run thing you ever saw in your life'.[45] The French emerged with honour. The Imperial Guard fought a memorable battle, the cavalry attacked the enemy with flair, and they inflicted terrible casualties on their opponents. For Waterloo was truly a murderous battle, with some two hundred thousand men concentrated in a confined area barely two and a half miles square. The most reliable casualty figures list the losses in Wellington's army at three and a half thousand dead, three thousand three hundred missing and some ten thousand two hundred wounded – with the Prussians suffering a further twelve hundred dead, all in a single day.[46] But for all Napoleon's tactical skill, the battle was lost, and with it his imperial ambitions.

His first instinct on the morning after the battle, however, was to fight on, to engage the British and Prussian armies yet again, and turn defeat into victory. He insisted that it had been a glorious defeat from which his troops emerged with credit and honour, and that is how it would enter French collective memory. To Victor Hugo, Waterloo was a *morne plaine* forever shrouded in mist and gunsmoke;

Charles Péguy summarised the regrets of his generation when he wrote of Waterloo that it was one of those rare defeats which 'more than any victory, and more positively than any victory, fix themselves in the memory of men, in the common memory of humanity'.[47] Though Napoleon remained in denial, it signalled the end of his Empire and the end of a dream. For whereas he seemed eager to fight on, demanding that Joseph raise a further hundred thousand men, the two Chambers were overtly hostile, understanding only too clearly that peace would be unattainable as long as France continued to harbour military ambitions. The deputies also knew that the Allies would have no truck with Napoleon, and that the best they could now hope for was peace on Europe's terms. In the Chamber of Deputies the unthinkable was being said, that the Emperor's abdication was an essential precondition of peace, and Napoleon returned to Paris to face a wall of hostility. To save his Empire would require drastic measures: he would have to dissolve the two Chambers, assume dictatorial powers and turn to the army, steps that would risk plunging the country into civil war.

A few of his advisers, notably his brother Lucien, advised this course of action but, perhaps mindful of what had happened after the Eighteenth of Brumaire, Napoleon had no appetite for a war against France. On 22 June, informed by the Chambers that he must abdicate or be deposed, he addressed 'the French people' for the last time: 'In opening war to support national independence,' he declared, 'I counted on a union of all efforts and all wills. Circumstances seem to me to have changed. I offer myself in sacrifice to the hatred of the enemies of France.' Expressing the somewhat forlorn hope that the Allies aimed only at destroying the person of the Emperor, he named his young son as his successor. 'My political life is over,' he told them, 'and I proclaim my son, under the title of Napoleon II, Emperor of the French.'[48] But the time for dynastic ambition was long past. It was a prospect that neither the Chambers nor the Allies were prepared to contemplate.

13

Years of Exile

Following his second abdication, Napoleon understood that he could have no political future in Europe, and he took advice on where to seek refuge. One idea was the United States, the Americas being a favoured destination for Bonapartists and imperial officers looking to escape from France; and in June, he and his close collaborators made for Rochefort with the apparent intention of embarking for the New World. The French government was complicit in these plans, the naval minister sending instructions to the prefect in Rochefort and assigning two frigates to accompany the expedition.[1] But the Royal Navy had blockaded France's Atlantic coast, cutting off any possible escape route. Napoleon chose not to risk running the blockade, preferring to board a British warship, the *Bellerophon*, and ask for refuge in England. He himself seemed almost satisfied with that solution, which had the virtue of offering international protection from his more vengeful enemies at home, and it is clear that he expected the British government to treat him honourably: to imprison him or keep him under house arrest in England, somewhere where he could retire from public life and concentrate on writing his memoirs. Or so he mused. After his recent adventures, however – his escape from Elba had plunged Europe once more into a bloody war – this was nothing more than a utopian dream. His former adversaries were not in a conciliatory mood, and, in Britain just as in Prussia or Russia, unforgiving voices called for exemplary punishment that would teach both the former Emperor and the French people a powerful lesson. To keep him in England would create a political outcry as well as pose insuperable problems of state security.

To the British public Napoleon was more a criminal than a victim, and it became fashionable for cartoonists to portray him as England's prisoner, suffering the humiliation of defeat or appearing before the London populace in the guise of a caged beast. In July 1815 Rowlandson drew him disguised as a harlequin and imprisoned in a small cage mounted on a cart drawn by two mules. The caption proclaimed him to be 'A Rare Acquisition for the Royal Menagerie', a former potentate who now had no other function than to amuse and divert the King and his guests.[2] Politicians joined journalists and artists in demanding his exclusion from Europe, some even proposing that he be tried as a warmonger and sentenced to death. The Francophobe editor of *The Times*, John Stoddart, had no time for clemency and argued that Bonaparte and those who had rallied to him should be exposed to the full rigours of the law.[3] Others expressed the view that he should have been left to the mercy of the Bourbons and the French courts. The political problem, of course, was acute – the same as for any deposed ruler, whether Bonaparte or Louis XVI. If he were to be executed by order of his enemies he would become a political martyr and a hero to his admirers, an outcome which the Allies wanted to avoid if at all possible. If, on the other hand, he were to be imprisoned on British soil, or in a nearby country, he risked becoming the focal point for future insurrection, a leader waiting to be recalled to power. All were agreed that Napoleon could not be trusted, and that his promised good conduct – 'I would have given my word of honour to have remained quiet and to have held no political correspondence in England,'[4] he said – was wholly worthless. The apprenticeship in exile that was Elba had demonstrated how tight security would have to be if he was not to escape for a second time. If he were imprisoned, escape must be impossible; there must be no second *vol de l'aigle*.

These considerations led the British government to alight, as a place of exile, on Saint Helena, an impoverished and windswept outpost of Empire cut off from the world in the far South Atlantic. Battered by Atlantic storms, it was a bleak and inhospitable island – especially during the long winter months – a rocky outcropping in a distant ocean, dominated by the mountain peaks which punctured the low clouds that greeted Napoleon and his party – High Peak to the west, and the twin peaks of Actaeon and Diana nearer to the centre of the island and dominating the house at Longwood where, after the early months, Napoleon would take up residence. When Charles Darwin landed on Saint Helena in 1836 it was the bleakness that he emphasised: 'the habitable part is surrounded by a broad band of black desolate rocks, as if the wide barrier of the ocean were not sufficient to guard the precious spot'.[5] The island had no native population, but it was an important staging post for ships of the East India Company and sustained a population of up to five thousand, including a British garrison, a large number of slaves from Madagascar, and Chinese indentured labourers; it serviced and supplied around a thousand ships every year.[6] Jamestown, the capital, was 'a village squeezed between two mountains', without port installations, where ships lay at anchor off the coast and passengers were brought ashore in open boats.[7] Assurances from the British government that the island's climate was healthy were more than a little deceptive. Summers were semi-tropical, but in winter Saint Helena was exposed to fierce storms that regularly piled in from the Atlantic, and there was a pervasive damp that clung to walls and seeped into the foundations of buildings.[8]

The journey from Europe to the South Atlantic was dull and seemingly endless, introducing the former emperor to something of the boredom that would afflict him once he reached Saint Helena. First the *Bellerophon* brought him to Plymouth, from where he would begin his voyage into exile. He was transferred to the seventy-eight-gun British warship *Northumberland*, which would take him to the South Atlantic, along with the French entourage that would become famous through their association with him: Bertrand, with his wife and three children; the Montholons, husband and wife; the young general, Gaspar Gourgaud, and the only civilian among them, Comte Emmanuel-Joseph de Las Cases, who was appointed Napoleon's chamberlain and was accompanied by his young son. Others would have gone, too, but the British authorities had no wish to create a thriving Bonapartist colony on Saint Helena and were especially determined to avoid any military concentration there. Of the fifteen army officers who had accompanied Napoleon from France, only three were allowed to share his exile. He was also given the right to take twelve servants, including his personal valet, Louis Marchand, a young man of twenty-four who had served in the imperial household since 1811 and had been with Napoleon on Elba. The servants included a cook, a butler, and, most famously, the devoted Saint-Denis, who had followed the Emperor across Europe and was universally known as Mameluke Ali.[9] As his doctor on Saint Helena he chose an Irish naval surgeon, Dr Barry O'Meara.

Conditions on board the *Northumberland* were cramped and rather Spartan, and the ship's captain was adamant that Napoleon should be granted only the space appropriate to a state prisoner; he was no longer an emperor, and could no longer bank on special privileges. When he came aboard he was greeted with the honours appropriate to a general, but not to a head of state. He did not complain, comparing conditions on board to those in the bivouacs he had endured on campaign. The ship itself, though it had been extensively refitted for the voyage and appeared resplendent with an admiral's ensign, was old and creaky. There were some one thousand and eighty men on board, many of them soldiers, and the ship was accompanied to Jamestown by two smaller troop ships, the *Ceylon* and the *Bucephalus*. The voyage from Plymouth took sixty-seven days, during which the little flotilla was battered by winds and high seas.[10] Despite claims that it was one of the best sailing ships in the Royal Navy, the *Northumberland*'s voyage to Saint Helena would be her last in active service. On her return from Saint Helena she was retired and converted to a hospital ship, in which capacity she would remain in service until she was sent to the breaker's yard in 1850.[11]

Bertrand, Montholon, Las Cases and Gourgaud would become Napoleon's closest companions on Saint Helena – they were commonly referred to as the 'four apostles', and each would leave his memories of the former Emperor's final years. They were in some ways a motley crew, united only by their loyalty to Napoleon and by years of service in his cause. Count Bertrand had risen to the rank of general on merit alone; he was a talented artillery officer who would stay with Napoleon until his death in 1821, as would the second of the 'apostles', the Count de Montholon. Although also a general, Montholon had not enjoyed a notable military career and, unlike Bertrand, was the scion of an old aristocratic family and a man of traditional tastes. Las Cases, a former *maître des requêtes* in the Council of State, had no military experience, but came to understand Napoleon well. He would become his confidant and memorialist on Saint Helena, noting down his intimate thoughts and discussing with him the high and low points of his Empire. For the British, indeed, the bond between Las Cases and the former Emperor was uncomfortably close, and when in November 1816 he was discovered smuggling his secret correspondence out of the island Las Cases was promptly deported. The fourth of Napoleon's companions, General Gourgaud, also left before Napoleon's death. In 1815 he was a young man of thirty-two who had enjoyed rapid promotion in the imperial army and whose talents had favourably impressed the Emperor. Unlike the others, he had volunteered himself for the expedition. Disappointed to be omitted from the official list of those who were to go, he pleaded to be included in an emotional tirade. 'He was', he shouted, 'a Baron of the Empire, a Lieutenant General; his life had been devoted to serving the Emperor! He had fought in thirteen campaigns, had received three wounds during that time, had even saved the Emperor's life at the Battle of Brienne, and had borne Napoleon's letter to the Prince Regent'.[12] Death, he said, was to be preferred to such an insult. Napoleon listened to the young man's pleadings, noted the strength of his devotion, and relented. Gourgaud got his way, but by 1817 Napoleon had had enough of his jealous outbursts, his quarrels with the others and his seemingly close relationship with the British governor, Hudson Lowe.

Gourgaud was fast becoming a disruptive influence, and Napoleon asked that he be removed.[13]

The presence of his French companions undoubtedly helped to make life on the island more bearable, as his exile would otherwise have condemned him to long periods of total solitude. With Las Cases, as with Bertrand, Napoleon built a solid foundation of trust, and it was to them that he vouchsafed his thoughts about his achievements, about his victories and defeats, and about the glories of his Empire. They spent hours closeted together, with Napoleon holding forth on some aspect of his reign or denouncing some *bête noire* he chose to blame for his failures. Las Cases and Bertrand would scribble away faithfully, recording their master's words and preserving them for posterity. Their presence supplied him with congenial company, which was itself important for him. They also gave him a sense of purpose in his exile, as he prepared his memoirs, embellishing and massaging his side of the story, his version of the events he had lived through and had so often dominated. In 1816, in his conversations with Las Cases, and thereafter with Bertrand, he offered a commentary on the past which he hoped would provide the master narrative for his contemporaries and for future historians of the Empire. Nothing that he wrote or dictated, however, should be read uncritically; every word was carefully chosen and its implications weighed. He remained a subtle propagandist, and his memoirs were to be a key tool in securing his place in history. He may also have hoped that British hatred of him would be assuaged, and that he might return to Europe from what he increasingly felt as a hateful exile. That hope was diluted by Bathurst's dismissive reply on behalf of the British government in 1817, then extinguished completely by the Allies in 1819 at Aix-la-Chapelle.[14]

Curiously little had been prepared for the Napoleon's arrival on Saint Helena. The house that had been identified as his place of captivity, Longwood, required considerable work before it was ready for occupation, while the temporary lodging allocated to him by the British government, Plantation House, was wholly unsuitable. In the first months on the island, he preferred to stay in a pavilion attached to a family house at The Briars, the same house where Wellington had lodged when he landed on Saint Helena back in 1805. The current owner, William Balcombe, employed as superintendent for public sales for the East India Company, agreed to the arrangement and made him as comfortable as he could, and, despite the simplicity of his surroundings, Napoleon later acknowledged that this was the happiest period of his enforced sojourn on the island. Yet already he was beginning to baulk at the petty restrictions imposed by his captors. He was subject to a curfew; if he left the garden he had to be accompanied by a British soldier; and if his friends came to visit, they were obliged to return to Jamestown by nine in the evening.[15] At Longwood, once Hudson Lowe had been installed as governor, the restrictions would become more numerous and Napoleon's contempt for them more unbridled. By 1816 his relations with British bureaucracy were tense and acrimonious, with Lowe the customary target of his anger. After August 1816 he refused all face-to-face discussions with the governor, and over time became more withdrawn and more depressed about his lot. Even when the British government recognised the inadequacies of Longwood and started building a new house for him, he refused to show any interest. No doubt he was aware that this was no generous gesture but the confirmation of what he most feared: that he would spend the rest of his days on Saint Helena.

Longwood was set among lava fields, what Louis Marchand would describe in his memoirs as 'volcanic terrain without a trace of vegetation'. Yet Napoleon admitted that he found the scenery haunting and rather inspiring. Behind the house was the forest of Deadwood, which contrasted vividly with the layers of cooled black lava. 'Pockets of soil spread by time gave birth to a few stunted trees and patches of greenery'. But the initial impression did not take long to wear off. 'For one who had remained at The Briars for six weeks without going outside', he wrote, 'this countryside was not without charm; but this favourable impression dissipated more and more the closer I approached the house. The trees forming a green roof were really very stunted, with such sparse foliage that they provided no shade. The lawn that appeared fresh was so only by comparison with the rocky ravines and volcanic land separating me from it.' His initial sense of a verdant landscape, of trees and lawns, did not survive close inspection. The foliage was stunted, the lawns dried and shrivelled. 'Scorched by the sun it was . . . more like a field of straw than of grass.'[16]

Longwood was a spacious residence by the standards of Saint Helena, though it hardly compared with the palaces to which Napoleon had become accustomed as Emperor. It contained a billiard room, a salon, a dining room and a library, as well as accommodation for Gourgaud, Las Cases and O'Meara, and family quarters for Montholon. Bertrand, at his wife's insistence, lived away from the main house, first at Hutt's Gate and later in a cottage the family built on ground opposite the front entrance to Longwood.[17] Longwood also had a substantial garden, set against the backcloth of volcanic rocks, where Napoleon was given to take the air and, in 1819, developed a brief passion for gardening. He declared his love of nature, planting trees and even raising a few sheep, but this was only a façade: for a man who had always been physically active his years of captivity proved a cumulative torture. In the first months of his stay at Longwood he took long walks or went riding to keep himself in good physical condition, but he became quickly bored, acutely aware that he was merely filling in the hours, and he began to lose interest. More and more, his time on Saint Helena was spent in reminiscence, looking back over his career and dictating his reflections to Las Cases or one of the other apostles. He also read profusely. He looked forward avidly to shipments of books from Europe, and enjoyed listening as Marchand or one of the others read to him of an evening.[18] His other great pleasure was to entertain visitors and indulge in good food and wine. We know that Napoleon's household greatly exceeded the domestic budget it was allocated by the British government, and that huge quantities of drink were consumed. In the last three months of 1816 alone, over thirty-seven hundred bottles of wine were delivered to Longwood, among them eight hundred and thirty bottles of Bordeaux.[19]

At his best, Napoleon had always been a social animal who enjoyed conversation and good company. In his early months at Longwood he appeared relaxed – even courtly – when he received visitors, even English ones, and he did not hesitate to discuss his past achievements, or the state of current affairs, or such changes as the future might bring. He was interested by stories of the outside world and struck visitors as well informed about what was happening in Europe. He particularly welcomed naval visitors, ships' captains and officers who put ashore from British vessels passing through on their way to India.[20] Throughout his life he remained something of a ladies' man, and was notably more welcoming to female visitors such as Lady Malcolm, the wife of Sir Pulteney Malcolm, a British admiral who came to Jamestown with the commissioners of the Allied powers and stayed there for some months in 1816 and 1817. Relations between the two men were amicable, and Lady Malcolm visited Napoleon at Longwood. A naval captain and diarist, Henry Meynell, was present at one of their meetings, taking notes on what he saw and heard. He was impressed by the variety and lightness of Napoleon's conversation, which clearly surprised him. 'On their arrival B. received Lady M. most graciously;' he notes, 'asked her several questions; how she bore so long a sea voyage; and if she was not very sea-sick? He then asked her if she was fond of hunting, as he understood that ladies in England were partial to that amusement.' Then, turning to another of his favourite topics, 'he talked to her much about Ossian's poems, which he had always admired'. His conversation was artistic, animated, and informed. 'He said he had seen two translations of them in French, that neither were good, but that the one he had seen in Italian was excellent and beautiful. He then asked Lady M. if she thought them genuine, that there had been many controversies about them, and whether she did not think that Macpherson had written them.' Napoleon showed he could listen too: 'Lady M. replied that she did not think Macpherson capable of writing them, that the Highland Society had taken much pains to investigate it and proved their authenticity.'[21]

But by 1817 these convivial social gatherings were becoming a thing of the past. Napoleon would spend long hours alone in his room at Longwood, skimming through a few books or lost in a depressive daze. There is little to suggest that he enjoyed solitude or adjusted easily to the constraints of his captivity. Over time Longwood took its toll: his capacity for conviviality dimmed and he grew increasingly self-absorbed. Lethargy overcame him, and he would sit alone or lie on his bed for hours, plunged in thought or simply doing nothing – classic symptoms of depression. By 1818 he was further isolated by the departure of a number of his contacts on the island: Gourgaud – whose departure he had requested – but also the Balcombes and his trusted physician, O'Meara, who was transferred by the British because he was seen as too friendly with their prisoner. He was saddened, too, by the death of one of his servants, his *maître d'hôtel* Cipriani, a fellow Corsican whom he liked and trusted. By the end of the year he had even given up work on his memoirs, which had previously given his captivity some shape and purpose.

The Napoleon who is depicted in the pages of Las Cases' *Mémorial* is not the workaholic who had once led great armies and presided over a continent. He appears diminished, both physically and mentally, increasingly resembling some colonial planter in his straw hat, wandering round his garden inspecting the produce.[22] This was the image that would be seized upon by cartoonists and pilloried by his opponents. It was the image of a man who was no longer young and vigorous, who tended to obesity, and was increasingly tortured by poor health – in short, a man who no longer posed any threat to his former enemies. By 1820 caricaturists could even allow themselves a degree of sympathy for him in his exile. An Irish cartoon of 1820, entitled 'The Sorrows of Boney', portrayed him in his terrible solitude, crouched on a barren rock, surveying the ocean and ruminating on the depths to which he has fallen. He had become a rather tragic figure, capable of eliciting pity rather than anger or condemnation.[23]

There was a degree of self-pity, too, as Napoleon relived his campaigns and lamented the defeats that had cost him his throne.

In particular he fought and refought the Battle of Waterloo, arguing about the reasons for the defeat, persuading himself that only a minor error had robbed him of victory. Usually, as was his wont, that error was not his but was attributed to one of his commanders, a marshal whose rashness or loss of faith had cost him the day. Bertrand records a number of his recurrent regrets: 'I made a great mistake in employing Ney. He lost his head. A sense of his past conduct impaired his energy.' Elsewhere the fault was Soult's. 'Soult did not aid me as much as he might have done. His staff, notwithstanding all my orders, was not well organised. Berthier would have done better service.' He would have done better with Suchet. Or the fault lay with the whole army. 'The men of 1815 were not the same as those of 1792. My generals were faint-hearted men. Perhaps I should have done better to have waited another month before opening the campaign to give more consistency to the army.'[24] Napoleon, it would seem, had become persuaded of his invincibility and sought scapegoats to explain his own failures. As he told Montholon, Waterloo could only be explained by the fact that fate had abandoned him. 'I did not lose the battle because the Allies had three times more men. I lost it because Soult had made a bad choice of officers of his general staff and one of them did not deliver my orders. If the messengers sent to Grouchy had not behaved like simpletons, if my orders had been carried to Guyot . . . the battle would have been mine.'[25] Always someone else was to blame.

In his later years at Longwood he was tormented by deteriorating health and reduced mobility, as a life of extraordinarily hard work and physical exertion, much of it spent in the saddle and in military quarters across Europe, finally took its toll. Despite his love of rapid military movements and taste for incisive decision-making,

Napoleon was a perfectionist who never lost his faith in careful planning. He had worked prodigiously over many years, both as a military commander in the field and as Emperor, planning his every move in meticulous detail, dictating huge numbers of letters and dispatches, and poring over his maps late into the night. Over a long military career that stretched from Toulon in 1793 to Waterloo in 1815, he had been wounded on several occasions, surviving two shell bursts and a series of minor injuries to his chest, his Achilles tendon and his left leg. He had never shirked from danger or avoided the thick of a battle; in the course of twenty-two years he had survived numerous attacks and had seen nineteen horses killed under him. At Arcis-en-Aube in March 1814, when a shell dropped to earth only a few feet from where he stood, Napoleon calmly rode over it. According to David Chandler's account of the incident, 'the shell exploded, the horse, disembowelled, went plunging down, taking its rider with it. The Emperor disappeared in the dust and smoke. But he got up without a scratch'.[26] There was no questioning his physical bravery. Increasingly, however, as the campaigns followed one upon the other in quick succession, he had suffered from sudden bouts of illness that contrasted with his normally robust good health and affected his capacity to lead his army in the field. Before Borodino he had difficulty breathing and his pulse rate was irregular; after Dresden he was assailed by vomiting and diarrhoea; at Leipzig he suffered acute stomach pains; and at Ligny he was incapacitated by illness immediately after the battle.[27] His frenetic lifestyle and refusal to rest his body had, it seemed, finally come home to roost.

On Saint Helena Napoleon was notoriously distrustful of doctors, especially once O'Meara left and he had only the physicians allotted to him by the British authorities. He dismissed as incompetent the doctor sent out by his family in 1819, the Corsican Francesco Antommarchi, who tended him during his final months and performed the official autopsy after his death.[28] In all, he had six doctors during his six years on the island, a rate of expenditure that reflected his fear of British perfidy – and of Hudson Lowe in particular – and his tendency to believe in plots and conspiracies where medicine was concerned.[29] This lack of trust has made it difficult for historians to establish reliable medical records for his last illness, though from the observations of those close to him it is clear that his health had been failing for some years. From 1817 he was suffering liver problems and stomach pains, possibly the result of cancer; or he may have been assailed by hepatitis, which was prevalent in Saint Helena's unhealthy climate.[30] By the autumn of 1820 he had taken to his bed, often in pain, unable to digest food, and growing steadily weaker. It is clear that he knew he was dying; indeed, he accepted death with a calm fatalism, comforting Louis Marchand with the thought that his death was pre-ordained and admitting to Bertrand that he would die with no belief in an afterlife. 'I am lucky not to believe,' he is quoted as saying, 'for I don't have chimerical fears of hell.'[31] He also found the energy in April 1821 to make a will, an elaborate document in which he left bequests to his family, as well as to Bertrand, Montholon and Marchand, whom he appointed as his executors, and to several of his former companions in arms. Even in his final illness he revived from time to time and had moments of astounding clarity, though they became increasingly rare. By the first days of May he was suffering increasing pain and was prescribed ever-larger doses of drugs.

Napoleon died on 5 May 1821, at the age of fifty-two. He was surrounded by those of his friends who had stayed with him to the last: Bertrand and Montholon and their children, and his two most loyal servants, Marchand and Ali.

This is probably not the place to resurrect the controversy that has raged over the causes of his death since traces of arsenic were discovered in the strands of his hair. These had been lovingly taken by Marchand as a keepsake after his master's death, and only much later subjected to scientific analysis. The evidence offered to suggest that Napoleon was poisoned seems, at best, circumstantial. There are other explanations that could account for the arsenic, including the effect of damp seeping into the wallpaper at Longwood. Napoleon's health was sufficiently poor to be considered life-threatening, and the doctors at the time attributed his death to hepatitis, stomach cancer and an ulcerated stomach lining. More recent medical opinion agrees. In the last days of his life there was clear evidence of gastric bleeding; some have talked of tuberculosis, others of long-standing renal problems which had weakened him throughout his life.[32] Napoleon had worn out and abused his body until it could take no more. It needed no external agency to kill him.

There remained the question of his funeral. Napoleon had expressed his wish to be buried in Paris, but there was scant chance of that being acceptable to either the British or the new French government. His other expressed wish was that his body should return to Corsica and be placed alongside his ancestors in the cathedral at Ajaccio. That, too, was rejected. Napoleon, it was agreed, must stay on Saint Helena; he could not be allowed to return to Europe where, even in death, his presence would be a threat to the new political order. Hudson Lowe did, however, grant Napoleon his choice of burial site, in the verdant Geranium Valley, under the willow trees and close to the spring where he had watched the

Chinese labourers loading drinking water for Longwood. For the funeral procession he authorised a level of ceremonial appropriate to an army general; again, the British government could not contemplate giving him the honours due to a head of state. Nonetheless, the funeral could not fail to make an impression on the islanders. The entire population lined the route as Napoleon's coffin was carried by twelve grenadiers to its final resting place; so did the two thousand or so British soldiers and sailors who were on duty on the island. The coffin was covered in blue velvet, and on it were placed his sword and the cloak that he had worn at Marengo; the tassels on the four corners of the pall were held by Bertrand and Montholon at the rear, and by Louis Marchand and Bertrand's eldest son, Napoleon, at the front. The coffin was followed by Napoleon's state horse, led by his groom, in front of the governor, the hated Hudson Lowe – resplendent in full-dress uniform – and a retinue of British staff and army personnel.

Amid the peace of Geranium Valley Napoleon's body was laid to rest beneath huge flat stones. Honour, it seemed, had been upheld, but there would be one last spat with the British over the inscription on Napoleon's tomb. The French wanted to commemorate him simply as Napoleon, his name when he was emperor; whereas the British, ever sensitive to the dangers of granting his Empire any vestige of legitimacy, insisted on Napoleon Bonaparte. And there the squabble rested. Rather than give ground on what they saw as a matter of principle, the French preferred to leave their former Emperor in an unmarked grave.[33]

14

Life after Death

Napoleon had shown repeatedly throughout his career that he was a master of persuasion and an arch-propagandist, aware of the power of words and phrases, images and music to win over public opinion to his cause. His victories at Toulon and Marengo, his venture into Egypt, his coronation and marriage to Marie-Louise, his relations with his men, his youthful experience as a revolutionary general, and his long hours spent as a ruler and legislator in the interests of his people – every aspect of his colourful career was carefully publicised in newspapers and bulletins to construct a heroic image that would be passed down to posterity.

Throughout his career, Napoleon had demonstrated an insatiable desire to project his chosen image, to reserve his place in history. And so, in exile he spent much of his time, especially during his early months on Saint Helena, with purpose and deliberation. There was at first no brooding over the past, no preparing for death, and no planning his return to Europe. What he engaged in was the black art of propaganda, of which he was a master, telling and retelling his story to make sure that his side of events would survive for future generations. He discussed past strategies, the outcomes of his campaigns, the ways he had intended things to work out, often justifying his actions, sometimes expressing regrets, and characteristically blaming others for their weakness or indecisiveness. That was the point of the long hours spent in his study, dictating his thoughts to his 'apostles' certain in the knowledge that they would record his views faithfully when his composition was complete. Of course, there was a more immediate purpose, too, in that they helped while away boredom and gave shape to his days. But his real aim cannot be in doubt: this was a tactical campaign as complex as any he had won on the battlefield.

On Saint Helena he convinced himself and his listeners that he had been consistent in his aims, that his had indeed been a liberal empire which he had created and governed in the interests of his people. The Emperor of these final years turned full circle to be reborn as the revolutionary of 1793, the man of the people who identified with the populace and remained loyal to the liberty and fraternity of the First Republic, breaking down privilege and spreading the values of individualism and economic freedom.[1]

His arguments and self-justifications, as they are recorded by Las Cases in the *Mémorial de Sainte-Hélène*, are less a record of his achievements than a plea to be understood as a son of the Revolution, a man of principle who had remained loyal to his republican ideals. Napoleon was carefully placing himself in history as a democrat who reflected the popular will and who listened to the French people, in stark contrast to the Bourbons and the politicians of the Restoration. He was, in a quite explicit way, making a pitch to be seen by the French public as a man of the Left, a man of democratic instincts. Las Cases records him talking of 'the irresistible rise of liberal ideas', for which he claimed that his Empire was largely responsible. The claim was bold and audacious. 'Nothing should henceforth destroy or efface the great principles of our Revolution', he declared, adding that they were noble truths that would last for ever, and that the glory with which he had embellished them had made them 'immortal'. In this process, revolutionary politics and imperial arms had played complementary roles. 'The product of the political rostrum, cemented by the blood of battles, decorated with the laurels of victory, saluted by popular acclamation, sanctioned by the treaties and alliances of rulers, they should never again be forced to retreat.' By carrying the torch for these ideals, he adds, he will forever be linked to them and to their success across the globe.[2] He talks the language of rights and of citizenship, and carefully presents this for export across Europe as the rights of peoples to win freedom from their empires and monarchies and establish themselves as nation states. He even alludes to the Empire as 'the regularisation of the republican principle'.[3]

Napoleon also took the opportunity in his discussions with his entourage to mount attacks on his critics, especially those intellectuals who had, whether through ideological conviction or personal spite, denounced his policies or denied his virtue. Napoleon might relish power, but he was vain enough to value his reputation, too. He cultivated artists and authors, and he resented the continual sniping that he suffered from one or two key literary figures – writers whom he had admired and whom he read. It should not be forgotten that he had been an omnivorous reader ever since his early days on garrison duty, when he confessed that he read novels as a means of killing boredom.[4] He was certainly far too conscious of the power of words not to recognise the damage they were doing him. Even on Saint Helena he could not let their criticisms rest unanswered.

Chateaubriand who, like Napoleon, had begun life as a young army officer in the Revolution, was a conservative and a royalist. He became quickly disillusioned as the monarchy gave way to the Republic and pluralism to authoritarian centralism. He joined the army of the counter-revolution and launched his literary career in exile in London. After 18 Brumaire, he briefly rallied to Napoleon before becoming angered and disgusted by the execution of the Duc d'Enghien, which drove him into opposition. By the end of the Empire his attacks on Napoleon had become unremitting, not least the venomous tract he published in 1814, within days of the Allied entry into Paris – a time when it could be calculated to do the greatest psychological damage. Here, he not only challenged the legitimacy of Napoleon's rule but hit at the heart of his military reputation, accusing him of being a mediocre general who had made crass decisions in the field and squandered the lives of his men. 'Born largely to destroy,' he wrote, 'Bonaparte carries evil in his breast just as naturally as a mother bears her offspring, with joy and a sort of pride.'[5] His most famous work, the *Mémoires d'outre-tombe*, was a passionate indictment of the Empire. For Napoleon this constituted an act of betrayal by a convinced reactionary. Yet he remained an admirer of Chateaubriand as a writer, even as he deplored his disloyalty and denounced the virulence of his prose. On Saint Helena Napoleon would insist that his 1814 pamphlet had been so vituperative and libellous that it could inspire only disgust, before adding, with surprising indulgence, that 'it is to be believed that he now regrets writing them', and that 'such a fine talent as his would not prostitute itself by reproducing them today.'[6]

The liberal Benjamin Constant also threw in his lot with the Restoration, making clear in a piece he contributed to the *Journal des Débats* just why his conscience would not allow him to compromise with the Empire. It represented, he suggested, the worst of compromises, since 'on the King's side are constitutional liberty, security and peace; on that of Bonaparte slavery, anarchy and war'. The contrast could not be emphasised more starkly, and Napoleon resented it deeply.[7] Benjamin Constant's conversion from liberalism to support for the legitimist monarchy had seemed dramatic – too dramatic not to arouse Napoleon's suspicions. Who could be responsible for this sudden *volte-face* and apparent betrayal of liberalism? Napoleon's animus focused on one of his long-term *bêtes noires*, the liberal author Madame de Staël who, over a career built on acerbic writing and brilliant salon conversation, had evoked a bitter hatred for Napoleon and all the values he stood for. Her major political works, which were published posthumously, were thinly veiled attacks on his regime.

Germaine de Staël resented almost everything about Napoleon: his origins in Corsica, his military background, and the manner in which he had seized power, all of which helped convince her that he was little more than a tyrant and a usurper. The political allusions and allegorical references to the Emperor that littered her texts were intended to be recognised across Europe, and thus to wound him.[8] In *De l'Allemagne*, arguably her most political work, Napoleon is portrayed as a new Attila, a comparison that caused the book to be pulped by the French censors. And though the subject focused on Germany rather than France, the German rulers were not its principal target. The book was a denunciation of tyranny, and to her European readers in 1810 the very use of the word 'tyrant' conjured up images of Bonaparte.[9]

Of greater significance than her dislike of tyranny, however, was a contempt that resulted from her personal vanity and her fierce family loyalty. Germaine was widely admired for her sparkling conversation, but not for her beauty; and Napoleon, on the few social occasions when they met, either treated her rudely or chose to ignore her altogether. For one of the most prominent socialites of her day, a woman who had had a succession of equally prominent lovers and may have set out with an infatuation for the young Bonaparte, his contempt was unbearable, and she alleged that Napoleon had no appreciation of women, that, indeed, he was uncomfortable in their company. Just as important was the resentment she felt towards a man who did not share her passionate belief in her father's genius. She was the daughter of Jacques Necker, the most reformist controller-general put in charge of France's finances under Louis XVI. Necker was not only her dear father, he was also her hero, and the offhand treatment he had received at Napoleon's hands shocked and angered her. She pursued him relentlessly throughout his reign, and so wearied Napoleon that he sent her into exile to rid himself of her attentions. On Saint Helena he continued to marvel how she had continued to 'fight with one hand and beg with the other'.[10] Of her family relations he remarked that hers was indeed a 'singular family': 'her father, her mother and herself, all three on their knees in constant adoration of one another, and breathing in reciprocal incense for the better edification and mystification of the public'.[11] It was, as so often, a well-aimed rapier-blow before the tribunal of History.

Like so many modern political memoirs, the *Mémorial de Sainte-Hélène* was an exercise in self-justification that presented the Emperor in the best possible light and gave coherence to his policies and decisions. It was a work of creative literature that gave a narrative overview to the period which impressed and excited its readers, since it bore the stamp of experience, the authenticity of Napoleon's own voice. First published in Paris in 1823, shortly after his death, it became an instant best-seller and was rapidly translated into a number of European languages, including English and German. The memoir became one of the most influential works of the first half of the nineteenth century, providing sustenance to those who had shared the Napoleonic dream and who regretted the passing of the Empire. It would also have a crucial political role in disseminating the Napoleonic legend across nineteenth-century Europe.

The *Mémorial* was the first, and by far the most influential, of the memoirs and autobiographical accounts to emerge from the years of exile. Montholon and Gourgaud published an account of Napoleon's Italian campaigns in 1823, whereas Bertrand's two-volume work on the war in Syria and Egypt only appeared in 1847, almost a generation later.[12] But their more personal accounts of Napoleon on Saint Helena and reflections on his years of exile had to wait much longer: Gourgaud's journal from 1815 to 1818, in two volumes, was published only in 1899; while, astonishingly perhaps, Bertrand's *Cahiers de Sainte-Hélène* lay undiscovered until after the Second World War.[13] Napoleon's two valets, Marchand and Ali, also published their memories of their master's exile, managing to work in some domestic anecdotes that betrayed their affection for their master.[14] Marchand, who was one of Napoleon's executors, gives considerable space to the terms of his will, and notes the air of sadness that engulfed Longwood when he died.[15]

Others who were not with him in his exile were also moved to contribute their reflections and memories. A Napoleonic publishing industry came into being, dispensing the Napoleonic myth both to veterans of the Empire nostalgic for the world they had lost, and to a new generation of young men, growing up after 1815 and avid for the glory and political excitement that Napoleon personified. If Chateaubriand and Mme de Staël sowed the seeds of a black legend, Napoleon and his apostles made sure that the world knew his side of the story, and their writings appealed to the romantic imagination of the nineteenth century. Bertrand, by this time reinstated in the Restoration army, phrased it memorably when he wrote that the Emperor 'remained our Standard, our rallying-point. The memory of our glorious past made us forget for a moment the miseries of our country, and we felt that our heart, with all our soul, went out to him, even though army discipline made us obedient to the White Flag.'[16] Even Britain was not immune from his appeal: a generation of poets and novelists, from Scott and Byron to Southey, de Quincey and Thackeray, fell under the spell of the Emperor. In the words of one leading literary critic, in their work is 'a desire that eschews abstinence and order in favour of indulgent fantasies of violent becoming – indeed, the very stuff of Napoleonic identity.'[17]

If Napoleon can claim credit for creating his new identity as a man of the people and the legitimate heir to the ideas of 1789, his enemies gave him huge assistance. Every action of the Restoration monarchy, it seemed, intensified the equation of Revolution and Empire in the popular mind: the encouragement given to Catholic missions, which toured southern villages annihilating every vestige of the Republic; the uprooting of liberty trees and banning of the tricolour; and the purging of men known for republican or Bonapartist sympathies from any form of public office, all symbolised the monarchy's determination to return to an old order where the people were once more subjugated and nobles and clergy were secure in their wealth and prestige.[18] In some parts of the south, White Terror returned as well, as those who had suffered the excesses of the Jacobin period joined forces with returned émigrés and newly empowered priests in a concerted campaign of denunciation and revenge killing. Against this background it was not difficult to develop nostalgia for a more egalitarian age, and Napoleon's apologists exploited those feelings with consummate skill. Political realities gave way to an idealised image of a time of equality and opportunity. In a particularly unrealistic portrayal of the Empire in 1840, the liberal novelist Frédéric Soullié wrote, 'Remember, that equality was the law under his reign. It is because of this that he is our hero; it is for this reason that he has remained so great and revered in our memories.'[19] Seldom has the history of a regime been so single-mindedly concentrated on that of a single man.

Prefects worried about the secret ambitions of former soldiers, now demobilised on half-pay, and throughout eastern France miniature statues of Napoleon and Marie-Louise were reported to be in high demand.[20] For some, unconvinced by the news of his death, he remained a living hero, a man who, they hoped, would play a part in the future life of the nation just as he had done in the past. Police and administrative reports made repeated references to individuals who claimed that he was not dead, some who expressed the hope that he would return, some who had even seen him in the flesh. Unsurprisingly, these were most common in peasant France, in the depths of countryside where superstitious beliefs remained widely held and where visions of the Virgin Mary were not unknown. In the Creuse, not far from the town of Guéret, a rumour spread that Bonaparte had appeared, almost Christ-like, 'escorted by angels', to a mother and her child at the very moment when the story of his return was being recounted.[21] Religious themes were often strong in the imagery surrounding these visions, as simple countrymen struggled to put their faith into words. Some even alleged that the tale of Napoleon's death had to be false since he was not as other men, and would not die. In 1815, indeed, in the Massif Central, one man was overheard to say simply that Napoleon was 'immortal', a belief that easily led to expectations of a Second Coming.[22] Such an event would be eagerly awaited, too, since the return of the Emperor would put bread on their tables and guarantee the return of prosperity, and the government was alert to the possibility that support for Napoleon lay at the root of sedition and conspiracy. The fact that many young conscripts, instead of turning in their weapons or breaking them to show their contempt for the new order, had preferred to keep them for future use, only added to the sense of emergency.[23]

In 1819 the government's approach became more repressive, following the murder of the Duc de Berry late at night in Paris as he accompanied his sick wife home from the theatre. He was the younger son of the Comte d'Artois, the King's brother and future Charles X, and though the murder was demonstrably the work of a lone fanatic intent on destroying what remained of the Bourbon line, it unleashed a huge political backlash, and police spies worked hard to unearth new plots.[24] In the years that followed they devoted particular attention to the activities of freemasons, and secret republican societies calling themselves *Carbonari* who combined an enlightened or progressive view of the state with a taste for intrigue and conspiracy. Romantics and neo-liberals were among those most prone to get caught up in such conspiracy, not least those who had served under the Emperor during his military career. But to the

Bourbons they represented an intolerable threat, and they were determined to eliminate every trace of Napoleonic sympathies. Youthful or romantic dreaming was not taken as an excuse by a government concentrated on repression. The Four Sergeants of La Rochelle, who had been arrested for membership of a secret society and for plotting against the monarchy in 1822, were among the most high-profile victims of this juridical campaign. Denounced to the authorities, they were offered no quarter, were summarily condemned to death, and were guillotined before the public's obvious sympathy for four romantic young soldiers risked becoming politicised. Their martyrdom could only play into the hands of the liberal opposition.[25]

The Paris crowd was especially feared by the authorities in view of its past record of political activism, both in the Revolution and during the Old Regime. Disillusionment with the restored monarchy combined with high levels of unemployment to heighten the appeal of the past, and here, in the bars and drinking dens of the capital, the cult of Napoleon rapidly took root. Singing was a favourite pastime among Parisian workers at the time: recalling his memories of his Parisian youth, Pierre Vinçard describes the years around 1818 as a time when singing societies (or *goguettes*) were being established in a number of working-class districts. These societies, he explains, were mainly composed of workers; they operated freely with tacit authorisation from the local police, and the songs they sang were those most popular in the workers' repertoire of the day, including many that were critical of the government and the Catholic church.[26] It was a time when singing was becoming increasingly political, a form of popular resistance to authority. And among the songs that were especially popular were nostalgic ditties about the

Empire, notably those written by Pierre-Jean Béranger and Emile Debraux, whose song sheets contributed significantly to the mood of nostalgia. The workers' voices rose in denunciation of the aristocracy and of a Church which they saw as a rampart of the social elite; they sang to the memory of Napoleon and of the armies he led; and they turned the Napoleonic legend against the authority of the restored monarchy. Debraux's verses about his exile on Saint Helena and Béranger's evocations of the spirit of the departed Emperor were emotionally highly charged; sentimental songs that brought tears to the eyes.[27] But they were as nothing compared to Béranger's most powerful and haunting lyric, sung with force and passion. The title, in the 1820s or 1830s, called for no explanation: 'He is not dead'. Or so they would convince themselves as they fantasised about their Emperor's return:

> We soldiers know, that from his jailer-band
> A ship at midnight carried him away;
> Since then, disguised, through his beloved land
> He wanders, lonely, hunted, day by day.
> That weary horseman, with his furtive glance,
> That poacher, hiding in the woods his head,
> 'Tis he, perhaps; he comes to rescue France!
> It is not true, oh God! He is not dead![28]

Where song sheets helped politicise workers in the towns, others consumed the Napoleonic legend in visual form, through popular woodcuts and *images d'Epinal*, the brightly coloured images that were so popular in the French countryside during the first half of the nineteenth century. The first images, produced in the Vosges by the workshop of Jean-Charles Pellerin, had dealt primarily with religious subject matter, pictures of saints and scenes from the Bible, along with moral tales about human behaviour. By the early nineteenth century these had become part of popular culture, sold at markets and country fairs to a largely peasant audience. And their range had increased exponentially, however much they relied on a staple of traditional themes and well-worn visual clichés like *The Ages of Man* and *The Wandering Jew*. Pellerin was an admirer of Napoleon and, with his team of artists and engravers, devoted great energy after the 1830 revolution to popularising images of the Empire. Those of François Georgin are probably the best-known: a series of detailed battle scenes that evoked all the glory of the imperial armies, from the Battle of the Pyramids during the Egyptian Campaign through to the touching moment when Napoleon took his final leave of the army at Fontainebleau. There were more than forty in all, produced in large format and offering a memorable tribute in pictures to the Grande Armée. They represented good business for Pellerin, too, as they sold in huge numbers across the country and were reprinted many times in the course of the century. In the countryside especially, they had an important role in spreading the imperial myth.[29]

After 1830 the cult of the Emperor became more open and respectable; it was no longer something that had to be practised in secret, concealed from the authorities. His former soldiers now spoke openly of their affection for him, in cafés and *cercles* and in those places where old soldiers met to reminisce. He was spoken of with awe as well as affection, the awe that soldiers have for a great leader, but one whom they considered as one of their own. He had brought them victory, respect and glory, and had rewarded them with medals and battle honours. He had led them to the end of Europe, to the ends of the world as they knew it, and had opened their eyes to different cultures and exotic civilisations. It had been – as they saw it twenty years later – a wonderful adventure, a moment when they had been present at the making of history. Even the fact that it had ended in defeat and disappointment, and that Napoleon had lived out his final years in solitary exile, added to the poignancy of his legend, turning their Emperor into yet another of those tragic heroes of war the French treasure so much – a hero undone by his enemies, badly treated by his captors, and left to rot and die in the dank wilderness of Saint Helena. Defeat, in other words, became part of his legend, a necessary ingredient in a romantic hero, and one that placed him – as it would in the school textbooks of the Third Republic – in the exalted company of those other French heroes and heroines of war, Roland, Duguesclin, Bayard and Joan of Arc.[30] In the paintings of the period these comparisons were often made quite explicitly, as in Delacroix's great canvas on the death of Charles the Bold before the walls of Nancy, a work that hinted at the dangers of vaulting ambition and was seen by many as a direct reference to Napoleon's own career.[31]

With the fall of Charles X in 1830, the government no longer lived in fear of the Emperor's legacy, and a new generation of political leaders competed for the honour of appealing to his memory. They actively sought to share in the public esteem that flowed from associations with the First Empire, going to ever-greater lengths to link the memory of the Empire to their current political cause. Following the 1830 revolution the Bourbon monarchy had finally ended, and power passed to the Orléans line and to the 'bourgeois monarchy' of Louis-Philippe. The new king had reached adulthood around the outbreak of the French Revolution, in which his father had briefly become a popular hero before being arrested and guillotined under the Terror. The son, however, did not break with the Revolution, serving bravely as an officer in the republican armies, which allowed him to appear in later years as a man of compromise who could, perhaps uniquely, unite warring factions and avoid unnecessary bloodshed after 1830.[32]

Louis-Philippe was well aware of the power of Napoleonic symbolism, and he did not hesitate to cultivate the notion that he was the real heir to the imperial tradition. At his coronation in 1831 he was ostentatiously surrounded by four Napoleonic marshals; in 1833 he approved the placing of Seurre's iconic statue of Napoleon atop the Vendôme Column, a permanent reminder to Parisians of the man who had once been their Emperor; in 1836 he inaugurated the Arc de Triomphe at the top of the Champs-Elysées to honour the memory of the Napoleonic legions; and in 1837 he admitted Napoleon to his cultural showpiece, the Museum of the History of France at Versailles.[33] Even in death, it seemed, Napoleon continued to exercise as much influence and fascination over the French people – civilians and old soldiers alike – as he had during his lifetime. The huge and expectant crowds that lined the banks of the Seine in 1840 to welcome their Emperor home bore eloquent testimony to the awe and affection that he still commanded two decades after his death.

His reputation as a strategist and battlefield technician also seemed secure, with public and professional memory focusing on his victories rather than his downfall. It is interesting to look, for instance, at the course programmes at the French military academy at Saint-Cyr during the 1880s and 1890s, a time when the new republican government felt vulnerable to outside attack. Despite the intensely republican ethos of the school, and the widespread belief that France's debacle in the Franco-Prussian War of 1870 – when an army widely believed to be the best in Europe had been utterly overwhelmed by the Prussians in only a few weeks, leading to an ignominious surrender at Sedan and the collapse of the regime – had been caused by the abandonment of mass conscription in the course of the nineteenth century, it is interesting that the French revolutionary armies were presented more as a lesson in civic responsibility and public morality than as a tactical exemplar. Valmy was seen as a clarion call to arms, not as a model of battlefield tactics, and in the course on military history taught on the eve of the First World War, the royal army of the eighteenth century, pre-revolutionary tactics and the campaigns of the French Revolution were each dismissed in a single lesson. A fourth lesson was devoted to the transformation of the army in Italy by Bonaparte; then a further ten sessions were devoted to Napoleon's campaigns.[34] The professional perception was clear – that here was a great French general, from whose tactics and approach to war there was still much to be learned. If he was finally overwhelmed by superior numbers, he still had his place with the great generals of history, among whom they counted Alexander the Great from the Ancient world and Frederick the Great from their own.

That is also, largely, how the public sees him, even today; and how the history of the Empire continues to be presented in art, in the galleries of the Louvre or in the Great Gallery at Versailles.[35] Of course there is a tendency in any country to celebrate victories rather than bemoan defeats, especially in history painting, so this imbalance may not seem so surprising. But though Napoleon was defeated at Waterloo, it is interesting to reflect on how that battle-field is presented to the visitor today, and on what it is that the tourists who flock there want and expect to see. Neither Wellington nor Blücher is really the main attraction. The Butte, the mound constructed in 1826 to commemorate the battle with the Lion of Waterloo at its summit, and to some degree also the museum and visitor centre on the battlefield, are dedicated principally to the memory of the French, and of the Great Man whose imperial adventure ended there. The classic Belgian travel guide by Fierens-Gevaert expresses this admirably: 'There is no place more suited to dreaming of the majesty of Napoleon, to evoking the legendary grandeur of his reign, to appreciating with a look into the past the epic task of his soldiers, than the summit of this triangular tomb raised on the corpse of imperial heroism. I have seen many visi-tors, scorning their guides, sunk in prolonged contemplation of the mighty battlefield. Rarely have they turned towards Waterloo and the heights occupied by Wellington; almost always, their eyes were fixed on the bluish haze of the horizon where the imperial glory finally faded.' For the museum and its visitors, as for Euro-pean memory more generally, Waterloo was about Napoleon, his defeat, and the beginning of his myth.[36]

And so it remains for our own times, and not only for France. Just as Napoleon remained one of the towering influences in nineteenth-century literature, so he would be translated into the mass media of the twentieth, and especially to cinema, as a tragic hero and a giant on the European stage. Since the great silent movie by Abel Gance in the 1920s, through to modern French cinema and Holly-wood, the Emperor has continued to fascinate and confound audi-ences across the globe. The Napoleonic Wars featured in many of the films produced in Europe between the two world wars, when parallels could readily be drawn between the Napoleonic Empire and the problems of the present. In this period no fewer than fifty-five films on the subject were made in Germany, considerably more than in either France or Britain. All nations drew on the period to glorify their national histories, with Napoleon presented either as the hero of the nation or as the greatest threat to liberty and national identity. Audiences in France, for instance, enjoyed literary films about Napoleon and glorified accounts of veterans of the *Grande Armée*. But Germany was a case apart, a country becalmed by political and societal crisis, and here the Wars of Liberation against Napoleon became critical points of reference. As the contemporary film historian Oskar Kalbus explained, one reason for this interest lies in the uncertainties of life under the Weimar Republic and the Third Reich, as a result of which 'sentiment is more receptive to the great epochs of history and their men'. The entry of Napoleon on to the European stage, with the destruction and reconstruction it caused, was one such 'great epoch of history'.[37]

Napoleon also left a significant political legacy that continued to resonate in France and would inspire popular insurrections abroad, especially in Central and Latin America. Bonapartism remained a strong political tradition in France, one that was revived not only (and most obviously) by Napoleon III but also, in different ways, by General Boulanger in the 1880s and by Philippe Pétain and Charles de Gaulle in the twentieth century. The idea of linking strong personal authority to popular support, to a leader thrown up by the people, who would rule without constant interference from intermediary bodies or elected politicians, became an accepted, if for many rather threatening, theme in modern French politics.[38] If the July Monarchy was tempted to play on Napoleon's memory in order to curry favour with the electorate, it was playing with fire. In 1848, elections were held for the presidency of the newly declared Second Republic, elections which for the first time involved universal manhood suffrage. The result was staggering. The popular appeal of Louis-Napoleon Bonaparte – the appeal inherent in his great-uncle's name – was so great that the other candidates were swept aside, and he was elected by a substantial majority. Three years later, in 1851, he would imitate the great Napoleon by staging his own coup d'état, overthrowing the Republic to declare a second empire.

But there the parallel stops. Louis-Napoleon had none of the incisiveness of the first Emperor, no clear vision of the policies he wished to pursue. He had little of the personal charisma, either, that had contributed so much to Napoleon's success. A coup that was derided by Karl Marx as the 'Eighteenth Brumaire of Louis Bonaparte' did not herald a return to international glory, as Louis-Napoleon's supporters had hoped. Republicans were horrified to be robbed of the political gains they had fought so hard to achieve, and across France people took up arms, proclaiming revolutionary commissions in over a hundred communes and clashing violently, sometimes bloodily, with troops and gendarmes. Repression followed, and, if exception is made for Paris, it resulted in the most ruthless political purge between the Jacobin Terror of 1794 and the Resistance movement during the Second World War.[39] There would be no triumphant second coming in 1851. If history did repeat itself, as Marx inferred, it repeated itself as farce.[40]

Notes

1: PARIS, 1840

1. Jean Tulard, 'Le Retour des Cendres', in Pierre Nora (ed.), *Les lieux de mémoire*, part II: *La Nation*, vol. 3 (Paris, 1986), p. 103.
2. Jean Boisson, *Le Retour des Cendres* (Paris, 1973), pp. 11–13.
3. André Desfeuilles, *Autour d'un centenaire manqué* (Paris, 1950), p. 3.
4. Charles de Rémusat, quoted in Michael Paul Driskel, *As Befits a Legend. Building a Tomb for Napoleon, 1840–61* (Kent, Ohio, 1993), p. 56.
5. Jean-Marcel Humbert (ed.), *Napoléon aux Invalides. 1840, Le Retour des Cendres* (Paris, 1990), pp. 11–12.
6. Driskel, *As Befits a Legend*, pp. 1–2.
7. Todd Porterfield, 'Staging the future', in Todd Porterfield and Susan L. Siegfried, *Staging Empire. Napoleon, Ingres and David* (University Park, Pennsylvania, 2006), p. 185.
8. Decree of Louis-Philippe, 10 June 1840.
9. Adolphe Thiers, quoted in Gilbert Martineau, *Le Retour des Cendres* (Paris 1990), p. 88.
10. François Guizot, quoted in Martineau, *Retour*, p. 88.

11. Lord Palmerston, quoted in Martineau, *Retour*, p. 89.

12. Fernand Beaucour, *Le Retour des Cendres de Napoléon: ses causes et sa portée politique* (Paris, 1991), p. 9.

13. Martineau, *Retour*, p. 107.

14. Marie-Françoise Huyghues des Etages, 'L'expédition maritime et fluviale', in Humbert (ed.), *Napoléon aux Invalides*, p. 33.

15. Boisson, *Retour des Cendres*, p. 14.

16. Rémi-Julien Guillard, *Retour des Cendres de Napoléon. Procès-verbal d'exhumation des restes de l'empereur Napoléon* (Paris, 1841), pp. 1–2.

17. Ibid., p. 3.

18. Martineau, *Retour*, p. 125.

19. Boisson, *Retour des Cendres*, p. 326.

20. Georges Poisson, *L'aventure du Retour des Cendres* (Paris, 2004), p. 231.

21. Boisson, *Retour des Cendres*, p. 397.

22. André-Jean Tudesq, 'Le reflet donné par la presse', in Humbert (ed.), *Napoléon aux Invalides*, p. 88.

23. Françoise Waquet, *Les fêtes royales sous la Restauration* (Paris, 1981), p. 78.

24. I owe this description, and much of the detail of the procession that follows, to Jean-Marcel Humbert, 'Le parcours parisien et son décor', in Humbert (ed.), *Napoléon aux Invalides*, pp. 49–70.

25. Ibid., pp. 52–53.

26. Ibid., p. 71.

27. Boisson, *Retour des Cendres*, p. 430.

28. Ibid., pp. 448–49.

29. Jérémie Benoît, Agnès Delannoy and Alain Pougetoux, *Napoléon.*

Le Retour des Cendres, 1840–1990 (Courbevoie, 1990), p. 143.

30. Ibid., pp. 144–48.
31. Ibid., pp. 132–34.

2: CORSICAN BEGINNINGS

1. Stephen Wilson, *Feuding, Conflict and Banditry in Nineteenth-Century Corsica* (Cambridge, 1988), pp. 14–15.
2. Ibid., p. 91.
3. Ibid., p. 16.
4. Thadd E. Hall, *France and the Eighteenth-century Corsican Question* (New York, 1971), passim.
5. Ibid., p. 102.
6. Antoine-Marie Graziani, *Pascal Paoli* (Paris, 2004), pp. 103–11.
7. Michel Vergé-Franceschi, *Napoléon, une enfance corse* (Paris, 2009), p. 87.
8. William Doyle, *Aristocracy and its Enemies in the Age of Revolution* (Oxford, 2009), pp. 56–57.
9. Luigi Mascilli Migliorini, *Napoléon* (Paris, 2004), pp. 21–22
10. Doyle, *Aristocracy*, p. 224.
11. Jean Defranceschi, 'Charles Bonaparte', in Jean Tulard (ed.). *Dictionnaire Napoléon* (2 vols, Paris, 1999), vol. 1, p. 273.
12. Louis Madelin, *La jeunesse de Bonaparte* (Paris, 1937), p. 36.
13. Steven Englund, *Napoleon. A Political Life* (New York, 2004), pp. 24–25.
14. Arthur Chuquet, *La jeunesse de Napoléon* (Paris, 1897), p. 45.
15. Pierre Branda, *Le prix de la gloire. Napoléon et l'argent* (Paris, 2007), p. 18.

16. Joseph Valynseele, 'Bonaparte, généalogie', in Tulard (ed.), *Dictionnaire Napoléon*, vol. 1, p. 258.

17. Eric Le Nabour, *Letizia Bonaparte. La mère exemplaire de Napoléon Ier* (Paris, 2003), pp. 36–37.

18. Jean and Nicole Dhombres, *Lazare Carnot* (Paris, 1997), pp. 225–28.

19. James Marshall-Cornwall, *Napoleon as Military Commander* (London, 1967), p. 15.

20. Christian Amalvi, *Les héros de l'histoire de France* (Toulouse, 2001), p. 69.

21. Christian Amalvi, *Les héros de l'histoire de France* (Toulouse, 2001), p. 69.

22. James Boswell, *État de la Corse* (Paris, 1769), reprinted Marseille, 1977.

23. Bonaparte, *Correspondance générale*, vol. 1, p. 51.

24. Napoléon Bonaparte, 'Sur la Corse', in *Oeuvres littéraires et écrits militaires*, ed. Jean Tulard (3 vols, Paris, 2001), vol. 1, p. 42.

25. Madelin, *La jeunesse de Napoléon*, pp. 49–50.

26. Marshall-Cornwall, *Napoleon as Military Commander*, p. 16.

27. Napoléon Bonaparte, *Correspondance générale*, edited by Thierry Lentz, vol. 1: *Les apprentissages, 1784–97* (Paris, 2004), pp. 1339–45.

28. Antoine Casanova, *Napoléon et la pensée de son temps: une histoire intellectuelle singulière* (Paris, 2000), p. 28.

29. Philip Dwyer, *Napoleon. The Path to Power, 1769–1799* (London, 2007), p. 46.

30. Napoléon Bonaparte, 'Défense de Rousseau', in *Oeuvres littéraires et écrits militaires*, ed. Jean Tulard (3 vols, Paris, 2001), vol. 1, p. 52.

31. Cited in Englund, *Napoleon*, p. 30.

32. Nada Tomiche, *Napoléon écrivain* (Paris, 1952), p. 209.

33. Napoléon Bonaparte, *Souper de Beaucaire*, texte présenté par Jacques Bainville (Paris, 1930).

34. Annie Jourdan, *Napoléon, héros, imperator, mécène* (Paris, 1998), p. 59.

3 SON OF THE REVOLUTION

1. James Marshall-Cornwall, *Napoleon as Military Commander*, p. 18.

2. Ibid., p. 19.

3. Napoléon Bonaparte, letter to Joseph Bonaparte, 22 July 1789, *Correspondance générale*, vol. 1, pp. 78–79.

4. Napoléon Bonaparte, letter to Joseph Bonaparte, 9 August 1789, *Correspondance générale*, vol. 1, p. 81.

5. Napoléon Bonaparte, letter to Pascal Paoli, 12 June 1789, *Correspondance générale*, vol. 1, p. 76.

6. Antoine Casanova et Ange Rovere, *La Révolution française en Corse* (Toulouse, 1989), pp. 118–22.

7. Steven Englund, *Napoleon*, pp. 43–44.

8. Napoléon Bonaparte, 'Lettre à Matteo Buttafuoco', in *Oeuvres littéraires* (3 vols, Paris, 1888), vol. 1, p. 154.

9. Luigi Mascilli Migliorini, *Napoléon* (Paris, 2006), p. 49.

10. Archives Nationales, D-IVbis 6, Comité de Division, Corsica; decree of National Assembly on the division of France into departments, 9 December 1789.

11. Philip Dwyer, *Napoleon. The Path to Power, 1769–1799* (London, 2007), p. 128.

12. Jean Tulard, *Napoléon et la noblesse d'Empire* (Paris, 1979), pp. 17–18.

13. Napoléon Bonaparte, letter to Joseph Bonaparte, 22 June 1792, *Correspondance générale*, vol. 1, p. 113.

14. Migliorini, *Napoléon*, p. 58.

15. Samuel F. Scott, *The Response of the Royal Army to the French Revolution* (Oxford, 1978), p. 109.

16. Alan Forrest, *The Soldiers of the French Revolution* (Durham, North Carolina, 1990), pp. 15–25.

17. David A. Bell, *The First Total War. Napoleon's Europe and the Birth of Warfare as We Know It* (London, 2007).

18. Pascal Dupuy and Claude Mazauric, *La Révolution française. Regards d'auteurs* (Paris, 2005), pp. 173–81.

19. John A. Lynn, 'Towards an Army of Honor: The Moral Evolution of the French Army, 1789–1815', *French Historical Studies* 16 (1989), pp. 152–73.

20. J. David Markham, 'The Early Years and First Commands', in Philip Haythornthwaite *et al.*, *Napoleon: The Final Verdict* (London, 1996), p. 22.

21. Jean-Pierre Bois, *Dumouriez, héros et proscrit* (Paris, 2005), pp. 324–29.

22. Napoléon Bonaparte, *Souper de Beaucaire* (Paris, 1930), p. 44.

23. Bernard Ireland, *The Fall of Toulon. The Last Opportunity to Defeat the French Revolution* (London, 2005), pp. 301–02.

24. Spenser Wilkinson, *The Rise of General Bonaparte* (Oxford, 1930), pp. 19–26.

25. Dwyer, *Napoleon. The Path to Power*, p. 144.

26. Napoléon Bonaparte, letter to deputies Albitte, Ricord and Saliceti, 12 August 1794, *Correspondance générale*, vol. 1, p. 198.

27. Markham, 'The Early Years and First Commands', pp. 27–28.

28. Bronislaw Baczko, *Comment sortir de la Terreur. Thermidor et la*

Révolution (Paris, 1989), chapter 2, 'La fin de l'an II'.

29. 'Paul-François-Jean-Nicolas Barras', in Alfred Fierro, André Palluel-Guillard and Jean Tulard (eds), *Histoire et Dictionnaire du Consulat et de l'Empire* (Paris, 1995), p. 522.

30. 'Chronologie, 1795', in Napoléon Bonaparte, *Correspondance générale*, vol. 1, p. 1352.

31. Englund, *Napoleon*, pp. 74–77.

32. Matthew Shaw, 'Reactions to the French Republican Calendar', *French History* 15 (2001), pp. 4–25; James Friguglietti, 'Gilbert Romme and the making of the French Republican Calendar', in D.G. Troyansky, A. Cismaru and N. Andrews jnr (eds), *The French Revolution in Culture and Society* (Westport, Connecticut, 1991), pp. 13–22.

33. George Rudé, *The Crowd in the French Revolution* (Oxford, 1959), pp. 176–77.

34. Englund, *Napoleon*, pp. 83–87.

35. 'Joséphine (Marie-Joseph-Rose de Tascher de la Pagerie)', in Jean Tulard (ed.), *Dictionnaire Napoléon*, vol. 2, p. 86.

36. Christopher Hibbert, *Napoleon. His Wives and Women* (New York, 2002), pp. 10–14

37. Several editions have appeared of Napoleon's love letters to Josephine. Among the more recent is Jean Tulard (ed.), *Napoléon. Lettres d'amour à Joséphine* (Paris, 1981).

38. Frank McLynn, *Napoleon. A Biography* (New York, 1997),

39. Geoffrey Ellis, *Napoleon* (London, 1997), pp. 26–27.

4: BONAPARTE IN ITALY

1. Emmanuel de Las Cases, *Le Mémorial de Sainte-Hélène*, Marcel Dunan, ed. (Paris, 1951), pp. 117–18.

[2.] Geoffrey Ellis, *Napoleon*, pp. 22–23.

[3.] Napoléon Bonaparte, letter to Joseph Bonaparte, 20 October 1795, *Correspondance générale*, vol. 1, p. 271.

[4.] Napoléon Bonaparte, letter to Joseph Bonaparte, 1 November 1795, *Correspondance générale*, vol. 1, p. 273.

[5.] Steven Englund, *Napoleon*, p. 198.

[6.] Luigi Mascilli Migliorini, *Napoléon*, p. 86.

[7.] Jean-Paul Bertaud, *La Révolution armée. Les soldats-citoyens de la Révolution Française* (Paris, 1979), pp. 174–76.

[8.] Englund, *Napoleon*, pp. 99–100.

[9.] Alan Forrest, *The Soldiers of the French Revolution*, pp. 126–44.

[10.] Martin Boycott-Brown, *The Road to Rivoli. Napoleon's First Campaign* (London, 2001), p. 44.

[11.] Napoléon Bonaparte, letter to Chauvet, *commissaire ordonnateur en chef*, in Genoa, 27 March 1796, *Correspondance générale*, vol. 1, p. 301.

[12.] Philip Dwyer, *Napoleon: The Path to Power, 1769–1799* (London, 2007), pp. 200–01.

[13.] Jean Thiry, *Bonaparte en Italie, 1796–1797* (Paris, 1973), p. 351.

[14.] Spenser Wilkinson, *The Rise of General Bonaparte* (Oxford, 1930), p. 80.

[15.] Englund, *Napoleon*, p. 100.

[16.] Napoléon Bonaparte, *Oeuvres littéraires et écrits militaires*, ed. Jean Tulard (Paris, 2001), vol. 3, p. 109.

[17.] A full account of Napoleon's military campaign in Italy can be found in Alan Schom, *Napoleon Bonaparte* (New York, 1997), pp. 43–60.

[18.] Jean Tulard, *Napoléon. Les grands moments d'un destin* (Paris, 2006), p. 97.

19. Wilkinson, *The Rise of General Bonaparte*, p. 142.

20. Robert B. Holtman, *Napoleonic Propaganda* (Baton Rouge, Louisiana, 1950), pp. 244–45.

21. Marc Martin, 'Journaux d'armées au temps de la Convention', *Annales historiques de la Révolution française* 44 (1972), pp. 567–605.

22. Dwyer, *Napoleon: The Path to Power*, pp. 306–08.

23. Philip G. Dwyer, 'Napoleon Bonaparte as Hero and Saviour. Image, Rhetoric and Behaviour in the Construction of a Legend', *French History* 18 (2004), p. 386.

24. Jean-Paul Bertaud, *Guerre et société en France de Louis XIV à Napoléon Ier* (Paris, 1998), p. 147.

25. Nada Tomiche, *Napoléon écrivain* (Paris, 1952), p. 206.

26. Alan Forrest, 'Propaganda and the Legitimation of Power in Napoleonic France', *French History* 18 (2004), p. 433.

27. Jeremy D. Popkin, *The Right-Wing Press in France, 1792–1800* (Chapel Hill, North Carolina, 1980), p. 22.

28. Wayne Hanley, *The Genesis of Napoleonic Propaganda, 1796 to 1799* (New York, 2005), pp. 48–49.

29. *Journal de Bonaparte et des hommes vertueux*, issue 1, 18 February 1797.

30. Ibid., issue 8, 27 February 1797.

31. Jean-Yves Leclercq, 'Le mythe de Bonaparte sous le Directoire, 1796–1799' (*mémoire de maîtrise*, Université de Paris-I, 1991), p. 162.

32. Dwyer, *Napoleon: The Path to Power*, p. 319.

33. David O'Brien, *After the Revolution: Antoine-Jean Gros, Painting and Propaganda under Napoleon* (University Park, Pennsylvania, 2006), p. 39.

34. Hanley, *The Genesis of Napoleonic Propaganda*, p. 132.

35. Dwyer, *Napoleon: The Path to Power*, pp. 471–72.

5: LURE OF THE ORIENT

[1.] Napoléon Bonaparte, *Correspondance générale*, vol. 2 – *La campagne d'Egypte et l'Avènement* (Paris, 2005), p. 38.

[2.] Yves Laissus, *Description de l'Egypte. Une aventure humaine et éditoriale* (Paris, 2009), p. 7.

[3.] Philip G. Dwyer, *Napoleon. The Path to Power, 1769–99* p. 30.

[4.] Louis-Antoine Fauvelet de Bourrienne, *Mémoires de M. de Bourrienne, ministre d'état, sur Napoléon*, vol. 2 (Paris, 1831), p. 226.

[5.] Robin Harris, *Talleyrand. Betrayer and Saviour of France* (London, 2007), p. 99.

[6.] Emmanuel de Waresquiel, *Talleyrand, le prince immobile* (Paris, 2003), p. 243.

[7.] Vivant Denon, *Voyage dans la Basse et la Haute Egypte pendant les campagnes du général Bonaparte*, with introduction by Raoul Brunon (Paris, 1990), p. 57.

[8.] Jean-Marcel Humbert, 'Introduction', in *Bonaparte et l'Egypte: feu et lumières*, exhibition catalogue (Paris, 2008), pp. 40–43.

[9.] Steven Englund, *Napoleon. A Political Life*, p. 127.

[10.] A full list of the books Napoleon took with him to Egypt can be found in Luigi Mascilli Migliorini, *Napoléon* (Paris, 2006), p. 149.

[11.] Jean-Paul Bertaud, *Choderlos de Laclos* (Paris, 2003), pp. 512–13.

[12.] Frank McLynn, *Napoleon: A Biography* (New York, 1997), p. 161.

[13.] Englund, *Napoleon*, p. 127.

[14.] Luigi Mascilli Migliorini, *Napoléon*, p. 150.

[15.] Bonaparte, *Correspondance générale*, vol. 2, p. 311.

[16.] Henry Laurens (ed.), *L'Expédition d'Egypte, 1798–1801* (Paris, 1989), pp. 30–32.

[17.] Dwyer, *Napoleon. The Path to Power, 1769–99*, p. 343.

18. Timothy Wilson-Smith, *Napoleon and his Artists* (London, 1996), p. 75.

19. Englund, *Napoleon*, pp. 127–28.

20. Edward Said, *Orientalism* (New York, 1978); see Juan Cole, *Napoleon's Egypt. Invading the Middle East* (New York, 2007), p. 246.

21. Robert Asprey, *The Rise and Fall of Napoleon Bonaparte* (2 vols, New York, 2000), vol. 1, *The Rise*, pp. 310–12.

22. Jean-Yves Leclercq, 'Le mythe de Bonaparte sous le Directoire, 1796–99' (mémoire de maîtrise, Université de Paris-I, 1991), pp. 82–85.

23. Alan Forrest, 'Propaganda and the Legitimation of Power in Napoleonic France', *French History* 18 (2004), p. 433.

24. Frédéric Régent, 'L'expédition d'Egypte de Bonaparte vue par la presse parisienne, 1798–99' (*mémoire de maîtrise*, Université de Paris-I, 1992), p. 40. The quotation is from *La Décade philosophique*.

25. Wilson-Smith, *Napoleon and his Artists*, p. 79.

26. David O'Brien, *After the Revolution: Antoine-Jean Gros, Painting and Propaganda under Napoleon* (University Park, Pennsylvania, 2006), pp. 131, 136.

27. Ibid., pp. 90–91.

28. Laissus, *Description de l'Egypte. Une aventure humaine et éditoriale*, pp. 25–27.

29. Régent, 'L'expédition d'Egypte de Bonaparte', p. 42.

30. Nelly Hanna, 'Ottoman Egypt and the French Expedition: Some Long-term Trends', in Irene A. Bierman (ed.), *Napoleon in Egypt* (Reading, 2003), p. 11.

31. Jean-Paul Bertaud, 'Kléber, Jean-Baptiste', in Tulard (ed.), *Dictionnaire Napoléon*, vol. 2, pp. 116–17.

32. Jean-Edouard Goby, 'Menou, Jacques-François de Boussay, baron de', in Tulard (ed.), *Dictionnaire Napoléon*, vol. 2, pp. 301–03.

33. Englund, *Napoleon*, pp. 139–40.

34. Cole, *Napoleon's Egypt*, p. 245.

6: FIRST CONSUL

1. Napoléon Bonaparte, *Correspondance générale*, vol. 2 – *La campagne d'Egypte et l'Avènement*, p. 1088.

2. Philip Dwyer, *Napoleon: The Path to Power, 1769–1799* p. 444.

3. Juan Cole, *Napoleon's Egypt. Invading the Middle East* p. 244.

4. Jacques Bainville, *Napoléon* (Paris, 1931; nouvelle édition avec préface de Patrice Gueniffey, Paris, 2005), p. 129.

5. Bonaparte, *Correspondance générale, vol. 2*, p. 1089.

6. Steven Englund, *Napoleon. A Political Life*, p. 153.

7. Jean Tulard, *Napoleon: The Myth of the Saviour* (London, 1984).

8. Ibid., p. 70–71.

9. Bonaparte, *Correspondance générale*, vol. 2, pp. 1089–90.

10. Patrice Gueniffey, *Le dix-huit Brumaire : l'épilogue de la Révolution française* (Paris, 2008), pp. 160–61.

11. Bronislaw Baczko, 'Une passion thermidorienne: la revanche', in *Politiques de la Révolution Française* (Paris, 2008), pp. 165–338.

12. Bernard Gainot, *1799, un nouveau jacobinisme?* (Paris, 2001), p. 268.

13. Isser Woloch, *Jacobin Legacy: The Democratic Movement under the Directory* (Princeton, New Jersey, 1970), pp. 134–36.

14. Joseph Fouché, *Mémoires*, ed. Michel Vovelle (Paris, 1992), p. 93.

15. Germaine de Staël, *Considérations sur la Révolution française*

(2 vols, Paris, 1818), vol. 2, p. 4 ; the translation is taken from Malcolm Crook, *Napoleon Comes to Power. Democracy and Dictatorship in Revolutionary France, 1795–1804* (Cardiff, 1998), pp. 100–01.

16. Jean Tulard, *Le 18 Brumaire. Comment terminer une révolution* (Paris, 1999), pp. 9–10, 13–29.

17. D.J. Goodspeed, *Bayonets at Saint-Cloud: The Story of the 18th Brumaire* (London, 1965), p. 107.

18. Crook, *Napoleon Comes to Power*, pp. 1–3.

19. Jean-Luc Suissa, 'Lucien Bonaparte', in Jean Tulard (ed.), *Dictionnaire Napoléon*, vol. 2, p. 227.

20. Jacques-Olivier Boudon, *Histoire du Consulat et de l'Empire* (Paris, 2000), p. 457.

21. Ibid., p. 46.

22. Gueniffey, *Le dix-huit Brumaire*, p. 308.

23. Albert Vandal, *L'Avènement de Bonaparte*, vol. 1 – *La genèse du Consulat, Brumaire et la Constitution de l'an VIII* (Paris, 1902), pp. 408–09.

24. Thierry Lentz, *Le Grand Consulat, 1799–1804* (Paris, 1999), p. 151.

25. Jeffrey Kaplow, *Elbeuf during the Revolutionary Period: History and Social Structure* (Baltimore, Maryland, 1964), pp. 254–55.

26. François Furet, *La Révolution, 1 – 1770–1814* (Paris, 1988), p. 383.

27. Lentz, *Le Grand Consulat*, p. 74.

28. Quoted in Martyn Lyons, *France under the Directory* (Cambridge, 1975), p. 233.

29. Quoted in Crook, *Napoleon Comes to Power*, p. 117.

30. Jean Tulard, *Napoleon: The Myth of the Saviour*, pp. 86–87.

31. Irene Collins, *Napoleon and his Parliaments, 1800–1815* (London, 1979), p. 11.

[32] Crook, *Napoleon Comes to Power*, p. 66.

[33] Jean-Paul Bertaud, *La France de Napoléon, 1799–1815* (Paris, 1987), pp. 32–33.

[34] Lentz, *Le Grand Consulat*, pp. 118–19.

[35] Jacques-Olivier Boudon, 'L'incarnation de l'Etat de Brumaire à Floréal', in Jean-Pierre Jessenne (ed.), *Du Directoire au Consulat. 3: Brumaire dans l'histoire du lien politique et de l'Etat-Nation* (Rouen, 2001), pp. 333–34.

[36] Malcolm Crook, *Elections in the French Revolution* (Cambridge, 1996), pp. 190–91.

[37] Claude Langlois, 'Le plébiscite de l'an VII ou le coup d'état du 18 pluviôse an VIII', *Annales historiques de la Révolution française*, 1972.

[38] Michael Broers, 'Internal Conquest, 1799–1804: the Domestic History of the Consulate', in Vittorio Scotti Douglas (ed.), *L'Europa scopre Napoleone, 1793–1804* (2 vols, Alessandria, 1999), vol. 2, p. 1030.

[39] Howard Brown, *Ending the French Revolution: Violence, Justice and Repression From the Terror to Napoleon* (Charlottesville, Virginia, 2006), pp. 308–24.

[40] David Chandler, 'Adjusting the Record: Napoleon and Marengo', in Scotti Douglas (ed.), *L'Europa scopre Napoleone, 1793–1804*, vol. 2, p. 864.

[41] Clive Church, *Revolution and Red Tape: The French Ministerial Bureaucracy, 1770–1850* (Oxford, 1981), esp. pp. 145–74.

[42] Nicholas Richardson, *The French Prefectoral Corps, 1814–1830* (Cambridge, 1966), p.2.

[43] Annie Jourdan, *L'empire de Napoléon* (Paris, 2000), pp. 233–34.

[44] Georges Lefebvre, *Napoleon. From 18 Brumaire to Tilsit* (London, 1969), p. 152.

45. Jacques-Olivier Boudon, *L'épiscopat français à l'époque concordataire, 1802–1905* (Paris, 1996), pp. 11–14

46. Englund, *Napoleon*, pp. 180–85.

47. Claude Ducourtial, 'Introduction', to *Napoléon et la Légion d'honneur*, exhibition catalogue published as a special issue of *La Cohorte* (Paris, 1968), p. 3.

48. Pierre Branda and Thierry Lentz, *Napoléon, l'esclavage et les colonies* (Paris, 2006), p. 236.

49. Carolyn Fick, *The Making of Haiti: The Saint-Domingue Revolution from Below* (Knoxville, Tennessee, 1990), p. 236.

50. Yves Benot, *La démence coloniale sous Napoléon* (Paris, 1992), pp. 101–02.

51. Sylvain Pagé, *L'Amérique du Nord et Napoléon* (Paris, 2003), pp. 76–77.

52. Dwyer, *Napoleon*, pp. 506–07.

53. Christopher Hibbert, *Napoleon. His Wives and Women*, p. 106.

7: FROM CONSULATE TO EMPIRE

1. Isser Woloch, *Napoleon and his Collaborators: The Making of a Dictatorship* (New York, 2001), pp. 186–87.

2. Stuart Semmel, *Napoleon and the British* (New Haven, Connecticut, 2004), p. 20.

3. Ibid., p. 33.

4. Jean-Louis Halperin, 'Tribunat', in Jean Tulard (ed.), *Dictionnaire Napoléon* (2 vols, Paris, 1999), vol. 2, p. 873.

5. Woloch, *Napoleon and his Collaborators*, pp. 123–24.

6. Duff Cooper, *Talleyrand* (London, 1958), pp. 82–83.

7. Joseph Fouché, *The Memoirs of Joseph Fouché, Duke of Otranto, Minister of the General Police of France* (2 vols, London, 1896), vol. 1, p. 1.

8. Jean Tulard, *Figures d'Empire* (Paris, 2005), p. 631.

9. Martyn Lyons, *Napoleon Bonaparte and the Legacy of the French Revolution* (London, 1994), p. 118.

10. Jean Tulard, *Joseph Fouché* (Paris, 1998), p. 142.

11. Marcel Le Clère, 'Fouché', in Tulard (ed.), *Dictionnaire Napoléon*, vol.. 1, pp. 818–19.

12. Hubert Cole, *Fouché, the Unprincipled Patriot* (London, 1971), p. 121.

13. Howard G. Brown, *Ending the French Revolution: Violence, Justice and Repression from the Terror to Napoleon*, pp. 326–29.

14. Woloch, *Napoleon and his Collaborators*, pp. 66–79.

15. Thierry Lentz, *Le dix-huit Brumaire. Les coups d'état de Napoléon Bonaparte* (Paris, 1997), p. 411.

16. Elizabeth Sparrow, *Secret Service: British Agents in France, 1792–1815* (Woodbridge, 1999), p. 267.

17. Alan Schom, *Napoleon Bonaparte* (New York, 1997), pp. 273–81.

18. Thierry Lentz, *Le Grand Consulat, 1799–1804*, p. 537.

19. Jean-Paul Bertaud, *Le duc d'Enghien* (Paris, 2001), pp. 11–12.

20. Napoléon Bonaparte, *Correspondance générale*, vol. 4: *Ruptures et fondation, 1803–1804* (Paris, 2007), p. 648.

21. Lentz, *Le Grand Consulat*, p. 540.

22. Chateaubriand, *Mémoires d'outre-tombe*, quoted by Luigi Mascilli Migliorini, *Napoléon*, p. 236.

23. Comte de Las Cases, *Le mémorial de Sainte-Hélène*, edited by Marcel Dunan (2 vols, Paris, 1951), vol. 2, pp. 622–629.

24. Robert Asprey, *The Rise and Fall of Napoleon Bonaparte*, vol. 1, p. 344.

25. Antoine-Claire Thibaudeau, *Mémoires, 1799–1815* (Paris, 1913), pp. 70–71.

26. Jean-Jacques Cambacérès, *Mémoires inédits*, edited by Laurence Chatel de Brancion (2 vols, Paris, 1999), vol. 1, p. 633.

27. Malcolm Crook, 'Confiance d'en bas, manipulation d'en haut: la pratique plébiscitaire sous Napoléon, 1799–1815', in Philippe Bourdin, Jean-Claude Caron and Mathias Bernard (eds), *L'incident électoral de la Révolution Française à la Ve République* (Clermont-Ferrand, 2002), pp. 77–87.

28. Steven Englund, *Napoleon. A Political Life*, p. 219.

29. Thibaudeau, *Mémoires*, p. 69.

30. Napoleon's message to the Senate, 3 August 1802, in Malcolm Crook, *Napoleon Comes to Power*, p. 134.

31. Christopher Hibbert, *Napoleon, His Wives and Women*, p. 75.

32. Philip G. Dwyer, 'Napoleon Bonaparte as Hero and Saviour. Image, Rhetoric and Behaviour in the Construction of a Legend', *French History* 18 (2004), pp. 391–93.

33. Hibbert, *Napoleon, His Wives and Women*, p. 118.

34. William H.C. Smith, *The Bonapartes. The History of a Dynasty* (London, 2005), pp. 19–20.

35. Louis de Fontanes, *Parallèle entre César, Cromwell, Monk et Bonaparte, fragment traduit de l'anglais* (Paris, 1800).

36. Roger Barny, 'L'image de Cromwell dans la Révolution française', *Dix-huitième siècle* 25 (1993), pp. 387–97.

37. Annie Jourdan, 'La Hollande en tant qu'<objet de désir> et le Roi Louis, fondateur d'une monarchie nationale', in idem (ed.), *Louis Bonaparte, Roi de Hollande* (Paris, 2010), pp. 28–29.

38. Vincent Haegele, *Napoléon et Joseph Bonaparte. Le pouvoir et l'ambition* (Paris, 2010), pp. 73–74.

39. Ibid., p. 171.

40. Luigi Mascilli Migliorini, *Napoléon*, p. 233.

41. Archives Municipales de Nantes, I1–29, dossiers 18–20, 22.

42. Peter Burke, *The Fabrication of Louis XIV* (New Haven, Connecticut, 1992), pp. 71–83.

43. Thibaudeau, *Mémoires*, pp. 121–22.

44. Englund, *Napoleon*, p. 230.

45. Crook, *Napoleon Comes to Power*, p. 134.

46. Schom, *Napoleon Bonaparte*, pp. 336–41.

47. Lentz, *Le Grand Consulat*, pp. 568–69.

48. Schom, *Napoleon Bonaparte*, p. 336.

49. Ernest John Knapton, *Empress Josephine* (Cambridge, Mass., 1964), p. 227.

50. Sylvain Laveissière, *Le sacre de Napoléon peint par David* (Paris, 2004), p. 48.

51. Jean Tulard (ed.), *Napoléon: le Sacre* (Paris, 1993), p. xxxix.

52. Timothy Wilson-Smith, *Napoleon, Man of War, Man of Peace* (London, 2002), pp. 161–62.

53. E.E.Y. Hales, *Revolution and Papacy, 1769–1846* (London, 1960), pp. 165–66.

54. Ibid., p.159.

55. Laveissière, *Le sacre de Napoléon peint par David*, p. 50.

56. Proclamation of the Consuls to the French People of 15 December 1799, in John Hall Stewart, *A Documentary Survey of the French Revolution* (New York, 1951), p. 780.

57. Jean and Nicole Dhombres, *Lazare Carnot* (Paris, 1997), pp. 503–08.

8: QUEST FOR GLORY

1. Thierry Lentz, *Le Grand Consulat, 1799–1804* (Paris, 1999), p. 298.
2. Christopher D. Hall, *British Strategy in the Napoleonic War, 1803–15* (Manchester, 1992), p. 2.
3. See, for instance, Charles Esdaile, *The Wars of Napoleon* (London, 1995), esp. pp. 29–36.
4. Paul Schroeder, *The Transformation of European Politics, 1763–1848* (Oxford, 1994), pp. 235, 243.
5. Georges Lefebvre, *Napoleon. From 18 Brumaire to Tilsit* (London, 1969), p. 172.
6. Charles Esdaile, *The French Wars, 1792–1815* (London, 2001), p. 28.
7. Peter H. Wilson, 'The Meaning of Empire in Central Europe around 1800', in Alan Forrest and Peter H. Wilson (eds), *The Bee and the Eagle. Napoleonic France and the End of the Holy Roman Empire, 1806* (Basingstoke, 2009), p. 34.
8. See David Bell, *The First Total War* (New York, 2007); Jean-Yves Guiomar, *L'invention de la guerre totale, XVIIIe – XXe siècle* (Paris, 2004); Roger Chickering, 'A Tale of Two Tales: Grand Narratives of War in the Age of Revolution', in Roger B. Chickering and Stig Förster (eds), *War in an Age of Revolution, 1775–1815* (Cambridge, 2010), pp. 1–17.
9. Alan Forrest, Karen Hagemann and Jane Rendall (eds), *Soldiers, Citizens and Civilians. Experiences and Perceptions of the Revolutionary and Napoleonic Wars, 1790–1820* (Basingstoke, 2009), p. 2.
10. Robert Asprey, *The Rise and Fall of Napoleon Bonaparte*, vol. 1, pp. 481–87.

11. Jean-Paul Bertaud, Alan Forrest and Annie Jourdan (eds), *Napoléon, le monde et les Anglais. Guerre des mots et des images* (Paris, 2004), pp. 176–79.

12. Simon Burrows, 'The Struggle for European Opinion in the Napoleonic Wars: British Francophone Propaganda, 1803–1814', *French History* 11 (1997), pp. 41–53.

13. Simon Burrows, 'The War of Words: French and British propaganda in the Napoleonic Era', in David Cannadine (ed.), *Trafalgar in History: A Battle and its Afterlife* (Basingstoke, 2006), p. 51.

14. Louis Bergeron, *France under Napoleon* (Princeton, New Jersey, 1981), p. 64.

15. Fernand Beaucour, *Lettres, Décisions et Actes de Napoléon à Pont-de-Briques et au Camp de Boulogne* (Levallois, 1979).

16. Michael Duffy, 'British Diplomacy and the French Wars, 1789–1815', in H.T. Dickinson (ed.), *Britain and the French Revolution, 1789–1815* (London, 1989), pp. 139–41.

17. John D. Grainger, *The Amiens Truce: Britain and Bonaparte, 1801–03* (Woodbridge, 2004), pp. 180–81.

18. Roberto Conti, *Il Tesoro. Guida alla conoscenza del Tesoro del Duomo di Monza* (Monza, 1983), pp. 5–8; Alan Forrest, 'Napoleon as Monarch: A Political Evolution', in Alan Forrest and Peter H. Wilson (eds), *The Bee and the Eagle: Napoleonic France and the End of the Holy Roman Empire, 1806*, pp. 117–18.

19. Peter H. Wilson, 'The Meaning of Empire in Central Europe around 1800', ibid., pp. 22–41.

20. Esdaile, *The French Wars*, p. 33.

21. N.A.M. Rodger, 'The Significance of Trafalgar: Sea Power and Land Power in the Anglo-French Wars', in Cannadine (ed.),

Trafalgar in History: A Battle and its Afterlife, pp. 86–88.

22. Jay Luvass (ed.), *Napoleon on the Art of War* (New York, 1999), pp. 89–91.

23. Napoleon Bonaparte, *Proclamations, Ordres du Jour, Bulletins de la Grande Armée*, ed. Jean Tulard (Paris, 1964), pp. 45–46.

24. Jacques Garnier, *Austerlitz, 2 décembre 1805* (Paris, 2005), p. 403; Steven Englund, *Napoleon. A Political Life*, pp. 272–74.

25. Jacques Garnier, 'La bataille d'Austerlitz', in *Austerlitz. Napoléon au cœur de l'Europe*, ouvrage collectif, Musée de l'Armée (Paris, 2007), pp. 76–79.

26. The fullest recent discussion of the development of the battle is Jacques Garnier's study of *Austerlitz*, referred to above. For a succinct summary of the battle, see Charles Esdaile, *Napoleon's Wars: An International History, 1803–15*, pp. 226–28.

27. Michael Broers, *Europe under Napoleon, 1799–1815* (London, 1996), pp. 41–43.

28. Claus Telp, 'The Prussian Army in the Jena Campaign', in Forrest and Wilson (eds), *The Bee and the Eagle*, p. 166.

29. Sixty-fourth Bulletin, 2 March 1807, in J. David Markham, *Imperial Glory: The Bulletins of Napoleon's Grande Armée, 1805–1814* (London, 2003), p. 148.

30. Christopher Prendergast, *Napoleon and History Painting: Antoine-Jean Gros's La Bataille d'Eylau* (Oxford, 1997), pp. 1–19.

31. Pierre-François Percy, *Journal des campagnes du Baron Percy, chirurgien-en-chef de la Grande Armée* (Paris, 1904), p. 165.

32. Esdaile, *Napoleon's Wars: An International History, 1803–15*, pp. 295–99.

33. Napoleon Bonaparte, Fifteenth Bulletin, 22 October 1806, in Markham, *Imperial Glory*, p. 148.

34. Clive Emsley, *The Longman Companion to Napoleonic Europe* (London, 1993), p. 253.

35. Silvia Marzagalli, *Les boulevards de la fraude. Le négoce maritime et le Blocus continental, 1806–1813* (Villeneuve d'Ascq, 1999), p. 192.

36. Geoffrey Ellis, *Napoleon's Continental Blockade: The Case of Alsace* (Oxford, 1981), pp. 266–67.

37. Ibid., p. 271.

38. François Crouzet, 'La ruine du grand commerce', in François-Georges Pariset (ed.), *Bordeaux au dix-huitième siècle* (Bordeaux, 1968), pp. 500–02.

39. François Crouzet, 'Les origines du sous-développement économique du Sud-ouest', *Annales du Midi* 71 (1959), pp. 71–79.

40. Rory Muir, *Britain and the Defeat of Napoleon, 1807–1815* (New Haven, Connecticut, 1996), p. 6.

9: A VISION OF CIVIL SOCIETY

1. Louis Bergeron, *France under Napoleon* (Princeton, New Jersey, 1981), p. 64.

2. Emmanuel de Las Cases, *Mémorial de Sainte-Hélène*, vol. 1, pp. 1181–82 ; for comment see Robert Morrissey, *Napoléon et l'héritage de la gloire* (Paris, 2010), p. 172.

3. Louis-Antoine Fauvelet de Bourrienne, *Mémoires de M. de Bourrienne, ministre d'état, sur Napoléon* (10 vols, Paris, 1831), vol. 5, p. 32.

4. David P. Jordan, *The Revolutionary Career of Maximilien Robespierre* (New York, 1985), p. 86.

5. John A. Davis, *Conflict and Control. Law and Order in Nineteenth-Century Italy* (Basingstoke, 1988), p. 23.

6. Stuart Woolf, *Napoleon's Integration of Europe* (London, 1991), p. 21.

7. Ibid., p. 27.

8. Alexander Grab, *Napoleon and the Transformation of Europe* (Basingstoke, 2003), pp. 159–60.

9. Michael Rowe, 'Napoleon and State Formation in Central Europe', in Philip G. Dwyer (ed.), *Napoleon and Europe* (London, 2001), p. 209; Geoffrey Ellis, *The Napoleonic Empire* (Basingstoke, 2003), pp. 55–6.

10. Annie Jourdan (ed.), *Louis Bonaparte, Roi de Hollande* (Paris, 2010), pp. 423–24.

11. William Doyle, 'The Political Culture of the Napoleonic Empire', in Forrest and Wilson (eds), *The Bee and the Eagle*, p. 86.

12. *Précis de la vie politique de Théophile Berlier écrit par lui-même et adressé à ses enfants et petits-enfants* (Dijon, 1838), pp. 92–95, quoted in Isser Woloch, *Napoleon and his Collaborators. The Making of a Dictatorship*, p. 103.

13. Olivier Blanc, *Regnaud de Saint-Jean d'Angély. L'éminence grise de Napoléon* (Paris, 2002), pp. 67–72 ; Woloch, *Napoleon and his Collaborators*, p. 101.

14. Jean and Nicole Dhombres, *Lazare Carnot* (Paris, 1997), pp. 503–08.

15. Joseph Fouché, *Memoirs* (2 vols, London, 1896), vol. 1, p. 226.

16. Jean Tranié, *Napoléon et son entourage* (Paris, 2001), p. 83.

17. For the examples that follow, see Bergeron, *France under Napoleon*, pp. 73–79.

18. Nicole Gotteri, *Grands dignitaires, ministres et grands officiers du Premier Empire. Autographes et notices biographiques* (Paris, 1990), pp. 106–07.

19. Bergeron, *France under Napoleon*, p. 72.

20. Laurence Chatel de Brancion (ed.), *Cambacérès. Mémoires inédits* (2 vols, Paris, 1999), vol. 1, p. 714.

21. Nicholas Richardson, *The French Prefectoral Corps, 1814–1830* (Cambridge, 1966), p. 1.

22. Ellis, *The Napoleonic Empire*, p. 34.

23. Carla Hesse, *Publishing and Cultural Politics in Revolutionary Paris, 1789–1810* (Berkeley, California, 1991), pp. 235–36.

24. Steven Englund, *Napoleon*, pp. 309–11.

25. Martyn Lyons, *Napoleon Bonaparte and the Legacy of the French Revolution* (Basingstoke, 1994), pp. 96–102.

26. Annie Jourdan, 'La destinée tragique du "Bon Roi" Louis', in idem (ed.), *Louis Bonaparte, Roi de Hollande* (Paris, 2010), pp. 428–30.

27. Bergeron, *France under Napoleon*, p. 31.

28. Alan Forrest, *Conscripts and Deserters: The Army and French Society during the Revolution and Empire* (New York, 1989), pp. 219–37.

29. Michael Broers, *Napoleon's Other War: Bandits, Rebels and their Pursuers in the Age of Revolutions* (Oxford, 2010), pp. 81–83.

30. Michael Broers, *The Politics of Religion in Napoleonic Italy: The War against God* (London, 2002), pp. 188–89.

31. Michael Broers, *Napoleonic Imperialism and the Savoyard Monarchy, 1773–1821: State Building in Piedmont* (Lampeter, 1997), p. 276.

32. Michael Broers, *Europe under Napoleon* (London, 1996), pp. 180–82.

33. Grab, *Napoleon and the Transformation of Europe*, pp. 180–81.

34. John A. Davis, *Naples and Napoleon: Southern Italy and the European Revolutions, 1780–1860* (Cambridge, 2006), passim, esp. pp. 161–255, 259.

10: THE REINVENTION OF MONARCHY

[1.] Irene Collins, *Napoleon and his Parliaments, 1800–1815* (London, 1979), pp. 114–20.

[2.] Malcolm Crook, 'Confidence from Below? Collaboration and Resistance in the Napoleonic Plebiscites', in Michael Rowe (ed.), *Collaboration and Resistance in Napoleonic Europe: State-Formation in an Age of Upheaval, c. 1800–1815*, pp. 19–21.

[3.] Ibid., p. 34.

[4.] Jean Tulard (ed.), *Napoléon, Le Sacre* (Paris, 1993), pp. 59–60.

[5.] Thierry Lentz, *Le sacre de Napoléon* (Paris, 2004), p. 9.

[6.] This argument is more fully developed in Alan Forrest, 'Napoleon as Monarch: A Political Evolution', in Alan Forrest and Peter H. Wilson (eds), *The Bee and the Eagle: Napoleonic France and the End of the Holy Roman Empire, 1806* (Basingstoke, 2009), pp. 116–20.

[7.] Thierry Lentz, 'Napoléon et Charlemagne', in Thierry Lentz (ed.), *Napoléon et l'Europe: regards sur une politique* (Paris, 2005), p. 17.

[8.] Geoffrey Ellis, *The Napoleonic Empire* (Basingstoke, 2003), p. 54.

[9.] Roberto Conti, *Il Tesoro: Guida alla conoscenza del Tesoro del Duomo di Monza*, p. 6.

[10.] Michael Broers, *Europe under Napoleon* (London, 1996), p. 62.

[11.] Michael Kaiser, 'A matter of survival: Bavaria becomes a Kingdom', in Forrest and Wilson (eds), *The Bee and the Eagle*, p. 106.

[12.] Steven Englund, *Napoleon: A Political Life*, p. 203.

[13.] Annie Jourdan, *Napoléon: héros, imperator, mécène* (Paris, 1998), p. 117.

[14.] Christopher Hibbert, *Napoleon, His Wives and Women*, pp. 142–43.

[15.] Ernest John Knapton, *Empress Josephine* (Cambridge, Mass., 1964), pp. 233–34.

16. Ibid., p. 236.

17. Ibid., pp. 274–75.

18. Napoléon Bonaparte, letter to Josephine, 31 December 1806, *Correspondance générale*, vol. 6, pp. 1302–03.

19. Knapton, *Empress Josephine*, p. 245.

20. Henry Hall (ed.), *Napoleon's Letters to Josephine, 1796–1812* (London, 1901), p. 93.

21. Christine Sutherland, *Marie Walewska: Napoleon's Great Love* (London, 1979), pp. 84–87.

22. Ibid., p. 247.

23. Ibid., pp. 219–24.

24. Knapton, *Empress Josephine*, pp. 284–95.

25. Luigi Mascilli Migliorini, *Napoléon* (Paris, 2004), p. 357.

26. Englund, *Napoleon*, p. 360.

27. Knapton, *Empress Josephine*, p. 296.

28. Christophe Beyeler, *Noces impériales: Le mariage de Napoléon et Marie-Louise dessiné par Baltard* (Paris, 2010), pp. 7–10.

29. Peter Burke, *The Fabrication of Louis XIV* (New Haven, Connecticut, 1992), passim.

30. Alan Forrest, 'Propaganda and the Legitimation of Power in Napoleonic France', *French History* 18 (2004), pp. 437–38; for the later history of the festival see Sudhir Hazareesingh, *The Saint-Napoleon. Celebrations of Sovereignty in Nineteenth-century France* (Cambridge, Massachusetts, 2004).

31. Jourdan, *Napoléon*, pp. 109–10.

32. David O'Brien, *After the Revolution: Antoine-Jean Gros, Painting and Propaganda under Napoleon* (University Park, Pennsylvania, 2004), pp. 4–8.

33. David O'Brien, 'Antonio Canova's *Napoleon as Mars the Peace-

maker and the Limits of Imperial Portraiture', *French History* 18 (2004), p. 377.

34. Todd Porterfield and Susan L. Siegfried, *Staging Empire. Napoleon, Ingres and David* (University Park, Pennsylvania, 2006), pp. 9–10.

35. Udolpho van de Sandt, 'Le Salon', in Jean-Claude Bonnet (ed.), *L'Empire des Muses. Napoléon, les arts et les lettres* (Paris, 2004), p. 77.

36. Todd Porterfield, *The Allure of Empire. Art in the Service of French Imperialism, 1798–1836* (Princeton, New Jersey, 1998), p. 7.

37. Vivant Denon, *Voyage dans la Basse et la Haute Egypte pendant les campagnes du Général Bonaparte* (revised edition, Paris, 1990).

38. Terence M. Russell, *The Discovery of Egypt. Vivant Denon's Travels with Napoleon's Army* (Stroud, 2005), p. 102.

39. Béatrice Didier, 'La description de monuments: le *Voyage dans la Basse et la Haute Egypte*', in Francis Claudon and Bernard Bailly (eds), *Vivant Denon* (Chalon-sur-Saône, 2001), p. 218.

40. Russell, *The Discovery of Egypt*, p. 41.

41. Andrew McClellan, *Inventing the Louvre: Art, Politics and the Origins of the Modern Museum in Eighteenth-century Paris* (Cambridge, 1994), pp. 91–92.

42. Philippe Bordes, 'Le Musée Napoléon', in Jean-Claude Bonnet (ed.), *L'Empire des Muses*, pp. 79–80.

43. Englund, *Napoleon*, pp. 303–04.

44. David Chaillou, *Napoléon et l'Opéra: la politique sur la scène, 1810–1815* (Paris, 2004), p. 43.

11: FROM THE PENINSULA TO LEIPZIG

1. Tim Blanning, *The Pursuit of Glory. Europe, 1648–1815* (London, 2007), p. 658.

2. Luigi Mascilli Migliorini, *Napoléon* (Paris, 2004), pp. 301–03.

3. Vernon J. Puryear, *Napoleon and the Dardanelles* (Berkeley, California, 1951), pp. 168–69.

4. Rebecca Earle, 'The French Revolutionary Wars in the Spanish-American Imagination, 1789–1830', in Richard Bessel, Nicholas Guyatt and Jane Rendall (eds.), *War, Empire and Slavery, 1770–1830* (Basingstoke, 2010), pp. 186–93.

5. Michael Broers, *Europe under Napoleon, 1799–1815*, p. 144.

6. Charles J. Esdaile, *The French Wars, 1792–1815* (London, 2001), p. 39.

7. Steven Englund, *Napoleon. A Political Life* (New York, 20011), p. 325.

8. Silvia Marzagalli, *Les boulevards de la fraude: le négoce maritime et le Blocus continental, 1806–15* (Villeneuve d'Ascq, 1999), pp. 277–78.

9. Katherine B. Aaslestad, 'War without Battles: Civilian Experiences of Economic Warfare during the Napoleonic Era in Hamburg', in Alan Forrest, Karen Hagemann and Jane Rendall (eds), *Soldiers, Citizens and Civilians: Experiences and Perceptions of the Revolutionary and Napoleonic Wars, 1790–1820* (Basingstoke, 2009), pp. 118–19.

10. For a thorough discussion of the Peninsular campaigns see Charles J. Esdaile, *The Peninsular War: A New History* (London, 2002).

11. Jean Marnier, *Souvenirs de guerre en temps de paix* (Paris, 1867), p. 36.

12. Charles J. Esdaile, *Fighting Napoleon: Guerrillas, Bandits and Adventurers in Spain, 1808–14* (New Haven, Connecticut, 2004), pp. 111–13.

13. For details of these and other atrocities, see Jean-Marc Lafon, *L'Andalousie et Napoléon: contre-insurrection, collaboration et résistances dans le Midi de l'Espagne, 1808–12* (Paris, 2007).

14. John Lawrence Tone, *The Fatal Knot: The Guerrilla War in Navarre and the Defeat of Napoleon in Spain* (Chapel Hill, North Carolina, 1994), pp. 147–49.

15. Alan Forrest, 'The Logistics of Revolutionary War in France', in Chickering and Förster, *War in an Age of Revolution*, pp. 187–90.

16. Jonathon Riley, *Napoleon as a General* (London, 2007), pp. 34–35.

17. Jean-José Ségéric, *Napoléon face à la Royal Navy* (Rennes, 2008), p. 222.

18. Pierre Branda, *Le prix de la gloire. Napoléon et l'argent* (Paris, 2007), p. 485.

19. Georges Lefebvre, *Napoleon*, vol 2, pp. 52–53.

20. Adam Zamoyski, *1812: Napoleon's Fatal March on Moscow* (London, 2005), p. 37.

21. Alan Palmer, *Bernadotte: Napoleon's Marshal, Sweden's King* (London, 1990), pp. 185–90.

22. Clive Emsley, *The Longman Companion to Napoleonic Europe* (London, 1993), p. 17.

23. François Buttner, 'Grande Armée', in Jean Tulard (ed.), *Dictionnaire Napoléon* (2 vols, Paris, 1999), vol. 1, pp. 893–94.

24. David Gates, *The Napoleonic Wars, 1803–1815* (London, 1997), pp. 204–05.

25. Armand de Caulaincourt, *At Napoleon's Side in Russia* (New York, 2008), pp. 28–29.

26. Dominic Lieven, *Russia against Napoleon. The Battle for Europe, 1807 to 1814* (London, 2009), p. 124.

27. Thierry Lentz, *Nouvelle histoire du Premier Empire* (4 vols, Paris, 2002–2010), vol. 2 : *L'effondrement du système napoléonien, 1810–14* (2004), p. 268.

28. Alain Fillion, *La Bérézina racontée par ceux qui l'ont vécue* (Paris, 2005), p. 11.

29. Léon Hennet and Emile Martin, *Lettres interceptées par les Russes durant la campagne de 1812* (Paris, 1913), p. 228.

30. Zamoyski, *1812*, p. 409.

31. Richard Riehn, *1812: Napoleon's Russian Campaign* (New York, 1991), p. 395; Bates, *The Napoleonic Wars*, p. 221.

32. Riley, *Napoleon as a General*, pp. 199–200.

33. Emsley, *Longman Companion*, p. 16.

34. Englund, *Napoleon*, p. 378.

35. Gates, *The Napoleonic Wars*, p. 221.

36. Hezi Shelah, *Napoleon 1813* (London, 2000), pp. 78–79.

37. Emmanuel de Las Cases, *Le mémorial de Sainte-Hélène* (2 vols, Paris, 1951), vol. 2, p. 232.

38. Shelah, *Napoleon 1813*, pp. 90–91.

39. Emsley, *Longman Companion*, p. 19.

40. The fullest account of the military campaign is Michael V. Leggiere, *The Fall of Napoleon: The Allied Invasion of France, 1813–1814* (Cambridge, 2007).

41. Thierry Lentz, *Nouvelle histoire du Premier Empire*, vol. 2, pp. 522–50; see also Jacques Hantraye, *Le récit d'un civil dans la campagne de France de 1814: les 'Lettres historiques' de Pierre Dardenne, 1768–1857* (Paris, 2008), pp. lxix – lxxiii.

12: THE HUNDRED DAYS

1. F. Loraine Petre, *Napoleon at Bay, 1814* (London, 1914), pp. 199–200.
2. Dominique de Villepin, *Les Cent Jours ou l'esprit de sacrifice* (Paris, 2001), p. 10.
3. Alan Schom, *Napoleon Bonaparte*, p. 697.
4. Owen Connelly (ed.), *Historical Dictionary of Napoleonic France, 1799–1815* (London, 1985), pp. 3–5.
5. The phrase is from Guy Godlewski, *Napoléon à l'île d'Elbe: 300 jours d'exil* (Paris, 2003)
6. Neil Campbell, *Napoleon on Elba: Diary of an Eyewitness to Exile*, ed. Jonathan North (Welwyn Garden City, 2004), p. 31.
7. Ibid., p. 46.
8. Ibid., p. 57.
9. Catherine Clerc, *La caricature contre Napoléon* (Paris, 1985), p. 172.
10. Annie Duprat, 'Une guerre des images: Louis XVIII, Napoléon et la France', *Revue d'histoire moderne et contemporaine* 47 (2000), p. 500.
11. Schom, *Napoleon Bonaparte*, p. 697.
12. Henry Houssaye, *1814* (Paris, 1889), pp. 548–49.
13. Isser Woloch, *Napoleon and his Collaborators*, p. 222.
14. Henry Houssaye, *1815* (Paris, 1893), pp. 1–2.
15. Connelly, *Historical Dictionary*, p. 4.
16. Antony Brett-James (ed.), *The Hundred Days: Napoleon's Last Campaign from Eye-witness Accounts* (London, 1964), p. 2.
17. Christopher Hibbert, *Napoleon, His Wives and Women*, pp. 220–22.
18. Steven Englund, *Napoleon: A Political Life*, p. 420.
19. Campbell, *Napoleon on Elba*, p. 96.

20. Ibid., p. 130.
21. Quoted in Alan Schom, *One Hundred Days: Napoleon's Road to Waterloo* (New York, 1992), p. 1.
22. Thierry Lentz, *Nouvelle histoire du Premier Empire* (4 vols, Paris, 2002–10), vol. 4, *Les Cent-Jours, 1815*, pp. 194–97.
23. Frank McLynn, *Napoleon*, p. 604.
24. Englund, *Napoleon: A Political Life*, p. 428.
25. Lentz, *Les Cent-Jours*, p. 295.
26. McLynn, *Napoleon*, pp. 608–09.
27. Jean-Paul Bertaud, *Quand les enfants parlaient de gloire: L'armée au coeur de la France de Napoléon* (Paris, 2006), p. 176.
28. Robert S. Alexander, *Bonapartism and Revolutionary Tradition in France: the Fédérés of 1815* (Cambridge, 1991), p. 2.
29. *Acte additionnel*, in Frédéric Bluche, *Le plébiscite des Cent Jours, avril – mai 1815* (Geneva, 1974), pp. 134–35.
30. Bluche, *Le plébiscite*, p. 123.
31. Malcolm Crook, '"Ma volonté est celle du peuple": Voting in the Plebiscite and Parliamentary Elections during Napoleon's Hundred Days, April – May 1815', *French Historical Studies* 32 (2009), p. 628.
32. Woloch, *Napoleon and his Collaborators*, p. 231.
33. Englund, *Napoleon: A Political Life*, p. 430.
34. Michael Broers, *Europe under Napoleon*, p. 269.
35. Harold Nicolson, *The Congress of Vienna* (London, 1961), pp. 227–30.
36. Schom, *Napoleon Bonaparte*, p. 721.
37. David Gates, *The Napoleonic Wars, 1803–15*, p. 268.
38. Jacques-Olivier Boudon, *Napoléon Ier et son temps* (Paris, 2004), p. 93.

39. Hippolyte Taine, *Les origines de la France contemporaine* (2 vols, Paris, 1986), vol. 2, p. 432.

40. Jean-Paul Bertaud, *Guerre et société en France de Louis XIV à Napoléon Ier* (Paris, 1998), p. 74.

41. McLynn, *Napoleon*, p. 610.

42. Andrew Uffindell, *The Eagle's Last Triumph: Napoleon's Victory at Ligny, June 1815* (London, 1994), p. 23.

43. Ibid., p. 192.

44. The most recent account of the battle is Mike Robinson, *The Battle of Quatre Bras, 1815* (Stroud, 2009).

45. Andrew Roberts, *Waterloo: Napoleon's Last Gamble* (London, 2006), p. 120.

46. Alessandro Barbero, *The Battle: A History of the Battle of Waterloo* (London, 2006), pp. 419–20.

47. Charles Péguy, quoted in *Actes du colloque Napoléon, Stendhal et les Romantiques: l'armée, la guerre, la gloire* (Paris, 2002), p. 9.

48. Michael Thornton, *Napoleon after Waterloo: England and the Saint Helena Decision* (Stanford, California, 1968), pp. 4–6.

13: YEARS OF EXILE

1. Georges Bordenove, *La vie quotidienne de Napoléon en route vers Sainte-Hélène* (Paris, 1977), pp. 27–32.

2. A. M. Broadley, *Napoleon in Caricature, 1795–1821* (2 vols., London, 1911), vol. 2, p. 5.

3. Jean-Paul Bertaud, Alan Forrest and Annie Jourdan, *Napoléon, le monde et les Anglais: Guerre des mots et des images* (Paris, 2004), p. 191.

4. Michael J. Thornton, *Napoleon after Waterloo*, p.222.

5. Brian Unwin, *Terrible Exile: The Last Days of Napoleon on Saint Helena* (London, 2010), pp. 57–58.

6. Ibid, pp. 59–60.

7. Jean-Paul Kauffmann, *The Black Room at Longwood. Napoleon's Exile on Saint Helena* (New York, 1999), p. 8.

8. A range of descriptions and dramatic images of Saint Helena can be found in Bernard Chevallier, Michel Dancoisne-Martineau and Thierry Lentz (eds.), *Sainte-Hélène, île de mémoire* (Paris, 2005).

9. Frank McLynn, *Napoleon*, p. 638.

10. A contemporary account of the voyage by the captain of the *Northumberland* is *Buonaparte's Voyage to Saint Helena: comprising the diary of Rear Admiral Sir G. Cockburn, during his passage from England to Saint Helena in 1815* (Boston, 1833).

11. Gilbert Martineau, *Napoléon à Sainte-Hélène, 1815–1821* (Paris, 1981), p. 14.

12. Thornton, *Napoleon after Waterloo*, pp. 198–99.

13. McLynn, *Napoleon*, pp. 646–47.

14. Unwin, *Terrible Exile*, pp. 167–68.

15. Ibid., pp. 64–66.

16. Louis Marchand, *Memoirs*, translated as *In Napoleon's Shadow*, ed. Proctor Jones (San Francisco, California, 1998), pp. 368–69.

17. Unwin, *Terrible Exile*, p. xix.

18. Bertrand regularly lists the books that Napoleon read or cites the passages that were read to him. See Henri-Gratien Bertrand, *Cahiers de Sainte-Hélène, 1816–17* (Paris, 1959), passim.

19. Ibid., p. 118.

20. Ibid., p. 139.

21. Henry Meynell, *Memoranda of Conversations with Napoleon. Saint Helena, 1816* (Guildford, 1909), pp. 2–3.

22. Marcel Dunan, 'Introduction', in Emmanuel de Las Cases, *Le Mémorial de Sainte-Hélène* (2 vols, Paris, 1951), vol. 1, pp. x–xi.

23. Broadley, *Napoleon in Caricature*, vol. 2, p. 12; Alan Forrest, 'Propaganda and the Legitimation of Power in Napoleonic France', *French History* 18 (2004), p. 444.

24. Elizabeth Latimer, *Talks of Napoleon at Saint Helena with General Baron Gourgaud* (London, 1904), pp. 185–90.

25. Charles de Montholon, vol. 1, p. 469. xxxx

26. David Chandler, 'Foreword' to Sten Forshufvud and Ben Weider, *Assassination at Saint Helena: The Poisoning of Napoleon Bonaparte* (Vancouver, 1978), p. 2.

27. Ibid., p. 4.

28. Francesco Antommarchi went on to publish his account of Napoleon's final months as *Les derniers moments de Napoléon* (2 vols, Paris and London, 1825).

29. Martin R. Howard, *Poisoned Chalice: The Emperor and his Doctors on Saint Helena* (Stroud, 2009), passim.

30. Ibid., p. 53.

31. Jacques-Olivier Boudon, *Napoléon et les cultes* (Paris, 2002), p. 43 ; Englund, *Napoleon*, p. 454.

32. Albert Benhamou, *L'autre Sainte-Hélène: La captivité, la maladie, la mort, et les médecins autour de Napoléon* (London, 2010), p. 350.

33. By far the most moving accounts of Geranium Valley and the site of Napoleon's tomb are to be found in the work of historians who have visited, and often photographed, Saint Helena. The description of the funeral ceremony is taken from Unwin, *Terrible Exile: The Last Days of Napoleon on Saint Helena*, pp. 57–58

14: LIFE AFTER DEATH

1. Didier Le Gall, *Napoléon et Le Mémorial de Sainte-Hélène: analyse d'un discours* (Paris, 2003), p. 15.

2. Marcel Dunan, 'Introduction' to Emmanuel de Las Cases, *Le Mémorial de Sainte-Hélène* (2 vols, Paris, 1951), vol. 1, p. xiii.

3. Steven Englund, *Napoleon*, p. 453.

4. Peter Hicks and Emilie Barthet, 'Interpretation of *Clisson et Eugénie*', in Napoleon Bonaparte, *Clisson et Eugénie – a love story* (London, 2008), p. 41.

5. François-René de Chateaubriand, 'De Buonaparte, des Bourbons et de la nécessité de se rallier à nos princes légitimes pour le bonheur de la France et celui de l'Europe', in Chateaubriand, *Ecrits politiques, 1814–16*, ed. Colin Smethurst, p. 72.

6. Las Cases, *Le Mémorial de Sainte-Hélène*, vol. 1, p. 668.

7. Thierry Lentz, *Les Cent-Jours, 1815* (Paris, 2010), p. 313.

8. Angelica Goodden, *Madame de Staël: The Dangerous Exile* (Oxford, 2008), p. 262.

9. John Claiborne Isbell, *The Birth of European Romanticism. Truth and Propaganda in Staël's De l'Allemagne* (Cambridge, 1994), p. 93.

10. Las Cases, *Le Mémorial de Sainte-Hélène*, vol. 2, p. 190.

11. Ibid., vol. 2, p. 187.

12. Jacques-Olivier Boudon (ed.), *Napoléon Ier et son temps* (Paris, 2004), p. 227.

13. Englund, *Napoleon*, p. 531.

14. Henri-Gratien Bertrand, 'Les derniers jours de l'Empereur à Sainte-Hélène', *Les œuvres libres* 39 (1949), pp. 107–08.

15. *Mémoires de Marchand, premier valet de chambre et exécuteur*

testamentaire de l'Empereur Napoléon, ed. Jean Bourguignon and Henry Lachouque (Paris, 1985), pp. 567–613.

16. Natalie Petiteau, *Lendemains d'Empire. Les soldats de Napoléon dans la France du dix-neuvième siècle* (Paris, 2003), pp. 258–59.

17. Philip Shaw, *Waterloo and the Romantic Imagination* (Basingstoke, 2002), p. 3.

18. Alan Forrest, *The Legacy of the French Revolutionary Wars: The Nation-in-Arms in French Republican Memory* (Cambridge, 2009), p. 73.

19. Michael Paul Driskel, *As Befits a Legend: Building a Tomb for Napoleon, 1840–61* (Kent, Ohio, 1993), p. 39.

20. Robert Alexander, *Rewriting the French Revolutionary Tradition* (Cambridge, 2003), p. 95.

21. Sudhir Hazareesingh, *The Legend of Napoleon* (London, 2004), p. 68.

22. Bernard Ménager, *Les Napoléon du peuple* (Paris, 1988), p. 32.

23. J. Lucas-Dubreton, *Le culte de Napoléon, 1815–1848* (Paris, 1960), p. 21.

24. Munro Price, *The Perilous Crown: France between Revolutions, 1815–1848* (Basingstoke, 2007), pp. 106–07.

25. André Zeller, *Soldats perdus. Des armées de Napoléon aux garnisons de Louis XVIII* (Paris, 1977), pp. 319–41.

26. Pierre Brochon, *La chanson sociale de Béranger à Brassens* (Paris, 1961), p. 15.

27 Ibid., p. 22.

28 Lambert Sauveur (ed.), *Songs of France from Napoleon I to Louis-Philippe, by Pierre-Jean de Béranger* (Philadelphia, 1894), p. 100.

29. Henri George, *La belle histoire des images d'Epinal* (Paris, 1996), pp. 16–17.

30. Christian Amalvi, *Les héros de l'histoire de France* (Toulouse, 2001), pp. 68–71.

31. Christian Amalvi, 'Penser la défaite, le recours à une histoire analogique: de la chute de Napoléon à la chute de la Troisième République', in Patrick Cabanel and Pierre Laborie (eds), *Penser la défaite* (Toulouse, 2002), p. 10.

32. Munro Price, *The Perilous Crown: France Between Revolutions, 1814–1848*, p. 189.

33. Jean-Marcel Humbert, *Napoléon aux Invalides. 1840, Le Retour des Cendres* (Paris, 1990), p. 13.

34. Ecole Spéciale Militaire, Saint-Cyr, Programme des cours des élèves, première année d'études, 1913–14, histoire militaire (Archives de la Guerre, Vincennes, X0.16).

35. Yveline Cantarel-Besson, 'Les campagnes', in Yveline Cantarel-Besson, Claire Constans and Bruno Foucart (eds), *Napoléon, images et histoire: Peintures du Château de Versailles, 1789–1815* (Paris, 2001), pp. 110–213.

36. Philippe Raxhon, 'Le lion de Waterloo, un monument controversé', in Marcel Watelet and Pierre Couvreur (eds), *Waterloo, lieu de mémoire européenne, 1815–2000* (Louvain-la-Neuve, 2000), p. 159.

37. Wolfgang Koller, 'Heroic Memories: Gendered Images of the Napoleonic Wars in German Feature Films of the Interwar Period', in Alan Forrest, Etienne François and Karen Hagemann (eds.), *War Memories: The Revolutionary and Napoleonic Wars in Modern European Culture* (Basingstoke, 2012).

38. Robert Gildea, 'Bonapartism', in *The Past in French History* (New Haven, Connecticut, 1994), pp. 62–111.

39. Ted W. Margadant, *French Peasants in Revolt: The Insurrection of 1851* (Princeton, New Jersey, 1979), p. xvii.

40. Karl Marx, *Le 18 Brumaire de Louis Bonaparte* (Paris, 1969), p. 15.

Bibliography

Alexander, Robert S., *Bonapartism and Revolutionary Tradition in France: the Fédérés of 1815* (Cambridge, 1991).

Rewriting the French Revolutionary Tradition (Cambridge, 2003).

Amalvi, Christian, *Les héros de l'histoire de France* (Toulouse, 2001).

Antommarchi, Francesco, *Les derniers moments de Napoléon* (2 vols, Paris and London, 1825).

Asprey, Robert, *The Rise and Fall of Napoleon Bonaparte* (2 vols., New York, 2000).

Baczko, Bronislaw, *Comment sortir de la Terreur : Thermidor et la Révolution* (Paris, 1989).

Politiques de la Révolution Française (Paris, 2008).

Bainville, Jacques, *Napoléon*, nouvelle édition avec préface de Patrice Gueniffey (Paris, 2005).

Barbero, Alessandro, *The Battle: A History of the Battle of Waterloo* (London, 2006).

Barny, Roger, 'L'image de Cromwell dans la Révolution française', *Dix-huitième siècle* 25 (1993).

Beaucour, Fernand, *Lettres, Décisions et Actes de Napoléon à Pont-de-Briques et au Camp de Boulogne* (Levallois, 1979).

Le Retour des Cendres de Napoléon: ses causes et sa portée politique (Paris, 1991).

Bell, David A., *The First Total War: Napoleon's Europe and the Birth of Warfare as We Know It* (London, 2007).

Benhamou, Albert, *L'autre Sainte-Hélène: La captivité, la maladie, la mort, et les médecins autour de Napoléon* (London, 2010).

Benoît, Jérémie, Agnès Delannoy et Alain Pougetoux, *Le Retour des Cendres, 1840-1990* (Courbevoie, 1990).

Benot, Yves, *La démence coloniale sous Napoléon* (Paris, 1992).

Bergeron, Louis and Palmer, R. R., *France Under Napoleon* (Princeton, NJ, 1981).

Bertaud, Jean-Paul, *Choderlos de Laclos* (Paris, 2003).

Le duc d'Enghien (Paris, 2001).

La France de Napoléon, 1799-1815 (Paris, 1987).

Guerre et société en France de Louis XIV à Napoléon Ier (Paris, 1998).

Quand les enfants parlaient de gloire: L'armée au coeur de la France de Napoléon (Paris, 2006).

La Révolution armée. Les soldats-citoyens de la Révolution Française (Paris, 1979).

Bertaud, Jean-Paul, Alan Forrest et Annie Jourdan (eds.), *Napoléon, le monde et les Anglais. Guerre des mots et des images* (Paris, 2004).

Beyeler, Christophe, *Noces impériales: Le mariage de Napoléon et Marie-Louise dessiné par Baltard* (Paris, 2010).

Bierman, Irene A. (ed.), *Napoleon in Egypt* (Reading, 2003).

Blanc, Olivier, *Regnaud de Saint-Jean d'Angély. L'éminence grise de Napoléon* (Paris, 2002).

Blanning, T.C.W., *The French Revolution in Germany: Occupation and Resistance in the Rhineland, 1792-1802* (Oxford, 1983).

The Pursuit of Glory: Europe, 1648-1815 (London, 2007).

Blaufarb, Rafe, *The French Army, 1750-1820: Careers, Talent, Merit* (Manchester, 2002).

Bluche, Frédéric, *Le plébiscite des Cent Jours, avril – mai 1815* (Geneva, 1974).

Bois, Jean-Pierre, *Dumouriez, héros et proscrit* (Paris, 2005).

Boisson, Jean, *Le Retour des Cendres* (Paris, 1973).

Bonaparte, Napoléon, *Clisson et Eugénie – A Love Story* (London, 2008).

Correspondance générale (publiée par la Fondation Napoléon, 7 vols. to date, Paris, 2004-10).

Journal de Bonaparte et des Hommes Vertueux, 1797.

Lettres d'amour à Joséphine, ed. Jean Tulard (Paris, 1981).

Oeuvres littéraires et écrits militaires, ed. Jean Tulard (3 vols., Paris, 2001).

Proclamations, Ordres du Jour, Bulletins de la Grande Armée, ed. Jean Tulard (Paris, 1964).

Souper de Beaucaire, texte présenté par Jacques Bainville (Paris, 1930).

Bonnet, Jean-Claude (ed.), *L'Empire des Muses. Napoléon, les arts et les lettres* (Paris, 2004).

Bordenove, Georges, *La vie quotidienne de Napoléon en route vers Sainte-Hélène* (Paris, 1977).

Boudon, Jacques-Olivier, *Histoire du Consulat et de l'Empire* (Paris, 2000).

L'épiscopat français à l'époque concordataire, 1802-1905 (Paris, 1996).

Napoléon Ier et son temps (Paris, 2004).

Napoléon et les cultes (Paris, 2002).

Ordre et désordre dans la France napoléonienne (Paris, 2008).

Boudon, Jacques-Olivier (eds.), *Napoléon Bonaparte: discours de guerre* (Paris, 2011)

Bourdin, Philippe, Jean-Claude Caron and Mathias Bernard (eds.), *L'incident électoral de la Révolution Française à la Ve République* (Clermont-Ferrand, 2002).

Bourrienne, Louis-Antoine Fauvelet de, *Mémoires de M. de Bourrienne, ministre d'état, sur Napoléon* (Paris, 1831).

Boycott-Brown, Martin, *The Road to Rivoli: Napoleon's First Campaign* (London, 2001).

Branda, Pierre, *Le prix de la gloire. Napoléon et l'argent* (Paris, 2007).

Branda, Pierre et Thierry Lentz, *Napoléon, l'esclavage et les colonies* (Paris, 2006).

Brett-James, Antony (ed.), *The Hundred Days: Napoleon's Last Campaign from Eye-witness Accounts* (London, 1964).

Broadley, A. M., *Napoleon in Caricature, 1795-1821* (2 vols., London, 1911).

Brochon, Pierre, *La chanson sociale de Béranger à Brassens* (Paris, 1961).

Broers, Michael, *Europe under Napoleon, 1799-1815* (London, 1996).

Napoleonic Imperialism and the Savoyard Monarchy, 1773-1821: State Building in Piedmont (Lampeter, 1997).

Napoleon's Other War: Bandits, Rebels and their Pursuers in the Age of Revolutions (Oxford, 2010).

The Napoleonic Empire in Italy, 1796-1814: Cultural Imperialism in a European Context? (Basingstoke, 2005).

The Politics of Religion in Napoleonic Italy: The War against God (London, 2002).

Brown, Howard, *Ending the French Revolution: Violence, Justice and Repression* (Charlottesville, VA, 2006).

Burke, Peter, *The Fabrication of Louis XIV* (New Haven, CT, 1992).

Cabanel, Patrick et Pierre Laborie (eds.), *Penser la défaite* (Toulouse, 2002).

Cambacérès, Jean-Jacques, *Mémoires inédits*, ed. Laurence Chatel de Brancion (2 vols., Paris, 1999).

Campbell, Neil, *Napoleon on Elba: Diary of an Eyewitness to Exile*, ed. Jonathan North (Welwyn Garden City, 2004).

Cannadine, David (ed.), *Trafalgar in History: A Battle and its Afterlife* (Basingstoke, 2006).

Cantarel-Besson, Yveline, Claire Constans et Bruno Foucart (eds.), *Napoléon, images et histoire : Peintures du Château de Versailles, 1789-1815* (Paris, 2001).

Casanova, Antoine, *Napoléon et la pensée de son temps: une histoire intellectuelle singulière* (Paris, 2000).

Casanova, Antoine et Ange Rovere, *La Révolution française en Corse* (Toulouse, 1989).

Caulaincourt, Armand de, *At Napoleon's Side in Russia* (New York, 2008).

Chaillou, David, *Napoléon et l'Opéra: la politique sur la scène, 1810-1815* (Paris, 2004).

Chandler, David, *Dictionary of the Napoleonic Wars* (London, 1979).

Chappey, Jean-Luc et Bernard Gainot, *Atlas de l'empire napoléonien, 1799-1815* (Paris, 2008).

Chateaubriand, François-René de, *Ecrits politiques, 1814-16*, ed. Colin Smethurst (Geneva, 2002).

Chickering, Roger B. and Stig Förster (eds.), *War in an Age of Revolution, 1775-1815* (Cambridge, 2010).

Chevallier, Bernard, Michel Dancoisne-Martineau et Thierry Lentz (eds.), *Sainte-Hélène, île de mémoire* (Paris, 2005).

Chuquet, Arthur, *La jeunesse de Napoléon* (Paris, 1897).

Church, Clive, *Revolution and Red Tape: The French Ministerial Bureaucracy, 1770-1850* (Oxford, 1981).

Claudon, Francis et Bernard Bailly (eds.), *Vivant Denon* (Chalon-sur-Saône, 2001).

Clerc, Catherine, *La caricature contre Napoléon* (Paris, 1985).

Cockburn, George, *Buonaparte's Voyage to St. Helena: comprising the diary of Rear Admiral Sir G. Cockburn, during his passage from England to St. Helena in 1815* (Boston, 1833).

Cole, Hubert, *Fouché, the Unprincipled Patriot* (London, 1971).

Cole, Juan, *Napoleon's Egypt: Invading the Middle East* (New York, 2007).

Collectif, *Actes du colloque Napoléon, Stendhal et les Romantiques: l'armée, la guerre, la gloire* (Paris, 2002).

Collectif, *Austerlitz: Napoléon au cœur de l'Europe* (Paris, 2007).

Collins, Irene, *Napoleon and his Parliaments, 1800-1815* (London, 1979).

Connelly, Owen (ed.), *Historical Dictionary of Napoleonic France, 1799-1815* (London, 1985).

Cooper, Duff, *Talleyrand* (London, 1958).

Crook, Malcolm, *Elections in the French Revolution* (Cambridge, 1996).

Napoleon Comes to Power: Democracy and Dictatorship in Revolutionary France, 1795-1804 (Cardiff, 1998).

Crouzet, François, *L'économie britannique et le blocus continental, 1806-1813* (2 vols., Paris, 1958).

Davis, John A., *Conflict and Control: Law and Order in Nineteenth-Century Italy* (Basingstoke, 1988).

Naples and Napoleon: Southern Italy and the European Revolutions, 1780-1860 (Cambridge, 2006).

Denon, Vivant, *Voyage dans la Basse et la Haute Egypte pendant les campagnes du général Bonaparte*, with introduction by Raoul Brunon (Paris, 1990).

Desfeuilles, André, *Autour d'un centenaire manqué* (Paris, 1950).

Dhombres, Jean et Nicole, *Lazare Carnot* (Paris, 1997).

Dickinson, H.T. (ed.), *Britain and the French Revolution, 1789–1815* (London, 1989).

Doyle, William, *Aristocracy and its Enemies in the Age of Revolution* (Oxford, 2009).

Driskel, Michael Paul, *As Befits a Legend: Building a Tomb for Napoleon, 1840-61* (Kent, OH, 1993).

Ducourtial, Claude, 'Introduction', to *Napoléon et la Légion d'honneur* (Paris, 1968).

Dupuy, Pascal et Claude Mazauric, *La Révolution française. Regards d'auteurs* (Paris, 2005).

Dwyer, Philip G., *Napoleon: The Path to Power, 1769-1799* (London, 2007).

Napoleon and Europe (London, 2001).

Dwyer, Philip G. and Alan Forrest (eds.), *Napoleon and His Empire* (Basingstoke, 2007)

Ellis, Geoffrey, *Napoleon* (London, 1997).

Napoleon's Continental Blockade: The Case of Alsace (Oxford, 1981).

The Napoleonic Empire (Basingstoke, 2003).

Emsley, Clive, *The Longman Companion to Napoleonic Europe* (London, 1993).

Englund, Steven, *Napoleon. A Political Life* (New York, 2004).

Esdaile, Charles J., *Fighting Napoleon: Guerrillas, Bandits and Adventurers in Spain, 1808-14* (New Haven, CT, 2004).

The French Wars, 1792-1815 (London, 2001).

Napoleon's Wars: An International History, 1803-15 (London, 2007).

The Peninsular War: A New History (London, 2002).

The Wars of Napoleon (London, 1995).

Fick, Carolyn, *The Making of Haiti: The Saint-Domingue Revolution from Below* (Knoxville, TN, 1990).

Fierro, Alfred, André Palluel-Guillard et Jean Tulard (eds.), *Histoire et Dictionnaire du Consulat et de l'Empire* (Paris, 1995).

Fillion, Alain, *La Bérézina racontée par ceux qui l'ont vécue* (Paris, 2005).

Fontanes, Louis de, *Parallèle entre César, Cromwel, Monk et Bonaparte, fragment traduit de l'anglais* (Paris, 1800).

Forrest, Alan, *Conscripts and Deserters: The Army and French Society during the Revolution and Empire* (New York, 1989).

The Legacy of the French Revolutionary Wars: The Nation-in-Arms in French Republican Memory (Cambridge, 2009).

Napoleon's Men: The Soldiers of the Revolution and Empire (London, 2002).

The Soldiers of the French Revolution (Durham, North Carolina, 1990).

Forrest, Alan and Peter H. Wilson (eds.), *The Bee and the Eagle: Napoleonic France and the End of the Holy Roman Empire, 1806* (Basingstoke, 2009).

Forrest, Alan, Karen Hagemann and Jane Rendall (eds.), *Soldiers, Citizens and Civilians: Experiences and Perceptions of the Revolutionary and Napoleonic Wars, 1790-1820* (Basingstoke, 2009).

Forrest, Alan, Etienne François and Karen Hagemann (eds.), *War Memories: The Revolutionary and Napoleonic Wars in Modern European Culture* (Basingstoke, 2012).

Forshufvud, Sten and Ben Weider, *Assassination at St. Helena: The Poisoning of Napoleon Bonaparte* (Vancouver, 1978).

Fouché, Joseph, *The Memoirs of Joseph Fouché, Duke of Otranto, Minister of the General Police of France* (2 vols., London, 1896).

Fraser, Ronald, *Napoleon's Cursed War: Popular Resistance in the Spanish Peninsular War* (London, 2008).

Furet, François, *La Révolution, 1 – 1770-1814* (Paris, 1988).

Gainot, Bernard, *1799, un nouveau jacobinisme?* (Paris, 2001).

Garnier, Jacques, *Austerlitz, 2 décembre 1805* (Paris, 2005).

Gates, David, *The Napoleonic Wars, 1803-1815* (London, 1997).

George, Henri, *La belle histoire des images d'Epinal* (Paris, 1996).

Gildea, Robert, *The Past in French History* (New Haven, CT, 1994).

Goodden, Angelica, *Madame de Staël: The Dangerous Exile* (Oxford, 2008).

Goodspeed, D.J., *Bayonets at Saint-Cloud: The Story of the 18th Brumaire* (London, 1965).

Gotteri, Nicole, *Grands dignitaires, ministres et grands officiers du Premier Empire. Autographes et notices biographiques* (Paris, 1990).

Grab, Alexander, *Napoleon and the Transformation of Europe* (Basingstoke, 2003).

Grainger, John D., *The Amiens Truce: Britain and Bonaparte, 1801-03* (Woodbridge, 2004).

Graziani, Antoine-Marie, *Pascal Paoli* (Paris, 2004).

Gueniffey, Patrice, *Le dix-huit Brumaire: l'épilogue de la Révolution française* (Paris, 2008).

Guillard, Rémi-Julien, *Retour des Cendres de Napoléon. Procès-verbal d'exhumation des restes de l'empereur Napoléon* (Paris, 1841).

Guiomar, Jean-Yves, *L'invention de la guerre totale, XVIIIe – XXe siècle* (Paris, 2004).

Haegele, Vincent, *Napoléon et Joseph Bonaparte. Le pouvoir et l'ambition* (Paris, 2010).

Hagemann, Karen, Gisela Mettele and Jane Rendall (eds.), *Gender, War and Politics: Transatlantic Perspectives, 1775–1830* (Basingstoke, 2010).

Hales, E.E.Y., *Revolution and Papacy, 1769–1846* (London, 1960).

Hall, Christopher D., *British Strategy in the Napoleonic War, 1803-15* (Manchester, 1992)

Hall, Henry (ed.), *Napoleon's Letters to Josephine, 1796-1812* (London, 1901).

Hall, Thadd E., *France and the Eighteenth-century Corsican Question* (New York, 1971).

Hanley, Wayne, *The Genesis of Napoleonic Propaganda, 1796 to 1799* (New York, 2005).

Hantraye, Jacques, *Les Cosaques aux Champs-Élysées: L'occupation de la France après la chute de Napoléon* (Paris, 2005).

Le récit d'un civil dans la campagne de France de 1814: les 'Lettres historiques' de Pierre Dardenne, 1768-1857 (Paris, 2008).

Harris, Robin, *Talleyrand: Betrayer and Saviour of France* (London, 2007).

Haythornthwaite, Philip (ed.), *Napoleon: The Final Verdict* (London, 1996).

Hazareesingh, Sudhir, *The Legend of Napoleon* (London, 2004).

The Saint-Napoleon: Celebrations of Sovereignty in Nineteenth-century France (Cambridge, MA, 2004).

Hennet, Léon et Emile Martin, *Lettres interceptées par les Russes durant la campagne de 1812* (Paris, 1913).

Hesse, Carla, *Publishing and Cultural Politics in Revolutionary Paris, 1789-1810* (Berkeley, CA, 1991).

Hibbert, Christopher, *Napoleon: His Wives and Women* (New York, 2002).

Hocquellet, Richard, *Résistance et révolution durant l'occupation napoléonienne en Espagne, 1808-1812* (Paris, 2001).

Holtman, Robert B., *Napoleonic Propaganda* (Baton Rouge, Louisiana, 1950).

Houssaye, Henry, *1814* (Paris, 1889).

1815 (Paris, 1893).

Howard, Martin R. *Poisoned Chalice: The Emperor and his Doctors on St. Helena* (Stroud, 2009).

Humbert, Jean-Marcel, 'Introduction' to *Bonaparte et l'Egypte: feu et lumières* (Paris, 2008).

Napoléon aux Invalides. 1840, Le Retour des Cendres (Paris, 1990).

Ireland, Bernard, *The Fall of Toulon: The Last Opportunity to Defeat the French Revolution* (London, 2005).

Isbell, John Claiborne, *The Birth of European Romanticism: Truth and Propaganda in Staël's 'De l'Allemagne'* (Cambridge, 1994).

Jessenne, Jean-Pierre (ed.), *Du Directoire au Consulat. 3 : Brumaire dans l'histoire du lien politique et de l'Etat-Nation* (Rouen, 2001).

Jordan, David P., *The Revolutionary Career of Maximilien Robespierre* (New York, 1985).

Jourdan, Annie, *L'empire de Napoléon* (Paris, 2000).

Louis Bonaparte, Roi de Hollande (Paris, 2010).

Mythes et légendes de Napoléon (Toulouse, 2004).

Napoléon, héros, imperator, mécène (Paris, 1998).

Kaplow, Jeffrey, *Elbeuf during the Revolutionary Period: History and Social Structure* (Baltimore, MD, 1964).

Kauffmann, Jean-Paul, *The Black Room at Longwood: Napoleon's Exile on Saint Helena* (New York, 1999).

Knapton, Ernest John, *Empress Josephine* (Cambridge, MA, 1964).

Las Cases, Emmanuel de, *Le Mémorial de Sainte-Hélène*, ed. Marcel Dunan (2 vols., Paris, 1951).

Lafon, Jean-Marc, *L'Andalousie et Napoléon: contre-insurrection, collaboration et résistances dans le Midi de l'Espagne, 1808–12* (Paris, 2007).

Laissus, Yves, *Description de l'Egypte. Une aventure humaine et éditoriale* (Paris, 2009).

Largeaud, Jean-Marc, *Napoléon et Waterloo: la défaite glorieuse de 1815 à nos jours* (Paris, 2006).

Latimer, Elizabeth, *Talks of Napoleon at St. Helena with General Baron Gourgaud* (London, 1904).

Laurens, Henry (ed.), *L'Expédition d'Egypte, 1798–1801* (Paris, 1989).

Laveissière, Sylvain, *Le sacre de Napoléon peint par David* (Paris, 2004).

Leggiere, Michael V., *The Fall of Napoleon: The Allied Invasion of France, 1813-1814* (Cambridge, 2007).

Lentz, Thierry, *Le dix-huit Brumaire. Les coups d'état de Napoléon Bonaparte* (Paris, 1997).

Le Grand Consulat, 1799-1804 (Paris, 1999).

(ed.), *Napoléon et l'Europe: regards sur une politique* (Paris, 2005).

Nouvelle histoire du Premier Empire (4 vols, Paris, 2002-2010).

Le sacre de Napoléon (Paris, 2004).

Lefebvre, Georges, *Napoleon* (2 vols., London, 1969).

Le Gall, Didier, *Napoléon et Le Mémorial de Sainte-Hélène: analyse d'un discours* (Paris, 2003).

Le Nabour, Eric, *Letizia Bonaparte. La mère exemplaire de Napoléon Ier* (Paris, 2003).

Lieven, Dominic, *Russia against Napoleon: The Battle for Europe, 1807 to 1814* (London, 2009).

Lucas-Dubreton, J., *Le culte de Napoléon, 1815-1848* (Paris, 1960).

Luvass, Jay (ed.), *Napoleon on the Art of War* (New York, 1999).

Lyons, Martyn, *France under the Directory* (Cambridge, 1975).

Napoleon Bonaparte and the Legacy of the French Revolution (London, 1994).

McClellan, Andrew, *Inventing the Louvre: Art, Politics and the Origins of the Modern Museum in Eighteenth-century Paris* (Cambridge, 1994).

McLynn, Frank, *Napoleon: A Biography* (New York, 1997).

Madelin, Louis, *La jeunesse de Bonaparte* (Paris, 1937).

Marchand, Louis, *Mémoires de Marchand, premier valet de chambre et exécuteur testamentaire de l'Empereur Napoléon*, eds. Jean Bourguignon and Henry Lachouque (Paris, 1985).

Mémoires, translated as *In Napoleon's Shadow*, ed. Proctor Jones (San Francisco, CA, 1998).

Margadant, Ted W., *French Peasants in Revolt: The Insurrection of 1851* (Princeton, NJ, 1979).

Markham, J. David, *Imperial Glory: The Bulletins of Napoleon's Grande Armée, 1805-1814* (London, 2003).

Marnier, Jean, *Souvenirs de guerre en temps de paix* (Paris, 1867).

Marshall-Cornwall, James, *Napoleon as Military Commander* (London, 1967).

Martineau, Gilbert, *Napoléon à Sainte-Hélène, 1815-1821* (Paris, 1981).

Le Retour des Cendres (Paris 1990).

Marzagalli, Silvia, *Les boulevards de la fraude. Le négoce maritime et le Blocus continental, 1806-1813* (Villeneuve d'Ascq, 1999).

Ménager, Bernard, *Les Napoléon du peuple* (Paris, 1988).

Meynell, Henry, *Memoranda of Conversations with Napoleon. St Helena, 1816* (Guildford, 1909).

Migliorini, Luigi Mascilli, *Napoléon* (Paris, 2004).

Morrissey, Robert, *Napoléon et l'héritage de la gloire* (Paris, 2010).

Muir, Rory, *Britain and the Defeat of Napoleon, 1807–1815* (New Haven, CT, 1996).

Tactics and the Experience of Battle in the Age of Napoleon (New Haven, CT, 1998).

Nicolson, Harold, *The Congress of Vienna* (London, 1961).

Nora, Pierre (ed.), *Les lieux de mémoire*, part II: *La Nation*, vol. 3 (Paris, 1986).

O'Brien, David, *After the Revolution: Antoine-Jean Gros, Painting and Propaganda under Napoleon* (University Park, Pennsylvania, 2006).

Palmer, Alan, *Bernadotte: Napoleon's Marshal, Sweden's King* (London, 1990).

Percy, Pierre-François, *Journal des campagnes du Baron Percy, chirurgien-en-chef de la Grande Armée* (Paris, 1904).

Petiteau, Natalie, *Les Français et l'Empire, 1799-1815* (Paris, 2008).

Lendemains d'Empire. Les soldats de Napoléon dans la France du dix-neuvième siècle (Paris, 2003).

Napoléon, de la mythologie à l'histoire (Paris, 1999).

Voies nouvelles pour l'histoire du Premier Empire (Paris, 2003).

Petre, F. Loraine, *Napoleon at Bay, 1814* (London, 1914).

Poisson, Georges, *L'aventure du Retour des Cendres* (Paris, 2004).

Popkin, Jeremy D., *The Right-Wing Press in France, 1792-1800* (Chapel Hill, 1980).

Porterfield, Todd, *The Allure of Empire: Art in the Service of French Imperialism, 1798-1836* (Princeton, NJ, 1998).

Porterfield, Todd and Susan L. Siegfried, *Staging Empire: Napoleon, Ingres and David* (University Park, Pennsylvania, 2006).

Prendergast, Christopher, *Napoleon and History Painting: Antoine-Jean Gros's La Bataille d'Eylau* (Oxford, 1997).

Price, Munro, *The Perilous Crown: France between Revolutions, 1815-1848* (Basingstoke, 2007).

Puryear, Vernon J., *Napoleon and the Dardanelles* (Berkeley, CA, 1951).

Richardson, Nicholas, *The French Prefectoral Corps, 1814–1830* (Cambridge, 1966).

Riehn, Richard, *1812: Napoleon's Russian Campaign* (New York, 1991).

Riley, Jonathon, *Napoleon as a General* (London, 2007).

Roberts, Andrew, *Waterloo: Napoleon's Last Gamble* (London, 2006).

Robinson, Mike, *The Battle of Quatre Bras, 1815* (Stroud, 2009).

Rothenberg, Gunther E., *The Art of Warfare in the Age of Napoleon* (Bloomington, IN, 1978).

Rowe, Michael (ed.), *Collaboration and Resistance in Napoleonic Europe: State-Formation in an Age of Upheaval, c. 1800-1815* (Basingstoke, 2003).

From Reich to State: The Rhineland in the Revolutionary Age, 1780-1830 (Cambridge, 2003).

Rudé, George, *The Crowd in the French Revolution* (Oxford, 1959).

Russell, Terence M., *The Discovery of Egypt: Vivant Denon's Travels with Napoleon's Army* (Stroud, 2005).

Sauveur, Lambert (ed.), *Songs of France from Napoleon I to Louis-Philippe, by Pierre-Jean de Béranger* (Philadelphia, 1894).

Schom, Alan, *Napoleon Bonaparte* (New York, 1997).

One Hundred Days: Napoleon's Road to Waterloo (New York, 1992).

Schroeder, Paul, *The Transformation of European Politics, 1763-1848* (Oxford, 1994).

Scott, Samuel F., *The Response of the Royal Army to the French Revolution* (Oxford, 1978).

Scotti Douglas, Vittorio (ed.), *L'Europa scopre Napoleone, 1793-1804* (2 vols., Alessandria, 1999).

Ségéric, Jean-José, *Napoléon face à la Royal Navy* (Rennes, 2008).

Semmel, Stuart, *Napoleon and the British* (New Haven, CT, 2004).

Shaw, Matthew, *Time and the French Revolution: The Republican Calendar, 1789- Year XIV* (London, 2011).

Shaw, Philip, *Waterloo and the Romantic Imagination* (Basingstoke, 2002).

Shelah, Hezi, *Napoleon 1813* (London, 2000).

Smith, William H.C., *The Bonapartes: The History of a Dynasty* (London, 2005).

Sparrow, Elizabeth, *Secret Service: British Agents in France, 1792-1815* (Woodbridge, 1999).

Staël, Germaine de, *Considérations sur la Révolution française* (2 vols., Paris, 1818).

Sutherland, Christine, *Marie Walewska: Napoleon's Great Love* (London, 1979).

Thibaudeau, Antoine-Claire, *Mémoires, 1799-1815* (Paris, 1913).

Thiry, Jean, *Bonaparte en Italie, 1796-1797* (Paris, 1973).

Thoral, Marie-Cécile, *From Valmy to Waterloo: France at War, 1792-1815* (Basingstoke, 2011).

Thornton, Michael, *Napoleon after Waterloo: England and the St Helena Decision* (Stanford, CA, 1968).

Tomiche, Nada, *Napoléon écrivain* (Paris, 1952).

Tone, John Lawrence, *The Fatal Knot: The Guerrilla War in Navarre and the Defeat of Napoleon in Spain* (Chapel Hill, NC, 1994).

Tranié, Jean, *Napoléon et son entourage* (Paris, 2001).

Tulard, Jean (ed.), *Dictionnaire Napoléon* (2 vols., Paris, 1999).

Le 18 Brumaire. Comment terminer une révolution (Paris, 1999).

Figures d'Empire (Paris, 2005).

Joseph Fouché (Paris, 1998).

Napoléon, ou le mythe du sauveur (Paris, 1977).

Napoléon: le Sacre (Paris, 1993).

Napoléon. Les grands moments d'un destin (Paris, 2006).

Napoléon et la noblesse d'Empire (Paris, 1979).

Uffindell, Andrew, *The Eagle's Last Triumph: Napoleon's Victory at Ligny, June 1815* (London, 1994).

Unwin, Brian, *Terrible Exile: The Last Days of Napoleon on St. Helena* (London, 2010).

Vandal, Albert, *L'Avènement de Bonaparte : vol. 1 – La genèse du Consulat, Brumaire et la Constitution de l'an VIII* (Paris, 1902).

Vergé-Franceschi, Michel, *Napoléon, une enfance corse* (Paris, 2009).

Villepin, Dominique de, *Les Cent Jours ou l'esprit de sacrifice* (Paris, 2001).

Waquet, Françoise, *Les fêtes royales sous la Restauration* (Paris, 1981).

Waresquiel, Emmanuel de, *Talleyrand, le prince immobile* (Paris, 2003).

Watelet, Marcel et Pierre Couvreur (eds.), *Waterloo, lieu de mémoire européenne, 1815-2000* (Louvain-la-Neuve, 2000).

Wilkinson, Spenser, *The Rise of General Bonaparte* (Oxford, 1930).

Wilson, Stephen, *Feuding, Conflict and Banditry in Nineteenth-Century Corsica* (Cambridge, 1988).

Wilson-Smith, Timothy, *Napoleon, Man of War, Man of Peace* (London, 2002).

Napoleon and his Artists (London, 1996).

Woloch, Isser, *Jacobin Legacy: The Democratic Movement under the Directory* (Princeton, NJ, 1970).

Napoleon and his Collaborators: The Making of a Dictatorship (New York, 2001).

Woolf, Stuart, *Napoleon's Integration of Europe* (London, 1991).

Zamoyski, Adam, *1812: Napoleon's Fatal March on Moscow* (London, 2005).

Zeller, André, *Soldats perdus. Des armées de Napoléon aux garnisons de Louis XVIII* (Paris, 1977).

Acknowledgements

This was not a book I undertook lightly. The gradual transition that has taken me from the social history of the Revolution to a biography of Napoleon Bonaparte has been many years in the making, a transition that had its roots in the study of France at war, and of the conscription, banditry and resistance that marked the years from 1792 to 1815. I have not, of course, wholly abandoned the Revolution: the Emperor whom I discuss here remains, at least in part, the revolutionary general he had been, while the Empire he ruled over had its roots in the spirit of the enlightened age that went before. This book is about continuity as well as change, a change that was imposed by personal ambition as much as by the savage, grinding imperative of a war that lasted – in the case of France and her most persistent opponents, Britain and Austria – for more than twenty murderous years.

In making this transition I have unavoidably accumulated a large number of debts to fellow scholars and historians, who have been unstinting in making me feel welcome in their midst. Some, of course, understood very well the challenge I was facing: like John Lynn and Jean-Paul Bertaud, they too had started out from the

386

French Revolution and had followed something of a similar trajectory, seeing the war rather than any political regime as the defining period for France in this particular *fin-de-siècle*. Indeed, it is perhaps no accident that I have come to the Emperor through studying his armies. But I have benefited also from the friendship and collegiality of the community of Napoleonic scholarship itself, from historians in Britain, France and beyond, those who are at this moment rewriting the history of the Empire and doing it in novel and exciting ways. The extent of my debt to them will be clear from the text itself, but I should particularly like to mention Michael Broers and Geoffrey Ellis, Michael Rowe, Charles Esdaile, Peter Wilson and Sudhir Hazareesingh in Britain; Thierry Lentz, Natalie Petiteau and Jacques-Olivier Boudon in France; David Bell, Rafe Blaufarb, and Katherine Aaslestad in the United States; Johan Joor and Annie Jourdan in Holland; and Philip Dwyer in Australia. While writing this book it has been my privilege also to work closely, through an Anglo-German research project on the experience and memory of the Napoleonic Wars, with Karen Hagemann at Chapel Hill, North Carolina, and Etienne François in Berlin, and with three researchers in this country, Leighton James, Catriona Kennedy and Marie-Cécile Thoral. Our work together proved especially enriching, as did the experience of examining the period in a consistently comparative way. It is instructive, indeed, how much of the most innovative research on the Napoleonic era in recent years has been done by those who approach the subject from a European – or transnational - rather than from a national perspective, and whose major research interests lie outside the *hexagone*, in Germany or Italy or Spain.

The idea of writing a critical biography of Napoleon, and of writing for a general readership rather than a purely academic audience, was first put to me by Tony Morris, and though I may have hesitated at first, I am so glad that he pressed the idea on me. At Quercus Josh Ireland has proved an understanding editor and an enthusiastic collaborator in this venture; it has been a pleasure to work with him. But my greatest debt in writing this book lies closer to home – to my wife, Rosemary and my daughter Marianne, whose enthusiasm was critical in persuading me to undertake this project in the first place.

York, August 2011.

Index